.... an experienced corporate fina.... who worked in the City for twelve years. As a director of Lazard, one of the UK's pre-eminent merchant banks, he was involved in a significant number of high-profile public and private transactions raising billions of dollars and advising corporate and government clients worldwide. As a long-serving member of the Territorial Army, Andrew was called up to both Kosovo and then later Iraq.

In May 2003 he set up and headed the Economic Planning and Development Department within the interim government of post-conflict southern Iraq, with responsibility for all economic activity in the British-led sector. After his departure from Basra in June 2004 he remained in the Middle East and went on to establish Gulf Capital, a specialist UK firm that offers strategic consultancy and advice to a diverse range of clients in the emerging markets – particularly in the Middle East. He lives in London.

BANKROLLING BASRA

The incredible story of a part-time
soldier, $1 BILLION and
the collapse of Iraq

ANDREW ALDERSON

ROBINSON
London

Constable & Robinson Ltd
3 The Lanchesters
162 Fulham Palace Road
London W6 9ER
www.constablerobinson.com

This edition published by Robinson,
an imprint of Constable & Robinson, 2007

A copy of the British Library Cataloguing in Publication
Data is available from the British Library

ISBN: 978-1-84529-510-3

Printed and bound in the EU

1 3 5 7 9 10 8 6 4 2

For those friends who have made the greatest sacrifice whilst trying to do what they believed was right.

For my family, whose love and encouragement throughout many escapades has always been a beacon to guide me home.

CONTENTS

ACKNOWLEDGEMENTS

Writing this book, I have tried to recollect conversations and events as accurately as they occurred. Inevitably my own recollections and opinions may differ somewhat from those of others who may have been party to the same events either directly or indirectly, because there are always two sides to every story. However, although this narrative is far from exhaustive throughout this book I have tried to present a balanced view of events as I experienced them.

Over 14 months between June 2003 and August 2004, I was fortunate to serve with some very dedicated, passionate and brave people from the international community and also from the local Iraqi community. Some of these people made the greatest sacrifice and paid the highest price working alongside us, and it's my sincere hope that their contribution and their memory shall never be forgotten.

Even today almost all of the Iraqis who had any involvement with the international coalition and its associated actors face significant danger every day. Many of them continue to face persecution, torture and even death within Iraq because they elected to come and work with or be associated with us. Therefore, for their own safety and protection, their names have been changed to protect both them and their families.

During this period I was privileged to work with men and women from within the military, various civilian agencies, different national government departments, commercial organisations such as security firms and private contractors and I hope that this story serves to inform the reader about some of the challenges that we faced on a daily basis. Without these people, and especially the team that we brought together in Basra under the leadership of Sir Hilary Synott and later Patrick Nixon, there would be no story. Although the book is written from my perspective because it was important to have a common thread, it's just as much their story.

The assistance and support of many of the team, both Iraqis and international staff, has been invaluable and has allowed this book to be written and I would like to thank them all once again for their contribution, both in Basra at the time and, more recently, in providing many of the anecdotes that you find here. Sadly, without the book becoming impossibly long and confusing, it has been impossible to include everyone who was involved or to record their valuable personal contributions. Instead, the narrative travels along the timeline which saw the birth, faltering first steps, full operation and then dismantling of an interim government and its associated actors, and within this framework provides personal examples, anecdotes and illustrations to bring the story alive.

Others far better qualified will no doubt be able to provide subsequent analysis and academic precedent and research which can reinforce or undermine a particular point of view. After all, the subject of Iraq is an emotive one and a topic of much widespread conjecture and debate. But, as (often unwitting) participants, we had neither the time nor the luxury to spend weeks undertaking complex evaluation for or against a particular course of action, what was important was that we did *something*, even if at times this meant doing nothing. In such a high-pressure environment where, to quote General Eisenhower, whose experience of reconstructing post-war Germany at the end of World War II seems strangely similar, we 'lived ten years every day', it was inevitable that we made mistakes. My father always taught me that to make a mistake was human, and therefore forgivable, but that the real fault was to make the same mistake twice.

Given the chaotic and confusing situations that we faced within Iraq, I suspect that if the whole dreadful scenario was re-played all over again we might choose to do some things somewhat differently. Over the past three years, as a result of my continued exposure to the country and the region, my view of the overall situation has certainly developed and changed. However, I do believe that wherever possible we tried to do what we believed was right, or acted to highlight a decision whenever we thought it might be incorrect.

Anyone who has experienced the reality which is modern Iraq knows it's an emotive place, and in my experience there are very few people who have been involved, in whatever capacity, who have not been significantly influenced personally and felt that their lives have been changed.

Post-conflict Iraq is a subject that's already part of our modern history. Every day a new chapter is being played out in our newspapers and on our television screens and I believe that an increasingly suspicious general public – around the world – is increasingly sceptical of propaganda, media spin doctors and political rhetoric, and is beginning to wonder what really happened. My personal aspiration for this book is that my experiences and those of my team will provide an informative backdrop and some colour – by way of a 'sand-between-the-toes' narrative surrounding the events and related decisions that we faced – informing you the reader and allowing you make up your own mind.

I would also like to take this chance to thank Chelsey Fox of literary agents Fox & Howard and my editor at Constable & Robinson Becky Hardie for all their hard work and for helping my idea for a book become reality.

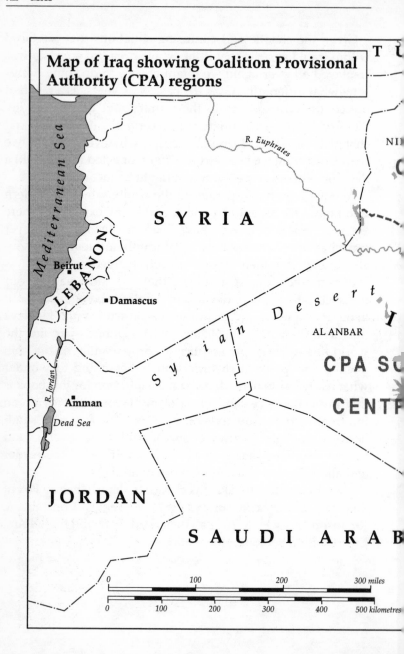

Map of Iraq showing Coalition Provisional Authority (CPA) regions

MAP xiii

1

ENTERING THE UNKNOWN

June 2003

Phil Smith sidled up to me in the corridor. 'Andrew,' he said quietly 'I think you should come and meet the brigadier.' I hesitated for a moment. I had met Phil the night before and he had seemed like a decent guy but I was puzzled. Why would the brigadier want to see me? And why now? However, before I could say anything Phil was already making his way along the corridor to a small conference room on the ground floor. I followed him.

He tapped on the door and we walked straight in. The room was whitewashed and spartan, with just four Formica-topped tables and a dozen white plastic chairs that looked as though they belonged in a garden. Brigadier Andrew Gregory was alone in the room. The first thing I noticed was his choice of outfit – a polo shirt, khaki trousers with a Guards regiment belt and desert boots. The second was that he was looking at me very intently.

'It's Major Alderson, isn't it?'

'Yes, Sir,' I agreed.

'Do you know anything about finance?'

'Well, yes,' I replied cautiously, 'I'm a former director of a merchant bank. It is quite a big field though, what is it you want to know?'

'We seem to have a problem with the Central Bank and Phil Smith suggested you might be able to help.'

This felt like trouble. I already had a job – with another brigadier altogether.

'Perhaps I could, Sir,' I said hesitantly. 'But the thing is, I'm already working for brigade HQ.'

'Don't worry about that,' said the brigadier breezily. 'Leave that to me. I shall speak to the brigade commander.'

With that he turned to Phil Smith. 'Where are the bankers?' he asked. 'When are they coming in?'

I realised I'd been ambushed. At 9.30 am I'd gone in to see the brigadier; by 10 am two rather nervous looking senior Iraqi officials from the Basra branch of the Central Bank of Iraq were being ushered in. Until a few minutes ago, I hadn't even heard of the Central Bank of Iraq. Now, just because I'd been a merchant banker in London, I'd been handed the task of sorting out an unspecified problem with a major financial organisation I knew nothing about.

Before we'd even sat down there was another tap on the door and after a brief conversation with a sergeant major the brigadier turned to us all and said: 'Gentlemen, I shall leave this in your hands – see what you can do.' With that he disappeared, taking his interpreter with him. So, not only was I expected to solve this problem, I was to do it without the aid of an interpreter. Still, I tried to look on the bright side. When I arrived in Iraq the army had told me I'd be sorting out local utilities. And to be honest I didn't know one end of a power station from another. At least as a City banker I did know something about finance – even if I hadn't quite been prepared for this meeting with two clearly important though scruffily dressed local officials.

'So,' I said optimistically, beaming across at the silent Iraqis. 'What seems to be the problem?'

The older and more senior of the two leaned across the

Formica table and looked me straight in the eye. 'You have stolen our money!' he declared.

I'd been in Iraq for just three days. It was a very different scene from the one I was used to. Since 1995 I'd worked for Lazard, the old-style blue-chip merchant bankers and advisers, part of the 'aristocracy' of the City of London. I'd helped advise on and negotiate multi-million pound deals and for several years my life had been fast and furious. My exhausting days routinely started at 7.30 am and often lasted till 10 pm. Though I was well paid for my efforts, by 2000 my enthusiasm for the lifestyle that went with the business was waning.

That year, I was involved in one of the biggest deals of my life – a multi-million pound contract with our clients, Granada. For three days I worked round the clock at my desk to help get this landmark contract through, only leaving it to go and buy fresh clothes. At 2 am on the last day, with the contract finally clinched, I drove home to my house in south-west London. Having just completed the deal of a lifetime I should have been over the moon. Instead I just felt flat.

Later that week I decided to leave early on Friday to visit my family in Edinburgh. Instead of simply saying 'OK' my boss asked 'why?' I pointed out that I'd worked for three and a half days without leaving the office that week, making a total of 35 hours by Wednesday morning, and had helped make the company a lot of money. That was a breaking point for me – the fact that I had to *ask* if I could leave early after working so hard made me angry and fed up. Why was I doing this? I knew then that I needed something else in my life.

Since university days when an injury forced me to give up rugby I'd been a member of the Territorial Army. And it was during a TA visit to Germany for a regimental ball that the chance of a new direction arose. I held the rank of captain at the time, and the morning after the rather boozy ball I was having a much-needed breakfast in the officers' mess. I spoke with Colonel David Allfrey, the commanding officer of the Royal Scots Dragoon Guards. We talked about my banking career and I told how him much I enjoyed the TA. 'I've always wondered what it would be like to go on an "operational tour",' I told him as I finished off my traditional army 'fat boy's' breakfast of sausage, bacon, egg and all the trimmings.

The colonel made no comment at the time but he had clearly been listening. A few days later, back at Lazard, I received a phone call. It was the colonel's adjutant reminding me of my talk with Colonel David – and the interest I had shown in going to Kosovo. I explained I hadn't actually mentioned Kosovo or indeed anywhere specific but the adjutant was undeterred. 'We're off on a tour of duty there as part of the KFOR peace-keeping force,' he told me, 'and we're one hundred and sixty-eight people short, including thirty-one officers. The colonel wondered if you were interested in joining us?'

I was at my desk so I automatically replied in banker mode. 'OK if you can send me a proposal I'll happily look at it,' I said, as if I was talking to just another client.

The army, I soon found out, had another way of working. Three days later the army's 'proposal' landed on my desk – in the form of mobilisation papers. Technically I could probably have wriggled out of it, but could I really say no? From the army's point of view I had volunteered my services and they were simply responding to that. They had called my bluff. I said yes.

My time in Kosovo opened my eyes to another world. In Podujevo I helped set up a national park, secured clean water supplies for the local people and for a time even became *de facto* managing director of a local waste disposal company. The chaos, the uncollected rubbish, the lack of infrastructure and the sheer stench appalled me. But I also found the work exhilarating. Making a huge difference to people's everyday lives was incredibly rewarding. But, as Colonel David observed: 'Andrew, having a merchant banker in the battle-group adds an entirely new dimension to what we can achieve. However, you're like a Labrador and must be kept firmly at heel. You do get ahead of yourself!'

There were a few moments of real drama. During trouble at a waste company when all the workers were on strike, it was my job to negotiate with the management. The manager's view of negotiation was a little at odds with my own. 'I can arrange to have you killed,' he said, staring at me menacingly. As soon as the interpreter relayed this message I pulled out my pistol and stared back at the manager.

'Let's start this conversation again, shall we?' I said. Fortunately, and with the help of my interpreter, we resolved the situation and got the company back to work.

On patrol on the border with Serbia, at that time one of the tensest military places not just in Europe but on the planet, I received a text message on my mobile. It was from my friend Jackie in the City, telling me that two planes had just flown into the Twin Towers in New York. We managed to pick up BBC World Service radio and listened in silence to an announcement from the Prime Minister, Tony Blair. He said that he had spoken to British armed forces around the world and that they were on a state of high alert. It was news to us. We may have been just a few hundred yards from the Serbian border, but we were all sitting around drinking tea. After the announcement was over I looked over to the leader of our patrol. He looked back at me. Finally I said: 'What are we to read into *that*?'

'Well I haven't heard anything from anybody,' he said thoughtfully. 'But I guess we all ought to put our helmets on.' And so we all did.

Later, I managed to speak to some Lazard colleagues in New York to check they were OK. One of them warned me to be careful. 'The world will change now. It's suddenly a much more dangerous place Andrew,' he said. I had no idea just how dangerous it might get for me in the near future.

During my six months in Kosovo I learned some valuable lessons. The most important was that the pen is sometimes mightier than the sword. Or to put it another way, that economics is often the best route to security; the better a country's economy functions the happier the people are and the more stable the nation becomes.

I returned to Lazard as planned. It was hard to leave Kosovo, as I'd become so passionate about my work there. But I'd known all along that this was simply a sabbatical and that I had to get back to my 'real' job. To be honest I also wanted to make sure I was back in time to collect my annual Christmas bonus; I'd suffered quite a pay cut to work as an officer in Kosovo.

But I found it hard settling back into office life. In Kosovo I'd been dealing with people who had lost their homes, destroyed by the Serbs. In the City people got worked up about getting a signature on a bit of paper. I realised I'd changed as a person and that now I really had to change my life too. In 2002 I quit my job at Lazard and went off to clear my head. I've always loved skiing so I decided to spend the winter on the slopes at Chamonix in France, helping friends out with their ski chalet business, with plenty of time on the slopes.

But while I was skiing, across the other side of the Atlantic the fallout from 9/11 was continuing. It was clear that George W. Bush, with the backing of Tony Blair, was now determined to invade Iraq to destroy their supposed arsenal of weapons of mass destruction. It was equally clear that British troops would be in action in Iraq. I wondered whether I might get called up.

In fact, like most other people in the world, I viewed the unfolding crisis in Iraq from the safety of an armchair. On

20 March 2003 I watched from my skiing retreat as President Bush announced that after the failure of any diplomatic solutions to the crisis, war with Iraq had started. A series of huge aerial attacks against targets in Iraq began, and soon afterwards coalition ground forces led by the US military began to move into southern Iraq. Few people were prepared for the swiftness of the coalition victory in the so-called Battle for Baghdad. By 9 April Saddam Hussein's regime had been toppled and on 1 May 2003 President Bush declared that major combat operations were completed. British forces had led the occupation of the south and had overseen the end of the old regime in Basra and surrounding provinces. The invasion was over in under six weeks. Or at least the fighting part was.

By now I was back from the slopes and doing a TA training course on Salisbury Plain to gain promotion to the rank of Major. One weekend in May, driving back to London for the weekend, I received a phone call from a fellow Major in the Queen's Own Yeomanry, my TA Regiment.

'Hi Andrew,' he said. 'You know you volunteered to do some TA work in Yorkshire …'

'Yes … ?'

'I don't think you're going,' he said. He paused. 'I think you're going to Iraq.'

'Are you sure?' I said, taken aback. 'I haven't heard anything about this!'

'I think you'll find your mobilisation papers when you get back home,' he said. 'Most of the TA staff in the regimental headquarters has been mobilised.'

I was in a reflective mood for the rest of my journey home. I'd assumed that the chances of me being called up for Iraq had gone, so the news came as a genuine shock. And all I knew about Iraq at the time was what I'd seen on the television – that it was hot, sandy and dangerous. And how would I tell my mother that her son was going to be posted to such a dangerous place?

The next few weeks raced past. I drove up to Catterick where 19 Brigade – the brigade I would be attached to in Iraq – was based so that I could hand over my CV in person to their chief of staff Major Hugh Eton. I knew from experience that in the army, unless you make sure people know what you can do, you end up doing any old job – being in charge of a telephone somewhere. Then I had to attend the Reserve Training and Mobilisation Centre at Chilwell near Nottingham. I had been to the centre before I went to Kosovo so I knew roughly what to expect. But the atmosphere was very different this time. The centre's sergeants, usually merciless over the slightest infringement of uniform regulations, were suddenly more forgiving. They were old hands. I guess they knew that some of us might never return.

As late June – the date for our departure – got nearer our nervousness increased. I'd teamed up with a fellow major from the Yeomanry I knew. Philip Ashton-Johnson, known to everyone as AJ, was an immensely popular man. It was good to see a familiar face and to have someone to crack jokes with. But our anxious mood wasn't helped by a delay in our flight to Iraq. After an extra nerve-racking night we were finally driven to RAF Brize Norton in Oxfordshire. Here on 29 June we were woken from our sleeping quarters at 2 am in readiness for our 7 am flight.

We were allowed to take just 64 kg of kit which had to contain all our belongings for six months. We boarded the Tristar jet by rank, colonels first. As officers we were directed into 'business class' but it was like no business class I'd ever seen before. All the passengers were in uniform and there was no in-flight service. Instead there was what is known in the army as the 'horror bag' – a paper box containing a pork pie, two cheese sandwiches on white-sliced bread wrapped in clingfilm, some bourbon biscuits, a bottle of orange squash and an apple that had clearly seen better days.

My mood had darkened. As far as I was concerned Kosovo had been an adventure. And although, as an adventure, it hadn't been without its perils, the Balkans weren't nearly as dangerous as Iraq. For a start hostile fire was coming back at us in Iraq. But it was the uncertainty of our mission that was the worst. We'd all heard President Bush say that the fighting was finished. And the UK media was saying that that the 'boys' – the British soldiers – had done well and were now coming home. So where did that leave us? What were *we* supposed to be doing out there?

As the plane finally took off AJ and I exchanged uncertain glances, as if to say, 'What the hell are we doing here?' Though of course no one said any such thing. Instead there was the usual military bravado and we did what soldiers nearly always do when they are nervous and don't know what else to talk about – we talked about our kit.

We arrived in Basra airspace just after midnight. As the plane made its final descent the pilot instructed us to put down the window blinds, to make sure we didn't make an inviting target for any attackers, and the jet made an instrument landing in near total darkness. As we stepped out of the plane we were met by another kind of enemy: a wall of heat. This was our first taste of the elemental force that is an Iraqi summer. Not many weeks before I had been skiing in sub-zero temperatures in the French Alps. It was quite a contrast.

Having found our kit we clambered aboard a requisitioned Toyota Hiace van and sped off into the darkness. By now I was seriously hot and desperate for water. It may have been night but it was still a stiflingly hot 35 °C and most of us were wearing full combat boots, socks, trousers, tee-shirt and combat shirt. I, though, didn't have a combat jacket – supplies had run out. However, I had little time to dwell on my thirst as one of our escorts explained the drill should the mini-convoy came under attack. Though we had our weapons, we had no bullets yet to go with them. So our instructions were simply to hide if we were ambushed. Great, I thought. Welcome to Iraq.

When we finally arrived at the brigade headquarters in the palace on the Shat Al-Arab waterway I didn't even care that the drinking water was so warm you could almost have boiled an egg in it. My clothes had been literally running with sweat and my feet, too, were soaking wet. After we'd quenched our thirst, AJ and I were shown in the darkness to our quarters, a sparsely decorated room we'd share with ten others. The beds were IKEA bunks that some enterprising quartermaster had bought as a job lot during a trip to neighbouring Kuwait. Feeling our way in the darkness AJ and I located a spare bunk as noiselessly as possible. As a merchant banker who had travelled the world I was used to staying in more luxurious accommodation. But by now I was too shattered to care and quickly fell asleep.

On my first morning in Basra I woke at 6 am, still tired and very hot, and took the chance to look round my new sur-roundings. The brigade was based in the vast presidential palace complex on the equally impressive Shat Al-Arab water-way that dominates much of Basra. This lavish, ornate palace was built by Saddam Hussein in 1990 on what was once a public park. Along one façade alone there were 56 windows, 18 huge rooms, 12 balconies, several bathrooms and wide sweeping marble staircases. And this was just one of the 15 vast buildings that made up this immense complex. Outside, the cooling waters of the Shat Al-Arab flowed around the walls, helping to keep down the temperatures in high summer as well as providing a natural security barrier. Inside, however, I soon found that appearances in the palace, as elsewhere in Basra, could be deceptive. The bathroom was almost as opulent as the rest of the building, even though it was part of the old servants' quarters. However, that didn't mean that there was any running water. As with so much of Saddam's legacy in the city, it looked impressive but that didn't mean it necessarily worked.

Having washed and shaved with bottled water I made my way to the officers' mess for breakfast. It was good to see a few familiar faces, both from the TA at home and also from my time in Kosovo. But I still had an overwhelming sense of being a new boy, as if it was my first day at school. And thanks to the flight delay back in the UK, AJ, myself and the rest of the recent arrivals were late new boys too. After breakfast I quickly made my way to the main palace building to find my new boss. I had met Major Hugh Eton, the brigade's chief of staff, at Catterick. He was in charge of allocating jobs for the military's CIMIC team – the initials stand for Civil-Military Cooperation. I had worked with such a team in Kosovo. As I strode towards the chief of staff's desk in the large Operations room overlooking the Shat Al-Arab, I saw another familiar face, the chief of staff of the outgoing brigade and whom I knew from Podujevo.

'Ah,' he said loudly and within earshot of the officers who were preparing to take his place. 'You guys are going to have the job of rebuilding the economy and he's just the kind of guy you want,' he said, pointing at me. 'He's an investment banker and he worked for us in Kosovo.'

Pleased if a little embarrassed at this commendation, I walked over to Major Eton and said hello.

'It's great to see you, Andrew,' he said looking up from his paperwork. But from his manner I could see something was wrong. 'Look, we'd earmarked you for that CIMIC job we'd discussed ... ' I didn't like the sound of this. ' ... but I'm embarrassed to say that this Danish officer has popped up and needs a job and we *are* supposed to be a multi-national force ... and you have arrived late and I've had to fill the posts. So I'm afraid you haven't got a job!' he concluded. I was bitterly disappointed. I had been compulsorily mobilised and told to go to Iraq – and yet when I got here there wasn't even a proper job for me. However, I tried not to show my feelings and listened as the major carried on talking.

'I see from your CV that when you worked in Podujevo you ran a utilities company and we think this will be an important area and will need quite a lot of work. So we wondered if you wouldn't mind doing utilities?'

This hardly made me feel any better. Yes, I'd worked with a utilities firm in Kosovo for nearly six months. But I'd had worked in finance for nearly 15 years – surely something in that sector would have been a more suitable alternative to the utilities job? But it seemed that even the potential finance post had already been allocated to someone else, a captain in the regular army with no experience. And just to rub it in, the position I had been given was a junior role – SO3 Utilities – that was technically a job for a captain. It felt as though they were just looking for any old job for me to do. It wasn't a great start.

My mood lightened slightly when AJ and I wandered over to the CIMIC desk and introduced ourselves to rest of the officers. Someone produced a table and two green canvas chairs and we sat down to join them. Suddenly, and for the first time, we began to feel part of a team. The Danish officer Michael Hostrup who had been given 'my' job, suggested that AJ and I should go and get kitted up with body armour, ammunition and other 'in theatre' stores we hadn't been issued with back in the UK. As we walked down to the front gates of the palace towards the quartermaster's stores, AJ and I chatted about the palace and our welcome, and I talked about my new role.

'It's OK for you, Sunny Jim, at least you have a job,' AJ said to me disconsolately. 'I have no idea what they want me to do – apparently because we arrived late they aren't sure they need us at all … '

I tried to cheer AJ up. 'Look on the bright side,' I said, 'it's all pretty chaotic and I'm sure that in true Yeomanry style we'll be able to find something to do.' TA Yeomanry officers are famous for being unpredictable and operating independently.

We walked on a little further and already we could see just how tough this heat would be for us. 'You realise that walking everywhere will get really boring,' said AJ as we sweltered in nearly 40°C. 'What we need is a staff car ... '

I stared at him. 'Where on earth are you going to get one of those?'

'Leave it to me, I'll ask around,' he said. Sure enough, just two days later AJ arrived at the HQ beaming from ear to ear and at the helm of a white Land Rover Discovery.

'Where the hell did you get that?' I asked.

'I spoke to a sergeant major I know at division and explained that I had been tasked with the job of liaison officer to the Battlegroup at Maysan,' said AJ. Maysan was another of the provinces in the south. 'And I explained that I couldn't possibly liaise with anyone one hundred miles away unless I had some transport. So he gave me one of these.' I looked at AJ in admiration.

'The best bit about being a liaison officer,' he joked, 'is that no-one really knows where you are – they both assume that you're liaising with the other!'

I spent my first couple of days getting to know more about the city and about my job. I was driven down to the offices of the new organisation that had been set up to help run the south until the Iraqis could take charge themselves. Initially it had been called the Office for Reconstruction and Humanitarian Assistance. This was because the coalition had feared the invasion might provoke a mass migration of people and a refugee crisis. But in June the name was changed to the Coalition Provisional Authority (CPA) to reflect the reality that in the absence of an Iraqi government – which had vanished – it had to run the country. In the south the organisation was CPA South or CPA(S) and was based in the centre of Basra, away from the palace. I think this was so that the people wouldn't associate it with the old regime. Before I arrived some officials had hoped to house the CPA in one of the fabulous waterfront properties further along the Shat Al-Arab. Unfortunately the United Nations got there first and claimed it as their base, so instead the CPA was housed in a large but run-down set of offices once used by the local electricity company. It was every bit as depressing a building as its previous use suggests.

As we drove through the streets I had my first real chance to see Basra. The rubbish, the pot holes, the sewage, all of it reminded me of Kosovo – only ten times worse. In particular, the smell of all that rubbish and waste in the heat had to be experienced to be believed. It was truly, hideously, vile. Another lasting impression was the number of donkeys and carts, mingling unhappily with a few clapped-out cars and vans. Many were stacked high with contraband furniture and equipment as government offices and facilities were system- atically looted. Generally, though, the mood was subdued.

It was an awful place to drive in. Drivers leaving the palace had to negotiate what was affectionately known among the soldiers as 'RPG alley'. This was a long, straight stretch of road that offered a superb range for anyone armed with a rocket-propelled grenade. The common belief was that if you drove fast your vehicle was harder to hit, so drivers used to slam on the accelerator and race away from the palace like bats out of hell. Yet going at high speed presented its own dangers. The thick metal manhole covers that punctuated the streets had become prized spoils of war among local people and many had been stolen. And when not dodging holes in the ground – a particular hazard at night when there were no street lights – the speeding motorist had to avoid slow-moving donkeys. Naturally, the traffic lights didn't work either, and every driver thought he had the right of way.

This was clearly a city that was run down and on the brink, brought to the edge of breakdown not only by the destructive war that had just finished but also by years of neglect by Saddam Hussein's government. Saddam and the ruling elite up in Baghdad were Sunni Muslims and they ran the country even though the majority of Iraqis are Sh'ias. In the south, including in Basra, the population is overwhelmingly Sh'ite. On top of the general mistrust that had existed between the different communities since the birth of Islam in the seventh century, there was a more recent reason why Saddam and the Sunnis had oppressed the Sh'ia. When the US-led coalition forces had forced Saddam out of Kuwait in 1991 and left much of his army in tatters, many of the Sh'ia had risen up in the south of Iraq hoping that the coalition would overthrow Saddam. When this didn't happen, and the Iraqi leader stayed in power, he took his revenge on the Sh'ia population. Thousands were massacred and many others were tortured.

It was back at the palace that I met Phil Smith for the first time. Phil was contracted to work for the British government's Department for International Development (DFID), via a private consultancy firm. He was an interesting character. In his 60s, Phil smoked incessantly, had a Russian wife and had run a business helping with accountancy issues for banks in Russia. He was in Basra working on small-scale funding projects in the finance sector. AJ introduced us because he knew I was an investment banker and figured that the two of us might have something in common. We were in fact destined to spend quite a lot of time working together. We chatted for a while about banking, and about my career at Lazard, about which Phil seemed unusually curious.

Two days later, when he took me for that fateful meeting with Brigadier Andrew Gregory, I understood the reason for Phil's close interest in my background. The CPA had come to realise that Basra's Central Bank had a key role to play in the south. Yet the Central Bank wasn't functioning. And, understandably enough, no one at the CPA or brigade HQ had much idea how a Central Bank worked – and certainly no idea how to fix one. Apparently an appeal had gone out: 'Does anyone here know anything about finance?' Once Phil Smith had met me he concluded I probably *did* know something about finance, so he told his boss Brigadier Gregory.

Which is how Phil Smith and I came to be sitting in the CPA conference room with the director general of the Iraqi Central Bank in Basra, a Mr Raffaq and his deputy. Mr Raffaq was a large man in his 50s with a round face, frizzy light brown hair and quite dreadful teeth. I later discovered he could be a jovial character but at this first meeting he sat there looking very stern, glowering at me. His deputy, who in contrast was tall and thin, said little and looked very nervous. Both wore rather battered looking and ill-fitting brown suits and deckchair-striped shirts with no ties.

As Phil and I spoke little or no Arabic and as the two bankers' grasp of English was far from perfect, it was hard for any of us to go into much detail. However, when Mr Raffaq accused the British army of having stolen his money I understood him well enough. I knew I had to play for time. 'I see,' I said, ostentatiously writing in one of the notebooks I had brought with me from the UK. 'That's clearly something I'll have to look into and get back to you about.' I wanted to make it clear that I wasn't accepting any responsibility for the 'stolen' money. I had learnt from Kosovo never to admit to anything in unexpected situations until you had the full facts. In any case their mood seemed to lighten slightly when I eventually succeeded in explaining that I too was a banker and had worked in the City of London. Maybe they thought that here at last was someone who could talk to them in their own language – the language of finance. I promised them I would get back to them the next day.

As I hurried back to the palace I took stock of the morning's events. I had arrived at the CPA building expecting to talk about diesel generators. Instead I had been asked to solve a problem with two bankers who seemed convinced that the army had walked off with their money. On top of that I now seemed to have inadvertently swapped commanding officers. In the morning I was reporting to the head of 19 Brigade Brigadier Bill Moore. But by lunchtime my new boss seemed to be Brigadier Gregory. How would I explain all *that* at HQ?

I walked swiftly into the Ops room back and towards my chair, desperately trying to keep my head down. I was intercepted by Major Hostrup who, to my relief, was grinning. 'I gather you have a new job,' he told me.

'Er yes,' I said cautiously, still wary about the protocol of all this. 'I wanted to talk to you about that … '

'Don't worry, we were just talking about it,' he interrupted. 'And we've re-organised the team.' I was to take over the finance officer job, while my old post was to be filled by another captain. 'So that's settled then,' said Hostrup with a smile, and off he went.

I congratulated myself on having escaped from a potentially awkward situation. But then I remembered I had a major problem on my hands. Just what had the bankers meant when they said we'd stolen their money? And where did I even begin to look for the answer? Now that I was officially liaising over 'finance' someone informed me that I needed to speak to Major Frances Castle, who was in charge of 19 Brigade's administration and pay and who was based in her own offices at the palace in a building next to the main HQ. I hurried over to see what I could find out. When I explained that I was now responsible for finance in the CIMIC team and had to sort out a problem with the Central Bank, initially Major Castle was a little wary. She clearly felt I was yet another unqualified and unwelcome person trying to meddle in complex financial issues.

'This wasn't my doing,' I tried to explain. 'I've been directed by Brigadier Gregory to get involved in this.'

Major Castle looked at me questioningly. 'So why did he ask you to help?' she asked, reasonably enough.

'I think it's because someone told him that I worked for a merchant bank,' I explained.

Instantly her mood began to change. 'So that means you understand banking and finance?' she asked me.

'Well some of it,' I replied, and went on to explain that I had met Mr Raffaq from the Central Bank just that morning. 'Mr Raffaq accused us of stealing all their money. I don't suppose you know anything about that?' I asked.

To my surprise she didn't bat an eyelid. 'Oh yes,' she said matter-of-factly. 'I may be able to help you there … we do have rather a lot of money for safekeeping. Here, you'd better have a look at this,' she added.

With that Major Castle took me outside where there were five large ISO shipping containers lying side by side. She unlocked one of them to reveal that it was full of sacks, plastic bags and bin liners. And every one was stuffed full of Iraqi dinar banknotes. I was dumbstruck. How in earth had they got here, I asked? The end of Saddam Hussein's rule, I was told, was greeted with widespread looting and the army had feared that the banks would be stripped of cash. The cash was brought back to the palace for safe-keeping until someone could think what to do with it. Millions of dollars' worth, all stashed away in five vast containers.

Well, this wasn't a bad result for my first real day of work, I thought, as Major Castle re-locked the container and its mountains of cash. At least I now had something to tell Mr Raffaq at our meeting the following day.

2

BASRA IS BANKRUPT

July 2003

Finding Mr Raffaq's money, I soon realised, had been the easy bit. I still had no clear idea what that cash was for or how the Central Bank in Basra operated. Over the coming weeks I was to undergo a crash course in state finance and centralised bureaucracy. What started out as an apparently straightforward task to locate some missing cash now led me deeper and deeper into the mysterious world of Iraqi economics. The country had a highly centralised command economy, run on similar lines to the old soviet-bloc models. At the centre was Baghdad, which handled the country's huge army of civil servants and state-sector workers. In fact, in Iraq there was hardly anyone who wasn't a state-sector worker. From oil and transport to teaching, health and the police, nearly everyone was employed and paid by the state. Though hopelessly inefficient, bureaucratic, technologically backward and cumbersome, this economy worked after a fashion – or at least everyone knew their place in it.

When the coalition troops came in and removed the head of this centralised economy, almost everything and everyone stopped working. Many civil servants and key ministers fled – worried they might be implicated in Saddam's crimes or become targets for retribution by disgruntled fellow Iraqis.

There was no one left to make any decisions and many of the files disappeared too. They were either destroyed or taken by the fleeing officials. Most important of all, no one was left to pay the state workers.

I soon learned how the Iraqis viewed this centralised system when I was introduced to my new interpreter, Abdul. 'Hello, I am Abdul,' he said by way of introduction. 'I am an interpreter and we are very pleased to welcome you to Iraq.' He came from a good family and when I first met him already spoke quite good English – in time it was to become superb. He had helped Frances Castle and her team deal with various pensioners and welfare groups who had been turning up at brigade HQ demanding money. Now he was going to help me.

'So what do you know about finance?' I asked.

'Well, nothing actually,' he cheerfully admitted. Then he added: 'Here everyone works for the government – so that makes things easier because everyone is the same, doesn't it?'

'Er, I guess,' I said hesitantly, not quite sure how to react. However, this proved to be the start of what became a long and wonderfully open relationship. Abdul seemed genuinely pleased that we were there. 'You will give us a new hope,' he explained, 'we are very pleased that the British are in Basra,' and he smiled. His enthusiasm was infectious.

Mr Raffaq also opened my eyes to the Iraqi view of government when I met him to explain I had 'found' his missing money. Far from it being stolen, Mr Raffaq now admitted he knew all along that the British military had stored it for safe keeping. The Iraqi Central Bank had even been given a key to the containers. So why hadn't he simply taken what he needed to pay the city's workers?

Mr Raffaq wearily informed me that the situation wasn't as simple as that. He had been told that he couldn't use the Iraqi dinars to make salary payments.

'Why not?' I asked, puzzled. 'The money belongs to the bank.'

'Yes, but Baghdad has told us to make the payments in dollars.'

'OK,' I said. 'So why don't you do that?'

'Because I don't have any,' came the perfectly reasonable reply. What a bizarre situation this was. The workers and pensioners in Basra had to be paid; the Central Bank had a stash of dinar notes sitting in Saddam's old palace; but a memo from the Central Bank in Baghdad specified that Basra had to pay salaries in US dollars. And Basra didn't have access to any dollars.

On the surface the instructions from Baghdad made sense. The Ministry of Finance in Baghdad and its American advisers wanted to keep a healthy balance of dinars in Basra to stabilise the economy. This meant any substantial payments should be made in dollars instead. This was great in theory. The trouble was Mr Raffaq had no US dollars – and he certainly wasn't going to ask for them. Because that isn't what you do in a command economy. You just follow instructions and wait to be told what to do next.

There was something else that puzzled me. Why had Mr Raffaq gone around saying the British army had 'stolen' his money if he knew all along where it was? This too soon became clear. Amid the chaos, looting and disorder of Basra, Mr Raffaq didn't want to be blamed for people not getting their wages. He had literally opened his bank doors and the vaults to show the disgruntled people on the streets that he had no money. Instead he could blame it on the British army who had 'stolen' it. It was quite understandable. It was a lawless society out there on the streets – many of the police had vanished – and had the bankers been suspected of hiding the cash they'd have been lynched. So as far as I could see the only people being paid in Basra – apart from the coalition – were the Central Bank staff, who mysteriously kept on receiving their salaries throughout this crisis. When it came to paying the rest of the city's workers Mr Raffaq and his colleagues were simply waiting for someone – us or Baghdad – to tell them what to do. I soon realised that the problem with the bank was absolutely central to the immediate future of southern Iraq.

On the streets tempers were beginning to boil. The daytime temperature was starting to hit the low 40s °C, while water supplies were intermittent and electricity supplies were still badly affected both by years of neglect and the recent war. Add to this the fact that none of the state workers had been paid for something like six weeks and you had an explosive situation. No wonder the CPA and the army were keen for someone to sort out the Central Bank. The only people who really understood the issue because they'd previously administered it – the old Iraqi Ministry of Finance – had long since headed for the hills.

Janet Rogan summed up what it was like for all of us in those early chaotic weeks. A Foreign Office official who had previously worked in the Balkans, Janet had volunteered to serve in Iraq and was the deputy regional co-ordinator for the southern region. She had arrived in Basra in June. 'We were all on a very steep learning curve at the time – everything had disappeared,' she said. 'This meant we were always reacting to events without knowing the bigger picture – for example when it came to realising who needed to be paid. Often we'd only know about local problems when people demonstrated. We only discovered later, for example, that each Iraqi ministry based in Baghdad also had a branch in Basra in the south.'

One person who witnessed the anger on the streets was Sergeant Major Ian McClymont, a regular army soldier in his 50s with vast experience all over the world. Ian was attached to 19 Brigade. However, the job he had been sent out to do – to look after any chemical or biological weapon threat – no longer existed. Instead, keen not to end up in a mundane job, he got himself seconded to the CPA building to help run the site. It turned out to be an inspired move.

Ian was worried that the CPA staff was hiding behind their closed gates, cut off from the Iraqi society that surrounded them. So he took it upon himself to stand outside the CPA building and become the visible link between the Iraqi people and the 'rulers' inside. He wore his uniform, but had no helmet, weapon or even hat while he stood out there – often in temperatures of 40 °C or more. He wasn't very big, standing at just 5' 7" tall. But what Ian did have was a natural air of authority and a priceless ability to communicate with people, even if he didn't himself speak Arabic. Aided by interpreters – including a courageous former Iraqi army brigadier called Sadiq – the sergeant major listened to people's complaints and relayed them to us inside.

Usually the anger of the crowds didn't spill over into direct violence. But one day he saw a group of about 60–70 Iraqi men hurrying down the road towards the old building. They were making a lot of noise and were clearly very upset about something. It turned out they were port workers who, like just about every other protestor who ever came to the gates, had a pay grievance. Ian had just warned the CPA sentries to be on their lookout when the crowd started pelting the front of the building with stones and rocks. He wisely ducked back inside the gates and pondered what to do next. Finally he looked at his interpreter and said, 'You ready, Sadiq?'

'No problem,' answered Sadiq and the two of them headed out to face down the crowd. At first they had to dodge a few rocks but soon the crowd stopped throwing things and started to quieten down.

'They were just standing there, staring at us,' said Ian. 'I'd just turned to Sadiq and said, "I think we're starting to get through to them," when a man picked up a large stone and hurled it at me. As I turned back to face the crowd I was hit smack bang on my forehead – the stone then exploded into tiny pieces!

'A big sigh went round the crowd. What they didn't know was that the stone was actually only a solid lump of sand, which is why it had exploded on impact without hurting me,' said Ian. 'Maybe they thought I was now indestructible ... who knows? But it certainly defused the situation.'

The level of anger Ian faced showed how urgent it was to sort out the payments issue. Now we'd overthrown Saddam and his henchmen, ordinary Iraqis naturally looked upon the coalition army as their new govenment. Most had genuinely celebrated the demise of the hated Saddam in Basra. But if we didn't pay them it might not be long before they took out their anger on the new 'rulers'. First, however, I had to figure out how the system worked. I told Mr Raffaq I needed to see some paperwork to show me how the money moved – where it came in and to whom it was paid. At first he shrugged his shoulders and told me all the paperwork had disappeared. However, as I got to know him and his Central Bank team, a series of vast old bank ledgers slowly and mysteriously began to appear in my makeshift office at the palace. These dusty tomes were written in Arabic and I needed Abdul to help me decipher them.

Fortunately I also had some new technology to help me make sense of the finances. During my trip to brigade HQ back in Catterick I'd persuaded the chief clerk to let me ship my laptop with cables, a printer, cartridges, batteries and a power cord. My time in Kosovo had taught me such items were in short supply 'in theatre'. And I knew it was unlikely that there would be a branch of WHSmith in Basra. So though my laptop sometimes suffered in the heat, now at least I could start to crunch some of the numbers I was getting from Mr Raffaq and his team. Many of the Iraqis had barely even seen a basic IBM 386 computer before and were completely over-awed by the technology they saw me using. But above all the Iraqi bankers seemed delighted that someone wasn't just talking but was actually *doing* something.

Despite the ledgers, Abdul's help and the laptop, it was still slow work. The two of us laboured for hours in a stiflingly hot office painstakingly sifting through the volumes. But I was still unclear about where all the money went when it was paid out. And as the tensions continued to rise in the heat, my biggest fear was that I wouldn't be able to work it all out before the city erupted in violence.

I'd discovered that Frances's predecessor had made two emergency payments of US $20 and US $40 to each and every civil servant, state employee and pensioner in April. One morning, after another day poring over the ledgers, I asked Frances if she had the paperwork. 'We have a spreadsheet somewhere,' she said and reached for a lever-arch file. Among the documents was an Excel spreadsheet.

It was a breakthrough. In typically military fashion someone had carefully logged every payment that had been made to every organisation that had asked for the emergency payment. Using this spreadsheet, it was now a relatively straightforward task to work out roughly how many people had been paid and what was owing. I was getting a crucial glimpse into how the economy of Basra worked. Now all we needed to do was understand how these payments fitted into the 'ministries' that we were beginning to hear about but didn't yet fully understand. Mr Raffaq and his two assistants from the Central Bank were a bit hazy too, as this was really the domain of the vanished Ministry of Finance. What they told us turned out later to be only 80 per cent accurate, but it was a start. I worked out that the groups of people to be paid were employed by a number of different Iraqi ministries. As far as I could see there was a total of 25 ministries in all. We hadn't yet fully determined where the money was supposed to come from – but we'd worked out who was throwing rocks at us at the front gate. They were all on file.

Finally after four hot, exhausting but ultimately rewarding days I had all I needed. I went to see Brigadier Gregory and told him I needed to discuss an urgent matter. I'd been feeling a bit left out of brigade life. While I was trying to find my way through a peculiar financial maze, all the other officers were embroiled in security operations around the city. I sensed my work was dismissed by the regular brigade staff as secondary to the main – to enforce security. So I was relieved to have something concrete to report to Brigadier Gregory, my chief of staff Hugh Eton and Brigadier Bill Moore, the brigade commander.

'We're forty-eight million dollars short, Sir!' I told the Chief of Staff in the palace Ops room.

'What? Who's stolen it?' he immediately wanted to know.

'No one has stolen it, Sir,' I replied. 'The money's in Baghdad – it's just not here.'

'So,' said Brigadier Moore, joining in the conversation, a slightly puzzled expression on his face. 'Who has it in Baghdad?' he asked.

'I think the Americans are likely to know something about it … ' I replied.

'So what do you suggest?' asked Major Eton.

I was now suddenly feeling very out of my depth. But I tried to sound confident. 'Well,' I said as matter-of-factly as I could manage, 'if this was my civilian job I'd get on aeroplane and go and see someone. I've always found these things are best sorted out face to face … '

Eton shook his head. 'We'll write a FRAGO to division … .'

Major Eton's idea was that the request for the required $48 million would first be passed on through the division to the next tier, the Coalition Joint Corps Headquarters, before finally being passed through to someone in the civilian author-ity in Baghdad. It was a perfectly logical response from a chief of staff of a brigade but my heart sank. I knew it wouldn't work. It wasn't hard to imagine the reaction of someone higher up the chain of command faced with a request from Basra for $48 million. 'Have they gone stark raving bonkers? Have they added three zeros or something?' they'd say. The simple truth was that this just wasn't the kind of order that comes out of a military HQ. The chain of command is vital in the military. But it has its limitations when dealing with non-military matters.

While Major Eton and I had been talking Colonel David Amos, in charge of Operations Support, had joined us and was listening in with interest. I was getting more and more frustrated. Although I knew I'd have little choice but to obey orders, I was trying to make it clear to Major Eton that the matter needed to be dealt with more urgently. I also knew, though, that I was just a TA major and that the regular army sometimes regarded TA soldiers as second-class citizens. After all, we were only part-timers, weren't we?

Towards the end of our discussion, Major Eton and Brigadier Moore were called away and Colonel Amos took me to one side. 'You're getting very agitated about this aren't you? What exactly is the problem?' I explained that the city's workers hadn't been paid for two months, that the money to pay them was sitting somewhere in Baghdad and that we needed to get our hands on it as fast as possible. Sending up an order via the chain of command wasn't going to do the trick.

'It'll never work – I can just see a clerk somewhere misunderstanding this request and it getting lost somewhere en route,' I said, as forcefully as I dared.

'OK,' he said, 'What do you want to do? What would you do now if you were a civilian?'

'I would go straight up to Baghdad, Colonel David,' I said.

'But you know that would cause some problems,' said the colonel, thoughtfully.

He was absolutely right, of course. Sending me to Baghdad to talk to the Coalition Provisional Authority would go against normal military protocol. To put this into context the CPA leadership in Baghdad was equivalent in seniority to a five-star general while even the most senior British Military Officer in Iraq was only at the level of a two- or three-star general. I, meanwhile, was just a part-time major who had been in Iraq for barely a week.

Colonel Amos considered the matter for a few moments. Then he winked. 'OK, put some civilian clothes on, use that phone over there and book a flight to Baghdad and go,' he said. 'I'll cover for you if need be,' he added. Delighted at the colonel's boldness I got straight on with carrying out my new instructions and booked a flight for Baghdad the very next day. I could hardly wait to get going.

Phil Smith didn't exactly share my enthusiasm, however, when I returned to the administration office to break the news to him. I found him hunched over his laptop and the Began satellite dish he used to send emails. He was swearing and chain smoking as he bashed out a message to his Russian wife. 'Do you know that she doesn't speak a word of English and I don't speak any Russian?' he said between drags.

I wondered what she'd make of the email but instead I asked: 'Do you know anyone in Baghdad?'

'Yes', he replied, but why did I want to know?

'Would you mind if I sent them an email? Because tomorrow we're going to Baghdad,' I explained.

Phil was horrified. 'Why do we bloody well want to do that? It's dangerous up there!'

'Yes,' I agreed. 'But we need to get the money!'

'Yeah OK but there are Americans up there and they shoot at people – I'm American and I wouldn't want to go there. So why do I have to go?' he complained.

'Because we need the money, Phil,' I repeated.

'Honestly what were you thinking … ?'

'We need to meet with the Ministry of Finance if we're to get that money,' I insisted. 'And anyway, it'll be a bit of an adventure, won't it?' Phil looked at me as if I was certifiable and realised he wasn't going to win the argument.

'Oh hell,' he said. 'I need another cigarette … '

I woke at 5.30 am the following day. The only safe way to get to Baghdad was by air and Phil and I had to catch an early morning RAF Hercules flight. Having had a quick wash and shave I gathered my belongings together as quietly as I could, trying not to wake my fellow officers. This was a sensitive mission and I didn't want to have to answer any awkward questions at this time of the morning.

I walked outside and looked across to the other side of the Shat Al-Arab waterway. The still waters reflected the huge red sun as it appeared slowly above the horizon. In a wooden skiff a fisherman was expertly casting his line while his son gently steered the craft with the current. The fisherman looked up and waved at me and I waved back. It was a scene that could have taken place at any time in this land's long and rich history, on this waterway where the ancient Euphrates and Tigris rivers meet. For a few tranquil moments it was almost possible to forget the recent chaos.

Colonel Amos's driver, Staff Sergeant Scott, raised his eyebrows when he saw me in my only set of civilian clothes though he politely said nothing. I was wearing chinos, polo shirt and a pair of deck shoes with a small green day sack slung over my shoulder, concealing my flak jacket, pistol, spare magazine, helmet and first field dressing. True, I hardly felt dressed to meet a Minister of Finance. But it was the best I could manage in the time. After Phil had puffed on his first cigarette of the day and I'd downed a quick coffee we climbed into the Mitsubishi Pajero and headed for the airport.

The streets of the city were nearly deserted as we drove out past the large teaching hospital, up the 'river route' along one of the tributaries of the Shat and met up with the dual carriageway that skirted the western edge of Basra. As we headed north our road took us towards the desert, which looked calm and peaceful in the soft morning light. Occasionally we overtook a dilapidated vehicle chugging painfully along the road, the occupants invariably waving and smiling at us as we passed. The children had learnt to copy signs they'd seen given by soldiers and greeted us with a thumbs up. Such greetings would become less common in the future. But for the time being I felt reassured that we were doing the right thing in their country.

It was only now that I saw evidence of the fighting that had ended just eight weeks ago. Burnt out 1950s Russian-made armoured personnel carriers and tanks littered the sides of the road. They'd clearly offered little resistance to the advancing British armoured-battle groups. As we left the outskirts and entered the desert I began to feel more relaxed. Any threat would be much easier to spot out here. In the distance I could see gas being burnt off from towers at an oil plant – I later learnt that it was the Shaibah oil refinery, some 20 km outside Basra.

At the airport the 'Arrivals' gate was surrounded by sand-bags stacked neck high and was the entrance to the military divisional headquarters. We drove in through the 'Departures' route and Phil and I were soon walking into the terminal's huge marble atrium. Here we checked in as in any airport the world over. There was a difference though: when the clerk asked if we had any baggage I indicated my small rucksack with the helmet and pistol inside. 'That can go as hand luggage, Sir,' she told me with a smile.

When our flight was called the pair of us walked out of the terminal towards the large grey hull of the waiting Hercules. I was excited at the prospect of the journey. Oddly it never entered my head that it could be dangerous – I've been fascin-ated by military planes since I was a small boy but had had little opportunity to fly in one. Phil and I, the only two 'civil-ians' on the flight, were surrounded by soldiers as we took our place on the red canvas seats and helped ourselves to the earplugs offered round. We soon realised why they were needed. The roar of the propellers made conversation impossible, and unless you were next to one of the tiny portholes there was little to see either. So despite the din I tried to sleep.

Most of the soldiers were dropped off at an airfield at Maysan and next we were cruising at 10,000 feet heading for Baghdad. It had been a smooth, uneventful flight. But suddenly, the plane dived sharply and began to corkscrew. My feet, below me one second, were above my head the next. For a few moments my stomach disappeared completely. Alarmed, I clung on to my seat, grateful for the belt that kept me in place. Were we under fire? I could see from the angle of the sun that we were in a steep downward spiral. Then there was a loud thud as we landed, almost colliding with the runway, and the plane eventually came to a halt. Nothing had been wrong. This was simply the way that planes landed at Baghdad airport to avoid being attacked.

The huge military operation on view at the airport dwarfed anything I'd seen in the south. There was row upon row of Blackhawk helicopters and Apache helicopter gunships as well as six or seven transport planes. You knew immediately you were in the presence of a military superpower. The British may have been partners in the coalition but we were very clearly the poor relations when it came to the scale of the military effort. Phil and I wandered towards the nearest Humvee, the distinctive US military vehicle. I asked a US soldier where we might find the Ministry of Finance. The sergeant looked at me in surprise and then said: 'You'll be wanting the palace' in a southern drawl that was clearly a long way from home.

'Thank you *so* much.' I replied very politely.

'Are you with the Brits?' he enquired.

The Americans hadn't been in Baghdad for long and bureaucracy still hadn't taken grip. So Phil and I quickly managed to hitch a lift to the city centre on a military convoy.

Our destination, we'd discovered, was the famous Saddam Palace, the headquarters of the Coalition Provisional Authority. We raced around the Baghdad airport perimeter road, with Phil and myself perched in the back of a light-blue Land Rover Discovery. Our first stop was Corps Headquarters, based at another magnificent palace close to the airport. Then we headed for downtown Baghdad.

The convoy was what is called 'locked and loaded'. We all wore helmets and flak jackets while the soldiers brandished short-barrelled and long-barrelled weapons, all cocked and safety catches applied – ready for a potential ambush. Soon I was feeling very uncomfortable. Plastic-lined body armour with ballistic plates trap the heat even in moderate temperatures. I was soon damp with sweat and again desperate for a drink of water. I could only imagine what the soldiers in the field must have felt like, wearing such protection all day as well as carrying their webbing and equipment in that sweltering heat.

Fortunately we drove quickly, heading along the 5 km stretch of the Baghdad airport dual carriageway lined with palm trees and dense vegetation. In time this route would become both very familiar for many of us from Basra and possibly the most dangerous road in the world. For now, however, the journey passed without incident and we drove under the city's landmark monument of the crossed swords to arrive at our relatively safe destination – Baghdad's Green Zone. This area is the closely guarded section of central Baghdad dominated by Saddam Hussein's former palaces. It became the centre of coalition activity and was turned into an effective fortress, protected by huge 16 feet-high concrete obstacles known as Texas barriers. Yet contrary to general belief it's not just westerners who occupy the Green Zone. Around 10,000 Iraqis live there as well.

Our ultimate destination was Saddam's main palace and it was an impressive sight. It seemed to go on forever. In fact I think it was something like a quarter of a mile long. Inside there was corridor after corridor and set of stairs after set of stairs. In all there were around 300 different rooms, each taped with a different number. Fortunately we had someone to help us find our way. The UK's liaison officer in Baghdad was Major Natasha Coxen, who had been in the regular British army. I'd known Tash since staff college days and it was great to see a familiar face in such intimidating surroundings. She kindly offered us a cup of tea, gave us a place to leave our weapons, helmets and flak jackets and then pointed us towards the Ministry of Finance, located in another wing. For ten minutes we stumbled up and down the maze of corridors, receiving several contradictory sets of directions from equally confused individuals. Eventually a quiet corridor revealed a sign saying 'Ministry of Finance' on a heavy panelled door. We knocked and went in, unsure what to expect.

Inside we met two British advisers, John and Jacob. Fortunately they were expecting us. I'd found their email address at brigade HQ and the previous evening had taken the precaution of sending them an email, taking advantage of the precarious satellite connection that Phil used. In the message I explained who I was and even sent them a copy of the all-important spreadsheet.

The meeting started well, as I explained to John and Jacob the situation in Basra. They seemed quite receptive. I was in full flow when a man in his mid-50s suddenly shuffled in and sat in a big chair next to our table. With his greying hair and gold-rimmed glasses he had a military bearing, though he was casually dressed in a white striped polo shirt, filthy-looking chinos, socks and sandals. I was still talking when he sat back in his chair, pushed up his glasses, looked to the ceiling and exclaimed: 'Five hundred! Oh my god, all I wanted was five hundred! I mean, doesn't the Appropriations Committee *understand*?' He was talking about the United States Senate Appropriations Committee and I quickly worked out that he surely didn't mean

$500 but $500 million. It was an impressive figure but nonetheless I felt irritated with this man for interrupting us. Fortunately I held my tongue, having just worked out that this was none other than David Oliver.

David R. Oliver Jr was a retired US rear admiral who had been the Principal Deputy Under Secretary of Defense for Acquisition, Technology, serving in both the Bill Clinton and George W. Bush administrations. Under the CPA's boss Paul Bremer, David Oliver had become the Director of Management and Budget for the coalition forces. In effect he was the main moneyman in Iraq. A tough, military character, he also knew his way around the corridors of the Pentagon and the White House – clearly one of the reasons why he'd been chosen for this difficult job. I'd heard of him and even seen his name on a couple of emails. But at the time there was no organisational chart on which you could see instantly who someone was and where they fitted into the scheme of things. Everything was so new and chaotic that you could spend three weeks trying to talk to someone only to find out, when you finally caught them, that they weren't really the person you needed, and so you would have to start all over again. I had known, however, that I needed to speak to David Oliver – and by luck here he was, sitting right in front of me.

'So who are you?' said David Oliver, suddenly aware of my presence and now staring straight at me.

'I'm Andrew Alderson,' I said, careful not to reveal my military rank. Baghdad was full of five-star generals and they were unlikely to want to pay much attention to me. 'I've just come up from Basra where the locals are a bit restless – I wondered if you could give us some money?' I couldn't see any point in beating about the bush and just hoped that Mr Oliver would take my request in the right way.

I was relieved to see that he smiled. 'Yeah I saw your name on an email, I think. You know what,' he added, still smiling, 'we figured that for forty-eight million dollars someone would get in an airplane and come to get it. I guess you did – so I guess we should give you the money.'

I could hardly believe it. Within a few minutes of meeting David Oliver here he was giving us the money – with no argument or discussion. I felt the familiar sensation of excitement and achievement you get as a banker when you make a trade – and here I felt $48 million was a very decent trade. My only aim now was for Phil and me to get out as soon as possible before he changed his mind. David Oliver was still talking, however. 'Can we do that John?' looking at his adviser, who nodded his assent. 'Yes,' continued David Oliver, 'that's right, we have this fund of one thousand million, so I guess we could take it out of that ... ?'

David Oliver was clearly a man used to dealing with large sums of money and, though it wasn't a negligible sum, the $48 million I was asking for certainly didn't faze him. I later discovered why when I saw their vaults downstairs. They were huge. But then they needed to be to house the $2 billion in cash that was routinely stored there. David Oliver and John discussed the logistics of sending the $48 million. It turned out that they'd be able to deliver the money the very next day. Oliver then asked me a little bit about myself and what I did in 'civvy street' so I told him about my time at Lazard. 'It's good to know we have a safe pair of hands down in the south,' he commented. I must admit I felt pretty good about life at that moment.

The journey back to the airport went smoothly and we managed to catch the last flight back to Basra. I was in good spirits when we were met by the two 4x4s that had been laid on by Colonel Amos to take us back to the palace. It was done quite discreetly as Phil and I were still supposed to be operating covertly. The main driver was again Colonel David's own driver Sergeant Scott or 'Scotty', and he was with John Godfrey, the officer I'd swapped places with to take over finance. We sped off into Basra.

Our mini-convoy was heading back towards the safety of brigade HQ when we took a wrong turn. Instead of skirting around the city we plunged straight into the centre of Basra old town, out of bounds to us without a properly armed patrol. Somehow we had to get out again. We drove slowly ahead and arrived at a market place. There must have been up to 5,000 Iraqis milling around. The evening light was starting to fade and suddenly some of the Iraqis started to bang on the roof of the vehicles demanding to talk to us. Phil and I were in our civilian clothes in the back seat and by now my companion was anxiously chain-smoking. John eventually let the window down a little and we started talking to the crowd. We could just about grasp that there was a gunman down the street, that someone had been shot and the crowd wanted us to do something about it.

As the crowd grew thicker I began to fear the worst. I thought of that horrible occasion when two British soldiers in civilian clothes had accidentally driven into the middle of a funeral procession in Belfast in 1988 and were first savagely beaten then shot to death. I also knew that six brave members of the Royal Military Police had been killed the previous month at Majar al-Kabir in Maysan province after they were trapped in a local police station. Today had been one of the biggest days of my life so far; now suddenly there seemed a real possibility it could be my last. Scotty turned round from the front seat and asked how many rounds we all had. John, Scotty and I had only a pitiful 20 bullets each, while as a civilian Phil had none. The three of us cocked our weapons. I'll always remember Scotty saying grimly: 'If we go, we're going down fighting. And you may want to save a round for yourself ... ' We inched forward, and though people banged on the roof we got through the market place unscathed. Eventually we found a familiar road and made our way back to the palace, very relieved. We were greeted by David Amos who wanted to know how we'd got on. Someone pointed out rather sheepishly to the colonel that we'd nearly been killed.

'I know,' said Colonel Amos. 'You were spotted. But how did you get on in Baghdad?'

'We had rather a big day,' I said with deliberate understatement and was just about to launch into an explanation of the meeting with David Oliver when a voice bellowed out from the back of the room.

'What is that civilian doing in my HQ?' The booming voice belonged to the brigade commander. It had been a high-octane day but the army has a good knack of bringing people down with a bump.

As I turned round, Brigadier Moore realised who I was, and I went over to the Chief of Staff to explain where I had been. To his great credit Major Eton congratulated me for my efforts even though my trip to Baghdad hadn't been his idea. 'We've had people trying to sort this out for several weeks … although I'll still only believe it when I see it!' he said. Then he looked at me. 'Incidentally what would have happened if we hadn't got the money?'

'The city is bankrupt and the salaries are due and there would have been violent demonstrations and more shootings,' I replied.

'Ah,' said Major Eton.

It turned out that on that earlier that day the mood of the protestors outside the military HQ had turned ugly. A group of 5,000 demonstrators had blocked the entrance road with a bus to stop an oncoming military convoy. In the heat and chaos one protestor had produced an AK47 assault rifle and fired off several rounds. A passenger in one of the military vehicles had meanwhile opened fire through the windscreen and the crowd had parted to allow the convoy into the camp. Fortunately no one was seriously hurt but the incident showed how tension was rising.

The sound of Chinook helicopter blades across the Shat Al-Arab the next day heralded the arrival of the cash. It was brought in from the airport on two large palettes straight into the palace compound. Officials from the Central Bank including Mr Raffaq and Frances's team loaded the bales of cash first into a lorry then into the shipping containers that were still standing in for a bank vault. Curious onlookers from the camp came to watch this transfer of cash. After all, it's not every day that $48.3 million in cash arrives at a military base. Brigadier Moore cheerfully noted at the evening briefing meeting that the money problem had now been 'solved'. One smart young officer begged to differ. 'Actually Sir, I was just thinking that Brigade HQ might suddenly become a rather bigger target than it was yesterday.' he said, to much laughter.

In fact the cash airlift had done the trick – for the time being. Word had raced around the city – via the Central Bank – that cash had arrived. People now genuinely believed they would at last get paid. An eerie quiet fell and, though the number of protesters at the main gate grew, there was now an air of expectation rather than hostility. The tension began to ease.

3

THE HONEYMOON IS OVER

August 2003

Now that we'd got our hands on the cash I had to work out exactly how to spend it. My 'map' of the local Iraqi system showed me that across the 25 economic ministries there were 168 different utility companies or state organisations. These ranged from water companies to the health service and from teachers to oil workers. Each of these groups was headed by a local manager or director general – DGs for short. I decided that I needed to call all the DGs in one by one. I had to find out how each of their payment systems worked and how many were on their payroll before arranging for them to be paid. Of course I knew there was a risk that some might not tell the truth or might try to massage their figures, but I also knew that 168 people couldn't all collude together – it was simply not possible. By comparing all their accounts, I hoped to be able to spot those whose practices or staffing numbers seemed out of step. There was another risk – that a DG might vanish with the cash. Or even that I might unwittingly hand over cash to an impostor. By meeting them all I hoped to be able to check their identities. In the end I relied on an honour system. I let it be known to a particular workforce that their money was coming. So if a DG considered running off with the money he knew he'd have a lot of very angry people after him.

In the next ten days alone we paid out $14 million to some 110,000 workers. I sat in a dingy little office in the CPA headquarters and met the DG and financial controller of each organisation to go through their payroll numbers. I would then meet them the next day at the palace where the money was stored and physically hand over the cash. On the whole the system worked well. Word quickly got around that there was money about and soon most DGs were lining up to see me. My aim was to keep as close to the old Iraqi way of doing things as possible so the process was something that the Iraqis themselves understood and were comfortable with. This wasn't an approach that the Americans always adopted in their sector, I discovered later.

I had to make some tough decisions. If a group belonged to a ministry they got paid; if they didn't, then they didn't. This didn't stop other groups coming forward and demanding to be paid anyway – the local unions, for example. I had no idea whether they'd been paid by the state or not in the past. There was no record if it. But then again, many records had simply vanished. In the same way I had to decide whether to pay artists when their representatives came knocking on my door. Again there were no records to guide me. In both these cases I decided not to make any payments.

Other cases were even less clear cut; should I pay war widows, pensioners, the sick, the invalided? All kinds of different groups came forward asking for money, some of them on the simple basis that if they didn't ask they'd never get anything. Sometimes the system stumbled because a DG failed to show up for our meeting. Curiously, a common excuse was that they were 'too tired' to come to see me. I never really knew what this meant.

Only once did one of the DGs try directly to defraud me. I'd allocated him $15,000, according to his staffing needs. The next day he reappeared at my office looking very crestfallen. 'Unfortunately I have to report that the $15,000 that you gave me yesterday has gone missing,' he explained via Abdul. 'It was stolen.'

'What do you expect me to do about it?' I replied, noting that the man was reluctant to look me in the eye.

'We need some more money,' he explained.

However, having translated this, Abdul quietly confirmed my suspicions by adding: 'Boss, I think he's lying, don't believe him.'

'I'm sorry there's no more money,' I told him briskly. 'If we followed this request for every organisation for which we're responsible, the budget would double and there wouldn't be enough money.' I thought for a moment and then added: 'Perhaps your work colleagues might be able to help you find the culprits, we can ask them to help you … ?' At this the DG looked genuinely frightened.

'Thank you for this meeting. Please do not worry, maybe we will find it somehow,' he said and hurriedly left. We never heard from him again.

Despite our initial successes the workload was mounting and we could barely cope. As well as Phil Smith and Abdul, Frances Castle and her staff gave me some assistance, but they had their own important work to do. Meanwhile I had a whole city to pay. However, I had a plan. I knew there were probably many TA officers and soldiers around with a range of useful civilian skills and with the help of Colonel Amos I put the word out for any such people to get in touch with me. Luckily one of the soldiers in the brigade tipped me off about a young TA corporal who used to work in a High Street bank in the UK. That was how Corporal Jude Dunn came to work with me. Jude, who was 33 at the time, is short with blonde hair, very athletic and seriously into sports. Like me she had come to Iraq as a member of the TA and like me she wasn't given the kind of role she had expected, thinking she'd be working in communications. Instead she had to fulfil a variety of other duties, ranging from sentry duty to filling sandbags.

She found the guard duty interesting even though it was incredibly hot standing up in the sentry tower in her full uniform, clutching her SA80 rifle. 'You could see right across the city from up there and even into people's backyards,' she said. 'We got the chance to talk with local people even though we weren't supposed to.' When she heard that I was interested in talking to her about finance work she jumped at the chance.

Jude was the perfect person to carry out the important task of paying Basra's wages. She was used to handling cash, even if not in quite the quantities that were lying around at the palace. 'I must admit it was bizarre walking in to find an ISO container full of money,' she said. 'And when I did my first cash check, finding that the sum was thirty million dollars!' But for her this was a chance to do challenging work. In the same way that I had by chance found myself working with the Iraqi Central Bank, now too by accident we'd stumbled upon a former bank manager who was ideal for the job in hand. In Jude I'd found a hard working, very able and loyal member of the team.

Jude and I soon decided that we ought to work full time from the CPA's dismal ex-electricity administration offices in the centre of Basra, the coalition's HQ in the south. It was a three-storey concrete office block with tiled floors and a central staircase into which the rudimentary air conditioning units fed. This made it like a furnace. As well as being the CPA staff's offices it was also their living quarters. These were equally appalling. For a while the CPA was utterly dependent on the good will of the military – it had nothing of its own, no operating budget, no access to food or equipment. The living quarters were very cramped with people sleeping many to a room wherever they could find space. The showers were adapted from old-style squat loos. Janet Rogan who had been one of the first women to live at the HQ said the portaloos when she arrived were of 'infamous levels of cleanliness'. 'It was so unsanitary that we ended up having a lot of people sick with diarrhoea and vomiting,' she said.

One of the challenges early on was coping when the various members of the coalition started sending teams of experts to help the CPA. These included volunteers from Japan, Denmark, Holland, Italy, Romania and the Czech Republic. 'Of course it was wonderful that they were willing to send these people so quickly. But we didn't always know that they were arriving, when they were arriving or what skills they had. We kept on getting more and more people, adding to a building that wasn't designed to be lived in and which was already full to over-crowding. It got to the point where we had to say "please do not send anyone else right now as we can't cope with them – there's nowhere for them to sleep, eat or work",' said Janet.

One of the problems was that the US contractors Kellogg Brown Root who were supposed to provide the CPA with its day-to-day necessities – what is known as its 'life support' – were unable to get into Basra from Kuwait. There was at the time no one to provide an escort for KBR and the route from Kuwait to Basra was judged not to be safe. In the meantime the CPA staff had to get meals from the Black Watch and later the Queen's Lancashire Regiment who were based next to the CPA building. In fact conditions were so difficult in the building that Janet joked that she was considering calling in the International Committee of the Red Cross to carry out an inspection. 'I decided they might find our circumstances worse than most prisons!' she said. Tash Coxen also told me that one doctor had seriously raised the question of getting the place closed down under health and safety rules. Some government departments – including those in the UK – were later reluctant to send more of their staff to work in such conditions, even though the volunteers from ministries such as the Department of Health had worked there uncomplainingly.

The CPA was led by a Danish ambassador called Ole Wohlers Olsen, a convert to Sunni Islam. His deputy was

Brigadier Gregory and his chief of staff was another Dane called Allan Rosenberg, who had worked for the Danish shipping company Maersk in the Middle East. Below them were the experts sent in from around the world. Though the CPA had lots of goodwill and talent, I felt it lacked shape and focus. In particular few people seemed to be looking at the big picture when it came to the economy.

The economy in southern Iraq had been brought to a near standstill by the invasion. I'd learnt from my time in Kosovo the importance of getting an economy back on its feet and people back to work. If people have jobs and a stable economy they are far more likely to feel they have a vested interest in working together for the future. Making sure people got their wages on time so that money could return to the local economy would have been a good start. Yet few people had time to focus on this. Instead, the CPA was mainly looking at small short-term projects. While useful in themselves, these didn't really help long-term economic development.

This issue came to a head at a meeting of CPA staff one morning. An American colonel called Jeff Smith was in charge of 'projects' for the south and the main finance person. Brigadier Gregory asked him what the situation was. The colonel started explaining in his heavy American drawl how this week he was spending about $100,000 on a particular project. I was quietly seething at the back of the room. This wasn't what finance should be about. Then the brigadier looked over to me. 'Is that it, Andrew?'

'Well actually, Sir, we have paid fourteen million dollars to one hundred and ten thousand people in the last ten days and we're broadly on track,' I said. The US colonel's expression changed. I think he suddenly realised that he was losing control of the 'finance' that he had cherished up to now. And, as a full colonel, he wasn't exactly pleased at being elbowed aside by a TA major.

That meeting was a seminal moment for me. Later Allan

Rosenberg encouraged me. He told me: 'Andrew, you have to remember that organisations gravitate towards those who get things done.' Janet too spoke to me about the possibility of taking on responsibility for broader economic issues. My role may have been growing, but as the new boy at the CPA I was given the last and worst office. It was barely six feet by five feet and had to house not just me but, Phil too. The room directly above was a bathroom that occasionally overflowed, so my office had the deeply unpleasant tell-tale traces of sewage bubbling down its painted walls. Iraqi visitors couldn't fathom this arrangement. One day the Governor of Basra province Judge Abdul al-Latif came to the building and saw me in my broom cupboard.

'Hello, Mr Andrew, how are you? I don't understand you English people – why is it that you have the most money but you have the smallest office. To us Arabs this cannot be right. Maybe you are not so important, after all … ' he laughed and lit a cigarette.

'Well I don't like to make a big fuss, Governor,' I replied.

Though the tension in the city had subsided after we'd started making our payments, we were still vulnerable in Basra. This was underlined late one July evening when I returned to the palace compound after another exhausting day down at the CPA building. As was my habit I'd gone off to the portaloos for my evening constitutional. (I preferred to use them when it was less hot because the smell was marginally less unpleasant.) At 11 pm it was still pretty hot as well as completely dark so I was clad in only my boxer shorts. I'd just settled down in the pitch blackness of the loo when all hell broke loose. I could hear and see trace rounds lighting up the sky as what seemed like the whole city went bonkers. At first it looked like 'happy rounds' – when people fire their weapons in the air in celebration. These are not by any means harmless – when the bullets come down they reach terminal velocity and can easily kill someone. Then I noticed something else. A gunman had started firing over the front gate of the palace and these rounds were dipping over the gates and spraying all over the compound. These are called 'gravity shots' and can be lethal. These bullets were now flying straight past my loo.

I was in a very dangerous situation. If a shot hit the loo there were only four thin sheets of plastic separating me from the bullet and I didn't fancy my chances. On the other hand with all those rounds going off I knew that running for shelter would be a lottery. I considered diving into the waters of the nearby Shat Al-Arab but realised I would probably be mistaken for an attacker and shot by one of our own sentries. For at least 60 seconds I weighed up these unappealing options. Then I made my decision. If I stayed, the chance was that I'd get shot while sitting on the karsy – not the stuff of Victoria Crosses! I know they say you should wear a clean pair of underpants in case you are suddenly killed. But I didn't want to be found in ONLY my underpants …

So with bullets still whizzing in all directions I opened the door and sprinted for cover. I headed towards the safety of the large pillars in front of the main accommodation block. I'd just got there and was gasping for breath when suddenly I looked up – and saw to my horror that many of my fellow officers were also standing behind the pillars. They were all in full battle gear. Captain John Godfrey took one look at me and remarked drily: 'Andrew, I think you're a touch under dressed for this.' By the time the laughter had subsided and I'd got into my uniform we heard the reason for the outbreak of 'happy rounds'. Just before 11 pm international TV news channels had broken the news that Saddam Hussein's sons Uday and Qusay had been shot and killed by US troops. The brothers were especially hated by the downtrodden Shi'ia population of Basra.

These were difficult days for the CPA in Basra, as it struggled to establish its authority and get a grip of events. The military certainly had a poor view of the interim administration. 'Dysfunctional' was one of the kinder descriptions flying about in army circles at the time. The military approach is to get out there and get things moving. Yet there was little sign of the CPA doing anything other than reacting to events. General Graham Lamb was head of the division and the senior British soldier in southern Iraq at the time. He was a tough, uncompromising man and a very talented soldier as you would expect from someone who's ex-Special Forces. When I met him at the bottom of the stairs in the CPA building we were introduced by his interpreter – an Arabic-speaking acquaintance of mine from officer cadet days – who explained I was working in finance in the authority.

'Yes I've heard about this,' said General Lamb. 'Look, I don't know what it is you're exactly doing around here but you're the only person who seems to be having any success at the moment – just keep doing whatever it is you're doing.'

The CPA's early problems weren't helped when in late July the boss, Danish Ambassador Ole Olsen suddenly announced he was leaving. Officially the ambassador said that it was a 'convenient' time for him to leave as the administration in Iraq was being re-organised. But Mr Olsen still had three and a half months of his six-month stint to run. His abrupt departure may have had to do with his criticism of the authorities in Baghdad, particularly of what he saw as a lack of support over the security issue. 'My people in the administration office have no security guards with them as they move around – and I'm not happy about that,' one media outlet reported him as saying. Others said there was a clash of personalities.

Whatever the real reasons for it, Ole Olsen's departure didn't help the organisation. However, I now sensed a real opportunity to make my mark. The payment of the wages was going as well as it could in the circumstances. But still no one else was looking at a strategic approach, establishing links between the various Iraqi organisations and trying to return the region to some kind of economic normality. I decided to make what I later called my 'land grab'. I went to see Allan

Rosenberg and he explained that he was helping to put together a chart of the new organisation. He wanted to know where I saw myself fitting in. I seized my chance. 'I'm not sure quite how to put this Allan,' I said to him. 'But though I could do just the finance bit I'd really like to look after all the economic ministries. I think I have got pay more or less under control and I'd like to spread out and look at the bigger picture and help with reconstruction.'

Allan seemed happy to go along with that. 'Fine,' he said. 'If that's what you want I'll put you in for it.' He was following his own maxim that organisations tend to get driven by the people who get things done. The news that my responsibility was about to be massively increased wasn't received well by everyone.

One colonel was overheard saying. 'But I'm a colonel and he's a major, he can't be made responsible for all this!' But Allan refused to be dissuaded.

The result was that as well as paying salaries, I was suddenly now to be responsible for all the so-called economic ministries – agriculture, irrigation, power, oil and gas, water, telecoms, housing and construction, finance, trade, industry and minerals, planning, health, education, transport, labour and social affairs. In other words the key functions that would make or break the economy. My task was to help completely rebuild these ministries and their departments in the south. I had to get them to a good enough state that they could then be taken over again by the people who should be running them – the Iraqis. I knew it would require money, time, lots of hard work and good luck; and of course the backing of the coalition authorities and the co-operation of the Iraqis themselves. But as I looked around me at the CPA offices there was one thing I knew I needed more than anything if I was to pull this off. And that was people.

*

Raneen had come with her brother, not wanting to arrive for the interview at the CPA building on her own. She'd heard I was looking for an assistant and had come to apply for the job. Raneen was in her mid-30s and had spent some time in Australia where she'd learnt her English, and had also worked for a United Nations organisation as an assistant, so she was relatively used to the western way of life. As I chatted with her in an upstairs room at the CPA building I initially had my doubts. Though her English was better than some of the other candidates I'd seen, she seemed very timid. However, the longer we spoke the more I realised there was something about her, and in her eyes I could see a quiet strength. So I hired her for the modest sum of $150 a month. Raneen was delighted. Like most Iraqis I met at the time she was very happy that the old regime had gone and was looking forward with optimism to the future of her country. She wanted to be part of that future by helping the CPA in its rebuilding work. Raneen turned out to be an inspired choice and worked loyally for me and the CPA for the next year. In time she would become more like an executive assistant. The only area in which she wasn't entirely comfortable was working as an interpreter. As a woman she always felt awkward dealing with the Iraqi officials who were all male.

Another key member of what would become my 'team' arrived about the same time. Phil Smith's tour of duty had ended and he was replaced by an Irishman called Pat McLoughlin. Pat is a chartered accountant and exactly the kind of person I was looking for. In time he became my right-hand man, my *de facto* deputy and we shared an office together for most of the next year. We were very different characters though. I was the optimistic one whereas he always saw the dark side of things and was very cynical. I called him 'Black Pat'. But he had a great sense of humour. A tall man, he was also very slim and despite the vast amounts of often American-style food that was on offer in our canteen he never put on an ounce – while some of us exploded in weight. In his mid-40s Pat also had the advantage of great experience; he had worked in 'post-conflict' situations in Kosovo and Montenegro so he knew what to expect and how to manage difficult situations. Over the next year he took over the financial side of things, in day-to-day charge of the large amounts of money that was moving around.

As well as people we also needed furniture. By now we'd moved to a slightly larger office on the first floor of the CPA building but we had no equipment and had to beg steal or borrow what we could. We may nominally have been in charge of the economy in southern Iraq but that didn't stop me from having to send out the interpreters to find a desk in the street that we could use. I couldn't even get hold of pencils. Though we were processing millions of dollars in cash for the city's workers, we never received any budget for equipment or supplies. It was an example of the kind of oversight that arose from the chaos and confusion after the invasion. So Pat and I devised a cunning plan.

The local Finance Ministry was still not up and running at this time but when it was it would need new equipment to replace what had been looted. So we wrote a project to fund these supplies even though the ministry officials weren't yet around. The idea was that we'd use the equipment while we waited for them to show up. As long as we kept a careful record of our spending I reckoned it would be OK.

Once the project was approved we had to find the supplies. We requested permission to drive to Kuwait for 24 hours to equip ourselves. Pat then called a member of the army supply staff in Kuwait and asked if we might make a visit. He also asked the man if he could lay his hands on a number of computers and some general office supplies. The local quartermaster agreed and we gave him our shopping list over the phone and arranged to meet him the following evening at the Marina Mall car park in the centre of Kuwait City. By now there were so many military convoys on the route to Kuwait that it was considered safe for civilian vehicles. So Pat and I resolved to drive there ourselves. First, though, we needed to find out how to get there. We asked around the CPA building and a Danish policeman – who was helping train local officers – kindly gave us directions. 'Head out of the city on the road south, over the bridge, then turn right at the two mosques and after an hour you will be at the border,' he told us. 'Kuwait city is an hour and a half through the desert to the south.' The Danish officer made it sound very easy. We hoped it would be – there wouldn't be many people to ask for directions out in the desert.

'Refuel in Doha on the way back and make sure to bring it back in one piece,' said the former sergeant major responsible for the CPA's vehicles as Pat and I finally set off in the large automatic GMC 'Suburban' we'd borrowed for the day. All we had was my pistol, a full tank of petrol, my UK mobile phone – and a small map. I'd volunteered to drive the first leg of the trip and I was suddenly feeling very nervous. We drove out of the CPA and followed the airport road before turning south and into the unknown.

With some relief we spotted the two mosques the Danish policeman had mentioned and headed off into the desert. The road was badly worn and at various intervals along each side we saw industrial buildings that I'd later discover were the assorted cement, petrochemical and fertiliser plants that would be such a focus of our work. Further south we could also see the flaming gas towers of the oil facilities and we used these as a navigational aid. Into the distance stretched mile after mile of electricity pylons, many of them leaning drunkenly in the desert heat. In many places the cables didn't appear to be connected.

There were no road signs until, just a few miles north of the border, we saw the name 'Kuwait' sprayed in large English letters on a concrete slab. At the border crossing I wound down the window and flashed my military ID card, allowing us to pass safely out of Iraq. In Kuwait, the contrast was immediately apparent. The road surface improved dramatically and the pylons were straight and painted red and white, their cables properly connected with each other. But in other respects the only distinction between the two places seemed to be that someone had literally drawn a line on a map, which translated into a score in the sand. On one side chaos ruled while on the other was one of the wealthiest states on the planet. Suddenly we were back in a first-world economy.

Pat and I followed the signs to Kuwait City and Jumeira Beach where some of the brigade staff had recommended that we stay in a three-star hotel they knew. The sight of garish advertising signs next to the road again reminded us of the extraordinary transition we'd made. So too did the offer of valet parking for our dusty, number-plate-less vehicle when we finally arrived at the hotel. We checked in using our own credit cards. 'I need a bath and running water then a good meal with metal cutlery,' announced Pat. It was exactly how I felt too.

The next morning we met our quartermaster contact, and together the three of us visited a Kuwaiti souk that specialised in electronics and IT equipment. After half an hour we'd chosen all we thought we needed and then went shopping for clothes with our own money. We found a branch of Marks & Spencer and we each bought a couple of sets of civilian clothes. On the way back to Basra we pulled off the main road to head for a large US military base. I showed my military ID card and the somewhat surprised guard let us through to the fuel pumps. 'We're just down from Basra,' said Pat smiling, 'can we get some fuel?'

'Where are you from again?' asked the soldier at the pump, 'Is that Basra … as in Iraq? I've heard it's dangerous there!'

'We're with the British,' said Pat in his broad Irish accent by way of explanation. I signed for a full tank, leaving my name, army rank and serial number and, after more shopping in the camp shop, we returned to Basra safely. Two days later our equipment arrived. At last we were in business. And we also had some new clothes, much to the delight of Abdul who had noticed that I'd been struggling sartorially. 'Boss, I think you could do with a couple more shirts,' he'd told me one day. So off he'd gone into the streets of Basra and had come back a few hours later laden down with shirts, jeans and shoes. I was very grateful for his efforts and the shirts and especially the jeans were very useful – I still have a pair. But I'd drawn the line at the shoes. These were typically Iraqi – as big as boats and more plastic than leather.

Apart from buying me clothes, Abdul's original role as interpreter had expanded to acting as a kind of gatekeeper, protecting me from people I didn't need to meet things I didn't need to hear. In one meeting three Iraqis had come in demanding to be paid a certain salary. They said that they were the martyrs of the Iran–Iraq War – the bloody eight-year conflict that ended in 1988 and cost a million lives. I explained through Abdul that they weren't on the list of people to be paid. One of then went off in a long tirade in Arabic that must have lasted five minutes. As the man eventually stopped to catch his breath I asked Abdul whether the visitor was all right. 'No,' was Abdul's simple one-word response, thoughtfully sparing me the vitriolic detail of what the man had said. Though I had no real idea what their precise claim was, I did include them in the list of pensioners and pay them. This was my usual policy, to include as many people as I could without setting any dangerous precedents. At least it would save me from getting another haranguing from this man in the future.

By now Jude, Pat and I had learnt to spot when people were trying it on. One day a director general came in and announced that he had had 300 more workers on his payroll than the previous month. 'But where on earth have they suddenly come from?' I asked.

'Last month they were sleeping,' he told me, with a straight face. It was typical of the many excuses we heard for variations in the payroll and this was where Jude played a major role. She was good at making sure that the DGs got paid only what they'd been paid before.

Despite our payments, there was still discontent on the streets. We were desperately short-staffed and it wasn't always possible to pay all the workers on time. Yet missing just one set of payments could instantly spark off strikes. Meanwhile water and electricity supplies were still patchy, the sewage system wasn't functioning properly, there were fuel shortages and the run-down health system wasn't working. On top of that there were the rising August temperatures. 'It is known as the month of revolutions in my country,' Abdul pointed out helpfully. It was also the month when Saddam Hussein had celebrated his own coming to power.

Despite the tensions there were occasional lighter moments. At the time Janet Rogan was *de facto* head of mission and she was worried – as we all were – about the constant protests that took place outside the CPA building as the heat got worse. 'Something changes climatically at that time of year and as well as extreme heat you get extreme humidity,' said Janet. 'And basically it's just unbearable.' However, she knew that local people had obeyed the law under the Saddam regime and figured that Iraqis must be generally law abiding. So she went to the British police officers with the CPA who were helping to train local officers. She asked them to write a short and simple public order regulation explaining to the Iraqis how to demonstrate peacefully. They produced one in 24 hours.

'It explained to the protestors that they were supposed to give 48 hours' notice of a protest, that there had to be wardens with armbands who were responsible for people's safety and so on. And it had a wonderful ending,' said Janet. 'It read "the waving of flags and the singing of songs is to be encouraged" I thought that was great!' The notice was translated into Arabic and read and approved by Governor Abdul al-Latif, who had been nominated to his post by a council of local dignitaries set up by the CPA. It was then distributed on leaflets before Friday prayers so that the message would get to as many people as possible. 'And the following day nothing happened – there was no demonstration!' said Janet. That day she worked late as usual and an Iraqi guard outside her office spent the entire evening singing. 'When I walked past him later he had a big grin on his face. I didn't speak Arabic, but I knew perfectly well that he was singing because he had read the ordinance.'

The tension continued to grow, however. One factor was oil, which is of course essential to the economy of Iraq. The south controlled about 75 per cent of the country's oil production. This made Mr Waleed a very important man. Mr Waleed was the director general of South Oil, the main production company in the south, and one of the most impressive Iraqis I met. A local sheikh, he was a well-built man in his late 50s with grey hair, a round face, very round eyes and a great sense of humour. He was also a very tough negotiator and a born survivor; he survived several attempts on his life while I was there. The first thing he said to me was: 'Mr Andrew, I am an important person and you will need to pay attention to me.' Then he paused. 'And anyway, why am I coming to your office instead of you coming to visit me in mine?' His second comment was no less direct. 'And by the way you owe me three million US dollars for our profits last year.' This was a problem that had been brewing for some time. Not all the state organisations worked in the same way. Departments such as health, for example, were non-profit making entities that couldn't raise money on their own and were entirely dependent on state payments. However, some state companies – such as the various oil companies – were able to raise finance to pay for equipment and day-to-day supplies. When the invasion happened all Iraqi bank accounts, including those of the oil companies, had been frozen and 'zeroed' by the

Americans, leaving them with a net balance of zero. Yet though this policy made sense – given that nearly all organisations were state-funded anyway – many Iraqis either were not aware of it or disagreed with it. The oil company had traditionally been allowed to pay its staff bonuses from its profits. And as far as the Iraqis were concerned these profits were now trapped in an inaccessible account. Mr Waleed had already raised this question with Brigadier Gregory. The brigadier had sought advice from Baghdad, who insisted that on no account were the oil bonuses to be paid. Brigadier Gregory's tour of duty had ended and he'd been replaced by Brigadier Bruce Brearley – but the answer on the bonuses had still been no. Now Mr Waleed was trying his luck with me.

'Mr Waleed, Baghdad has said you can't have them and your account has been zeroed, so there's nothing I can do,' I explained. But Mr Waleed was a forceful man and, not happy to accept this, demanded I do something. So I agreed to email David Oliver's office. As ever, however, the message came back that I wasn't to release the money.

In the meantime Mr Waleed was working on a separate strategy. He knew that there were two chains of command. One was the western one, under which I had to follow what my American counterparts in Baghdad were saying. The other was the Iraqi one in which Mr Waleed reported to his Iraqi bosses in the capital, many of whom had now returned or had recently been appointed. This chain of command reported everything formally in writing in Arabic and was therefore notoriously slow. There were no direct telephone links at this time between Basra and Baghdad as the telephone switches had been blown up. So, communications took place by letter or personal courier. It could therefore take up to four days for a message to be sent and replied to – and as long as ten days for agreement to be reached by the time several queries had been answered. Moreover, these parallel command chains didn't always talk to each other. This meant that different and often conflicting instructions were passed from Baghdad down the two communication lines.

Mr Waleed knew how to exploit this to his advantage. Unbeknown to me he had complained to the oil minister about the frozen bank accounts. He explained how it made his job very difficult and that they needed the accounts to operate more effectively for business. The minister duly raised this issue with the Americans. As Mr Waleed had planned, I now got an email from David Oliver's office in Baghdad instructing me to unfreeze South Oil's bank account. I got on the satellite phone to David Oliver's office.

'You know that as soon as the accounts are opened they will take those three million dollars for their bonus payments, don't you?' I told an official.

'They can't, because they are not authorised,' came the deadpan reply. Great, I thought, that's really going to stop them. So I put in my fears in an email. Of course I'd follow Baghdad's instructions, I said. But I said I could not be held accountable if, once those accounts were unfrozen, the company withdrew money to pay the very oil-worker bonuses that the same office in Baghdad had expressly forbidden. And it would also affect our work. If the oil workers withdrew the cash the Central Bank would be down by $3 million and we'd have no way to make up that shortfall to ensure other wages were paid. But Oliver's office was adamant.

So I followed Baghdad's orders and authorised the Central Bank to open the accounts. The next day I had a call from a British major at division HQ. The military had by now realised that paying people's wages on time made the security situation easier. This major wanted to make sure I knew the oil workers needed to be paid today. 'What do you think?' I replied. 'Given the fact that I'm in charge of paying them and that it was almost certainly me who told the division when they would be paid, I think there is a fair chance I do know, yes,' I continued, unable to hide my exasperation.

I then rang Mr Waleed. 'I have six million dollars waiting here to pay your staff their monthly wages,' I told him. There was a slight pause at the other end of the line.

'Er, thank you, Mr Andrew, but we are very busy today and we cannot collect the money.'

'Why is that?' I replied, by now guessing what was coming.

'Because we are still very busy counting out the three million you sent us yesterday,' he responded. 'Thank you very much – we will speak to you soon. Goodbye.' Mr Waleed had played a blinder. I had to admire him for that.

In the days after the invasion CPA staff had gone out to restaurants in the centre of Basra for meals. There was a regular group who used to go out most Thursday evenings at the start of the Iraqi weekend and sample the cuisine in some of the excellent local restaurants. Some officials had also stayed in city-centre hotels and gone out for lunches. By now such behaviour on the street of Basra was unthinkable. I wasn't alone in feeling an explosion was imminent.

Late one evening Colonel David Amos came to see me and found me exhausted, desperately trying to reconcile salary figures for yet another group of oil workers I hardly knew anything about. 'How's it going?' he asked.

'This is a losing battle,' I replied, 'because we just don't have enough people. And every time we think we've solved one thing, we discover another set of problems more complicated than the first.'

'What do you mean?' he asked.

I explained the problems. Though we were getting up to date with most of the salaries, we now discovered we needed to sort out operating budgets and bank accounts, and spares and equipment for all the different government departments. Some of these departments had no offices because they'd been bombed and looted – they didn't even have a desk or a telephone. And we wondered why nothing was working. 'Just to make it even worse, every time we think we've understood the problem there's another email from Baghdad with more detailed instructions. And these contradict those that we received from someone else the day before in the same department, as well as the Arabic version that has been sent down the Iraqi chain of command. Basically, I'm worried that we cannot keep it together and something is going to blow.'

'Andrew, you'll have to let it go,' said David. 'The only way that London will understand is if this starts to go wrong. You are hugely understaffed and don't have enough resources. When this goes off and hits the front page of the press then Whitehall will wake up and pay attention.'

The final spark was lit by the oil-distribution workers, unhappy that the staff at the South Oil Company were being paid more than them. An elaborate game had developed as each set of workers demanded to be paid more than the next. When one group received $60 a month the next wanted $80 and so on. The result was huge wage inflation. Even worse in the short term was that the oil distribution workers, led by a determined character called Mr Saed, now carried out their threats to go on strike. Already there was a chronic lack of electricity, medical supplies, cooking gas canisters, jobs, and education – soon there would be no petrol in the filling stations either. And this was guaranteed to make a bad situation even worse.

The first worrying indication came when the streets around the CPA building fell unnaturally quiet. It was the calm before the storm. Suddenly at about 10 am an angry crowd started to arrive carrying old car tyres, a sure sign that serious trouble was about to break out. Burning old tyres is a traditional protest action in Basra. Inside the CPA the military prepared to defend the building. There were few of them. The regiment based next door was already out in the city quelling potential trouble there. So at the CPA itself there was just a thin khaki line of senior officers working for the organisation – led by

Brigadier Brearley himself. The most junior rank on this exclusive defensive line was a sergeant major. There was an uneasy stand off as protestors came and went with some of them turning their attention to the nearby governor's building and lobbing missiles at it. Then we heard that trouble had broken out across the city with shots being fired as the army put armoured cars and armoured personnel carriers on street corners. The city was now 'locked down' meaning that all staff movement was restricted. The honeymoon in Basra was well and truly over.

When the riots started I was at the palace. But I had a problem. Yet another group of oil workers – this time belonging to Mr Waleed – needed to be paid. Unless this was done immediately they too would go on strike. But because of the lock-down Mr Waleed couldn't come to see me or I to go see him. Instead we hit on a plan. I was flown by Chinook helicopter to the divisional headquarters at Basra airport out of town, where Mr Waleed's representative was to meet me. I waited and waited for him, and had nearly given up on him when he finally arrived. He was very frightened as he told me what had happened. His car had been stopped and then set alight by a crowd of angry protestors along the way, his phone was stolen and he was roughed up. Fortunately he had been able to escape and had bravely made it the rest of the way on foot. But he was badly shaken. 'I thought I was going to die,' he told me. However, now at least we could arrange for his workers to be paid. I later learnt I'd been the only member of the CPA to move around the city that day.

The next day yet another payment crisis blew up. Some 12,000 port workers at the main port were threatening to go on strike if they didn't get their money on time. But the city was still in lock-down so how on earth could we get it to them? I was standing in brigade headquarters pondering this logistical headache when I decided to have another look at the map of the city. Getting from the palace to the port through the city was nigh on impossible. But the palace was surrounded by the huge Shat Al-Arab waterway and the port was just a relatively short distance upstream ... I decided it was worth a try. I asked the colonel of the engineers who were based at the HQ if I could borrow a couple of his rigid raiders, the large and very powerful landing craft used by the marines. Naturally enough the colonel asked why and I explained. I'd decided to take the port workers their money by boat.

Now all I needed were two volunteers to carry out the job. I explained to Jude and Captain Martin Dyson what needed to be done and they quickly agreed to help. The city may have been in lock-down but for them it was a chance to get out of the office and involved in some action. Around $1 million in cash was put carefully into four black bin liners and then aboard the two boats with Jude, Martin and the two crews. Within seconds they were racing away, underneath the temporary pontoon bridge built by the marines and up the waterway, past various half-sunken boats, including Saddam's former yacht lying forlornly on its side. Their first stop was the Central Bank which was helpfully sited right on the river. They ran inside, got the necessary paperwork signed off by a startled staff – fortunately they knew Jude though they were surprised to see her in uniform and armed – and then made off again up the Shat Al-Arab. Finally they reached the port where they made the local DG sign for the cash, dumped the four bin liners with him and sped off again back to the palace. That was one group of amazed but very happy port workers.

I also had two very happy volunteers post-mission. Jude especially was upbeat. 'It was an absolutely amazing experience,' she recalled later. 'Here I was going up a river in military attire with armed marines and a million dollars in black bin bags. It was surreal – almost like a James Bond film; the sort of thing you might see on TV but not the kind of thing you ever expect to get involved in!' she said.

The riots continued, fuelled by more power shortages. A former Ghurkha soldier working for the United Nations was shot as he drove through the city. He was immediately taken to the CPA building nearby and given emergency treatment in a corridor right outside Janet Rogan's office. The man had only been in the region for two weeks, and despite the desperate first aid he died. 'On one side of his identity card he had a photograph of green wooded hills and mountains, obviously a picture from home,' recalled Janet. 'The thought of this man from the mountains of Nepal coming all this way to Iraq to die from a random sniper bullet in a dusty corridor in the CPA building struck me as immensely sad.'

As David Amos had predicted, the stories of riots and deaths in Basra made headlines around the world and Whitehall suddenly began to pay closer attention to the situation in the city. Up to that time the occupation of the south by the British and other coalition nations had seemed relatively trouble free, at least compared with the American sector around Baghdad. The riots in Basra changed all that.

4

MAKING A PLAN AMID THE CHAOS

September 2003

One of the most senior British officials in Iraq was an experienced civil servant called Andy Bearpark. He was director of operations for the Coalition Provisional Authority in Baghdad and one of Paul Bremer's right-hand men. His brief was to help oversee the transition of the regions to Iraqi government. In August Andy flew back to London and returned to Baghdad with the latest thinking on the future of the coalition effort in the country. Janet Rogan then called in the CPA Basra staff for a meeting. She explained what the plan was. And for me it came as huge shock.

Iraq had traditionally been divided into 18 different governorates or provinces. In the south, the British and other non-US nations' sector, there were four in all. These were Al-Basra where we were based, Dhi Qar to the north-west and whose main city is Nasariyah, Maysan governorate to the north, where the main settlement is Al-Amarah and finally the vast desert lands of Al-Muthanna governorate to the south. Its main town is Samawah. Together these four provinces contain nearly a fifth of Iraq's total population of 28 million.

Janet explained that the plan was to mirror the Iraqi system in our own structure. This meant that instead of trying to administer southern Iraq as a region from Basra there would be separate governorate teams set up in the four provinces. These would all report directly to Baghdad. As for the CPA South itself, that in theory was to disappear. I was appalled. It may have sounded great in theory to follow the Iraqi system. But one of the reasons why the centralised Iraqi government hadn't worked well was precisely because they had 18 different groups reporting into the centre to be told what to do. I'd also found it hard enough finding a small team of three to run the finances for Basra, so where would we suddenly find another nine – three for each of the other governorates? Moreover, for every front-line person there would need to be up to ten support staff, providing logistics, security, food, communications and technical support. I wondered if anyone had thought this through.

Baghdad's answer was that the governorate teams or GTs would be embedded into the military bases that were already in the different provinces. They would give the GTs the support and logistics they needed. But I felt this would send out entirely the wrong message. The interim civilian government was supposed to be reaching out directly to the Iraqis. But how could they do that if they were hiding away in military bases? It seemed to me that this was the voice of Washington speaking through their mouthpieces in Baghdad and that the British sector – the southern region – was being sidelined. I left the meeting shaking my head in disbelief. Ole Stokholm Jepsen, the Danish adviser on farming and irrigation issues, agreed and called the plan nuts.

Later I had an argument with Janet about it all. 'This makes no sense – we're establishing a mirror command or soviet-style administration identical to the one that the Iraqis have, and which we know doesn't work … ' I complained.

'We have to fix what the Iraqis have, before we can change it.' Janet explained.

I was incredulous. 'So the capitalist free-market champions of the western world, the UK and the US, are proposing to rebuild a soviet economy?'

'Yes,' she said.

'This is crazy,' I said.

Meanwhile the British military's patience with the CPA was growing thin. Since May some officers had been scathing about the ineffectiveness of the CPA and its apparent inability to deal with the chronic shortages of water, electricity, the problems with sewage and so on. I heard General Lamb describe working with the CPA as 'like being forced to dance with a dysfunctional partner, wedded at the hip, with flailing arms and legs constantly in the way'.

In its defence the CPA had very few staff. The British military, on the other hand, had something like 15,000 men and women in southern Iraq at the time. And it was now that a Colonel Tim Grimshaw from division came forward with a plan. Colonel Tim – affectionately nicknamed 'Grim Tim' by some of his staff – was a man on a mission. Since his arrival he had been busy sending out his engineers to see what needed to be done to the country's infrastructure. They visited power stations, water pumping stations, sewage plants and other key areas to see what could be fixed. As a result he drew up what became known as the Emergency Infrastructure Plan or EIP. Colonel Tim reckoned that with $105 million of Whitehall cash he and his engineers could solve many of the immediate infrastructure problems facing southern Iraq.

In many ways the plan was a great idea. It showed the military at its best: getting things done in a difficult environment. And with so many Iraqis angry at the lack of progress swift action was needed. However, I had my misgivings. The plan focussed heavily on kit and machinery. There was little provision made for the ongoing running costs of the utilities that the army were to fix. The plan envisaged precious little engagement with the Iraqi people, yet without the involvement of the Iraqis themselves few projects had any long-term chance of survival. However, the plan began to make its way up the chain of command towards Whitehall and they got excited by it. Colonel Tim was a very determined operator.

No one disputed that the utilities infrastructure needed fixing. Ed Lock, a British army captain who was seconded to my team told me: 'What wasn't destroyed in the Iran–Iraq war was bombed by us in Gulf War One and anything that was still working after that has now been looted by the Iraqis.' The key question was how to co-ordinate its reconstruction in a way that was practical, sustainable and fitted in with the needs of the economy. Though the military in southern Iraq had 1,500 engineers their work didn't necessarily take that into account. For example, the military installed or repaired several diesel generators in Basra. This was a short-term engineering solution – what the military called a 'Quick Impact Project'. Yet these projects were ultimately unsustainable, because Iraq was a net importer of diesel and the local director generals understandably didn't want to spend precious operating budgets on expensive diesel fuel. Nor were operating budgets in Baghdad changed to allow for the extra money needed to keep such installations going. Moreover, though the military engineers had a great deal of experience, being able to repair or rebuild 1,000 MW power stations and national water and telephone networks was quite a different matter.

Meanwhile, my job wasn't getting any easier. In theory I was still in charge of working with the many economic ministries. But I had very few staff to do this and the plan to re-organize the CPA into provinces seemed about to abolish my organisation anyway. My task got even harder when early one evening Nei-San, the head of the nine-strong Japanese mission at the CPA, sought out Allan Rosenberg in his office. Nei-San, a delightful softly spoken man, politely sought permission for himself and his team to leave for Kuwait. Japanese public opinion had been shaken by the violence in Baghdad and Basra and the government in Tokyo was now reluctant to put its staff at further risk. Allan could hardly refuse the request and so at around 6pm the Japanese contingent loaded their vehicles and set off, never to be seen again.

The departure of the Japanese was a big loss. They were hard-working and skilled engineers and had made detailed drawings and assessments of many of the essential utilities in southern Iraq. Not only had we lost nine staff, we'd also lost much of their knowledge of the electricity network, the telephone network and basic utilities – one of the core activities for which I had responsibility. This just left Ed Lock, a British army captain, Colin McBride, a TA major and myself with responsibility to oversee 'utilities and essential services' for CPA South.

It was a low point for the CPA. The next day the new head of CPA south Sir Hilary Synnott was due to arrive. I wondered exactly what he would make of his inheritance. At the same time Janet had been urging me to set out how many people I needed for my team and what their job descriptions or Terms of Reference – TOR – should be. 'We're speaking to several UK government departments and asking them to send people to help, which is why I need you to write TORs for each post,' she explained.

'Who are they sending?' My heart sank at the thought of more civil servants. Janet said they were speaking to various government departments in Whitehall. But they couldn't decide who to send until I'd written the job descriptions.

'You must be joking … ' I said irritably. 'I'm spending 18 hours a day trying to keep this thing together, paying everyone to stop us getting killed. We reckon we need 50 staff for the economic activities alone – I don't have time for writing detailed job descriptions for every one of them.' By now I was getting quite angry. 'We don't need more bureaucrats, we have enough of a dysfunctional Iraqi government already. I need specialists from the private sector. This is a second-world economy that needs to be re-built, not an aid programme.' I knew Janet was right about one thing, however. I did need to establish exactly who I needed for my team.

Ed Lock and I found ourselves sitting in the CPA utilities office. On the flaking pale yellow walls were military maps and satellite images of Basra, Nasariya, Maysan and Al Muthanna detailing the various key installations that had been examined by the Japanese. Their research had begun to uncover what was needed to repair the telecommunications network, the power stations, the distribution grid, the fresh-water system and the sewage network. Each clutching a mug of coffee, Ed and I looked around at the now empty desks and considered our dilemma. 'We have the division and its engineers running around under Colonel Tim, totally separate from us and trying to deal direct with CPA in Baghdad themselves,' said Ed. 'And because I'm a captain and he's a colonel, it's rather tricky.'

'Well,' I said, 'we have a new ambassador arriving tomorrow and I think the first thing he's going to ask me is what *we* need.'

'It's obvious,' said Ed, 'we need more warm bodies who know what they are doing … and this time do you think we could get some that speak English too?' I grinned and took out my notebook. Not all of the coalition volunteers had spoken great English which sometimes made communications hard.

'So what do we need?' I asked. I turned to the back of the book and started writing. 'Electricity' was my first heading.

'Well, there's power generation, the transmission network and the distribution network,' said Ed, who was an expert in this area. 'There are three organisations and they are organised regionally.'

'OK,' I said. 'So we need at least one specialist for each department because they are different disciplines?' I queried. He agreed. 'So that's three people in the electricity team, ' I said. Next I wrote 'Water'.

'There's Reverse Osmosis water [where salt water is made drinkable], water for drinking, networked water for washing and cleaning, black water or sewage and also solid waste,' Ed explained. 'A big issue, so we need more people for this.'

'OK – two people for each specialism then?' I suggested. 'That makes eight people for the water team. What's next?'

In this way Ed and I gradually worked our way through the various utilities sectors – electricity and power generation, water and sanitation, oil and gas, and telecoms. For each team we then worked out the need for interpreters, a team leader, drivers and security. Having 'done' utilities, Ed and I moved on to 'Finance Trade and Industry' – the second of my three areas of responsibility. For these we carved out departments of finance, Central Bank, trade, industry, transport, agriculture, housing, roads and construction. By the time the sun had set we'd finished the first two areas and were at approximately 24 additional members of staff. The trick in our staffing request to Whitehall was to balance what was practically required with what was realistically possible. If we set our target too high, they would reject our proposal out of hand. On the other hand we didn't want to sell ourselves short.

The whole department needed a director, who I imagined would be me, so I sketched out a quick job description that, strangely enough, seemed suited to someone with my background. By now we were hot, tired and hungry. 'Let's grab some supper and continue this later,' I suggested. We hadn't yet covered the final section, which included health and education. 'I don't think I can face trying to sort out social affairs right now,' I said to Ed. 'I've only got this group anyway because everyone reckoned I was the youngest and most enthusiastic at the meeting with the chief of staff.'

The next morning I was summoned to meet the new ambassador. Sir Hilary Synnott had been due to retire when he agreed to take on the role as head of CPA South. His last posting had been as the British High Commissioner in Pakistan and he had also worked in Jordan so he had a good under-standing of Muslim countries. Sir Hilary made an immediate and striking impression on me and many others at the CPA. In his early 60s, he was slightly balding with white-grey hair; he wore glasses but had the most piercing blue eyes. We could all sense that here was man with a sharp intellect and a very effective operator.

'Hello,' he said after I'd knocked on his door. 'Come in.' He beckoned me to sit on the garish locally made blue sofa in his office, whilst he sat in a similar looking armchair. Leaning forward he peered at the latest version of CPA South's ever-changing organisation chart. 'I see you have a rather large department and responsibility.' he noted, his voice sounding a little sceptical. 'Is this not too large a portfolio?'

'It sort of grew as we went along, but it's exciting and I think I'm up to the task.' I replied as confidently as I could.

'Excellent,' he replied, peering at me through his silver-rimmed spectacles. 'That's the sort of reply I like to hear. Now, I'm writing to Number Ten tonight, and I need to make my observations – and also to tell them what we need.'

Suddenly, I wished that Ed and I had actually got round to finishing our staffing list. Despite our best intentions we hadn't done so. 'We've been devising a plan,' I said, trying desperately to complete it in my head.

'So do you need money?' he asked.

'Absolutely not,' I replied, 'we're awash with the stuff. What we need are people – and not generalists but specialists.'

It was true. Iraq was an oil producing country that wasn't short of cash. The oil fields were producing about two million barrels a day and this money was being pumped back into the economy via the wages we were paying. I was now getting a regular supply in cash of about $80 million a month from Baghdad for those payments. Meanwhile I was frantically cal-culating the staffing numbers. I had approximately thirteen staff already – including the finance team. And we'd established that two-thirds of the plan required an additional 24 staff. Therefore using my best maths I worked out that social affairs section would need a further 12 people, and that I'd require an assistant.

'So how many more do you need?' asked Sir Hilary.

'Thirty-seven,' I replied. Sir Hilary peered doubtfully at me again. 'This is a very precise number,' he said, 'are you sure it's not thirty-six or thirty-eight?'

'No, it's thirty-seven front-office staff, with the corresponding number of security teams and logistics support. Then we'll have a fully functioning economic team of about fifty able to handle the day-to-day ministries business.' I explained confidently.

'Good', he replied, 'I shall tell London that this is the first part of our staffing plan, and that the other departments will follow.'

From now on we'd become known unofficially as 'the 37' back in Whitehall in London. In reality, however, my team – officially known as Economic Planning and Development – when combined with the staff we had already in theatre only varied between 48 and 51 staff over the next 12 months.

Sir Hilary sent off a DipTel – diplomatic telegraph – asking for the extra staff. I was to be the group's director. It was about now that I became known in some circles in Whitehall as 'that merchant banker in Basra'. Apparently people thought it brilliant management to have an experienced investment banker 'running the economy in Basra' as some put it. No one seemed to realise it had all happened quite by accident. Sir Hilary was to prove a major ally in our plans to help kickstart the economy in southern Iraq. He was also able to counteract some of the ideas that came out of Washington, Baghdad and Whitehall – like, for example, the notion that we'd 'un-invent' ourselves by November. In fact, Janet Rogan later said to me that it was always clear to her and others that we needed to keep the body of expertise that we were building up at the CPA in Basra, at least until the handover to the Iraqis. One advantage of our new boss was that he reported straight to the top. Sir Hilary had direct access to Sir Nigel Sheinwald in the Cabinet Office – Tony Blair's chief adviser on foreign policy. Sir Hilary also combined a steel trap of a mind with old-world charm and a delightful lightness of touch. In one of his wonderful reports back to Whitehall read: 'We may not know exactly what we need yet but whatever it is, we will need three of them …'

But despite Sir Hilary's arrival every day was still a fight against chaos in the CPA building. We had only a few cars at our disposal – a few from the Americans, some borrowed from the army and others from the Danes – so we had to have a rule about 'booking' a car. And for security reasons we always travelled in pairs, which meant having to take a colleague with you if you went anywhere because we had no drivers. This was of course usually a complete waste of their valuable time.

On a more mundane personal level life was pretty chaotic for me too. Until now I'd returned every evening from my work at the CPA to sleep at the brigade HQ. This fact wasn't lost on the brigade. One day an officer came to me and said: 'Andrew you seem to be working full time at the CPA, these days.'

'Yes,' I said, 'so?'

'Er, well, it's just that we're a bit short on space. So now you're working there we'd rather like you to clear your things out of here and stay there altogether.' So I had to pack my belongings and find new quarters down at the CPA building. It was true the brigade was genuinely getting short of beds, but I was dismayed and again struck by the way that turf wars develop in such situations.

On top of this disappointment I was also pretty exhausted. I'd been working 18 hours a day for as long as I could recall, rarely getting to bed before 2 am. The loss of the Japanese had made a tough job even harder. I was confident that if we could get more staff in – and quickly – we could still make a big difference to the future of southern Iraq. But what I needed more than anything else was a break. Though I'd been ousted from my military HQ I was still technically part of the military set-up and was now overdue some military leave. So I decided to take a week away from Iraq to re-charge myself for the battles I knew lay ahead.

It felt strange being back in the United Kingdom. I flew to see my parents in Edinburgh, so tired that I slept for about two days. When I awoke my mind was buzzing with all I'd seen, felt and experienced and all the plans I'd made. Yet I found it very hard to talk about my experiences, even to my family. It all seemed too far removed from life back in Britain. The rest of my brief leave I spent down in London, thinking it important to visit Whitehall officials, who were to be me and my team's *de facto* employers. Given their fixation upon Colonel Tim's quick-fix plan I was worried that my recruitment drive might be at risk. My fears proved well founded. I'd arranged to see two senior civil servants at their newly refurbished offices in White-hall, a stone's throw from Buckingham Palace. I waited for 20 minutes while the receptionist tried to locate my hosts. They turned up eventually, explaining that they'd been double-booked. As a result the future of southern Iraq was discussed in their cafeteria, over tea in plastic cups. It wasn't a great start to the meeting and it went downhill from there.

Immediately I could see that their main interest was in the Emergency Infrastructure Plan – after a brief exchange of pleasantries it was the first thing they mentioned. 'But that's only half the story,' I protested and went on to describe my plan for 37 new staff to help get southern Iraq back on its feet. They both looked blank.

'We haven't seen anything like that,' they said. I was surprised. Not only had Sir Hilary contacted Whitehall about it, but I'd also sent a copy of the plan through to civil servants the back of the infrastructure proposal. Either it had just got lost or it had been parked somewhere by someone and ignored.

'The bottom line is we need people,' I said. But the two civil servants kept talking about the $100 million plus they were about to spend on the army engineers' plan. 'We are spending significant sums of money,' they said. 'And we have had to re-allocate our budgets to find that money,' they added, perhaps expecting me to be grateful. I was in fact thinking that $100 million was hardly a significant amount of money in Iraq – more than double that had already passed through my hands. In cash.

The civil servants were behaving as if this was another donor-aid programme. Indeed it struck me as odd that the British government was implementing an aid programme as part of its reconstruction efforts in Iraq. The lead role had been given to DFID, whose mission statement is pretty clear. It reads: 'The Department for International Development (DFID) is the part of the UK Government that manages Britain's aid to poor countries and works to get rid of extreme poverty.' With the world's second largest reserves of oil, Iraq wasn't really short of money. What it needed were people and expertise and above all some help to rebuild its economy. 'We are the government down there, this is not an aid programme,' I told them. 'I'm effectively running all the finances down there.'

'But that's not your job,' said one. 'The Iraqis should be doing it.'

'Well,' I said. 'The Iraqis are NOT doing it so someone has to.' I tried to explain. 'We aren't trying to run the whole thing but to run it hand in hand with them.' But I was struggling to get my message through. Two worlds were colliding. I was a merchant banker and part-time soldier and they were 'developmentalists'. I'd come to their offices because I wanted to be able to look in their eyes and feel confident when I was back in Basra that I was getting their support. But that was far from the feeling I was getting. This was a key issue of British foreign policy and I thought its civil servants should hear the views of people on the ground. As for the Iraqis what they wanted was to get their life and economy back on track again. Eventually I extracted a promise that the question of the 37 staff would be looked into. Yet I left the meeting with a sense of deep despondency about Whitehall's view of events in southern Iraq.

When I arrived back in Basra the contrast was extraordinary. The Whitehall civil servants may have been, like Sir Hilary, employees of Her Majesty's Government but as far as I could see all similarity ended there. In London I'd sensed the heavy hand of bureaucracy. In Iraq Sir Hilary had brought energy and direction to the CPA in Basra. Each evening at 6 pm the heads of the various departments – the ministries, politics, regions, utilities and security – held what was known as the 'head of pillars' meeting. Sir Hilary chaired these with real drive. He had a habit of holding out the palm of one hand and tapping it with the other saying: 'What does this mean, right here, right now?' You could see that he really cared about what was going on.

However, I was still worried that Whitehall was too focussed on the quick-fix plan and not enough on the wider economic picture in southern Iraq. I became even more worried when I learnt that the military wanted to bring in the engineering group Mott MacDonald as consultants. This told me that the army engineers lacked the capability to do all the work. In which case why were they in charge of this project at all? I told the ambassador of my fears that the Iraqis would not be very involved in the British military project. Sir Hilary stressed the need to harness the army's enthusiasm. It turned out that Whitehall couldn't give money directly to the army so they had given Tim's funding to Sir Hilary and CPA South to administer instead.

For my part, I'd still have concerns about it being an overtly military project and the development of a 'them and us' mentality with the army. But at least the CPA had some control of the purse strings.

The need to get more staff was becoming more desperate – partly because of the departure of the Japanese staff but also because my workload was growing. By now David Oliver had designated me 'our man in the south'. This meant that I was the main focal point in Basra for the Baghdad machine that handled money issues. The problem was that there were so many different sources of funding and so many complex rules about getting to them. Though I have worked in finance all my working life, I had trouble at first understanding all the many different forms, regulations and headings. In these early months the lack of understanding between ourselves and Baghdad over funding rules was a constant source of tension between the British and the Americans. Of course no one person was at fault, and the rules were devised for good reasons. But this didn't stop me getting bogged down at times in the accountancy quagmire.

An example of the confusion is contained in an email I sent to one of the senior American finance people in Baghdad:

Sherri,

It's me again …

Apologies but I have just spoken to our new contracting officer to help me fill in the blanks on the 6953 and 1034 and he seems to think that I need to fill in a form 7700. I am now totally confused (yet again)! Attached are the forms you asked me to sign, duly completed. The problem is that Sir

Hilary does not want to sign the DA3953 as the approving officer because there are too many blank spaces! I can get someone else to do so as a third party but I really need to know what each form does to understand the system.

I think it is as follows:

Form 5000 – request for replenishment of funds – forwarded to you?
Form 1034 – receipt for physical delivery of funds on the day – forwarded to Col Hough?
Form 3953 – ?? (something to do with contracting?)
Form 7700 – ?? (eek!? No idea!)

Sorry to be a menace but I want to get this right once and for all and everyone is telling me different things down here.

As Winnie the Pooh once said, "I am only a bear with little brain"!

HELP!!

Andrew

On top of day-to-day issues such as the payment of salaries, other problems came out of nowhere. For example in the middle of September I was told that under the Saddam Hussein regime all workers got an extra month's pay – a 13th month – to be paid at the time of the Muslim festival Ramadan. This was news to me. To make such a payment would have completely blown the budget. So I wrote to David Oliver in Baghdad to check if these payments were going to be made – and if so where the money would come from. It turned out there was no such convention. But it was another reminder we were all working in uncharted territory.

On another memorable day we received an urgent message from David Oliver's office asking how much the overall reconstruction in southern Iraq would cost. This didn't mean the existing essential services plan – that was simply a sticking plaster to get us through the next few months. It meant the large-scale reconstruction work to be funded by the forthcoming international donors' conference in Madrid in October. We were given just ten days to come up with the figures, to figure out the cost of replacing damaged power stations, water works, electricity pylons, telephone wires, roads, bridges, waterways, airports, ports, not to mention schools, hospital and factories – our multi-billion dollar shopping list for southern Iraq.

Our solution was to bring together what figures we already had. The rest we simply worked out in a notebook by little more than intelligent guesswork. I sat down with electricity adviser Ed Lock to work out our needs and the cost of achieving them. We put our fingers in the air and decided we needed two power stations for Basra. 'How much will that cost?' I asked Ed.

'About two hundred and fifty million dollars each,' he replied.

'How do you work that out?'

'Producing one megawatt costs one million so if we multiply that by two hundred and fifty then we get two hundred and fifty million dollars,' said Ed.

'Great we'll put that down,' I said.

And that was how we went on. We did the same with medical centres. We were already spending $50,000 per centre doing some of them up so we simply multiplied that figure by the total number in the region. It was strange to have to work out the cost of reconstructing the country by doing fag-packet calculations. But given the time we had, there was little choice. The Madrid conference was barely a month away.

One key area under my responsibility was agriculture. Although Iraq now imports about 80 per cent of its food, farming is still important, even in the dry and often harsh conditions of the south. Had I not seen it for myself, I wouldn't have believed that large swathes of the desert could support a green carpet of grass for several weeks after the annual heavy rains. Crops range from the age-old production of dates and wheat to more recent crops such as tomatoes, while a number of Iraqis keep flocks of sheep. In the marsh areas the local Arabs had traditionally tended herds of buffalo. Sadly Saddam Hussein's so-called Glory Canal, built to drain the marshes as part of his revenge on the south, put paid to them. One of the crucial issues was irrigation, usually done by flooding, using water pumped from rivers and canals or in the more remote sandy areas by drip irrigation from bore holes and wells. However, the irrigation infrastructure had suffered from a lack of maintenance and investment. Fortunately the CPA had an excellent man to deal with the agricultural matters in Ole Stokholm Jepsen, a Dane who had long experience of working in the Middle East. Though part of his time was spent in talks with international agencies and other people in Basra, Ole also got out and about talking to farmers and their communities.

One day he was visited by the boss of the Basra Cooperative Farmers' Union – an organisation Saddam Hussein had set up to control the farmers. The official was angry that we weren't paying his staff's salaries on the grounds that they weren't state employees. Ole recalled: 'The man said that they would organise a demonstration and throw stones at us. I made it clear that I would like to work with them to develop the agricultural sector – but if they chose to throw stones it was easy for me to go home.' Ole also discovered that Iraqis could be quite disparaging about themselves. A local sheikh, head of a community in Al-Basra province, came to see him complaining that because of the poor state of the irrigation both their soil and water were very salty. Ole agreed this was an important issue and offered to discuss it with the relevant Iraqi DGs.

'You shouldn't "discuss" this with these people, you should "order them",' replied the sheikh. Ole patiently tried to explain that the idea was to work together with local officials to find the best solutions. The sheikh's response was dismissive. 'But they are Iraqis!' he said.

The invasion had caused massive disruption to the region's farmers. The fighting occurred just when the spring crops should have been planted. The result was a very poor harvest. Farmers had to be given a grain subsidy both to survive and to be able to plant crops for the following year. They seized every opportunity to lobby senior officers from the army division and tell them they were desperately short of grain. Then someone at division would get on the phone to me: 'Andrew, you must do something about the grain subsidies – the farmers have no grain!' To which I usually replied: 'Listen, we don't get excited about military matters – so don't you get excited about economic matters! We'll deal with it.' There was no way I was going to have the army dictating grain policy in southern Iraq.

We quickly learnt how tempting it was to buy off trouble and protests with increased wages. But then another group would demand the same hike too and fairly soon inflation would spiral out of control. One of the groups who tried it on the most when it came to industrial action were the oil-distribution workers led by the indefatigable Mr Saed. I think he and his workers threatened to go on strike at least every month. They were always angry, and constantly moaning that other oil workers got paid more than them. But they were important. They distributed gasoline and diesel to petrol stations and other crucial places such as hospitals and water-treatment plants. Colin McBride, the head of utilities in our team, often dealt with them. Colin was a TA major who had worked as a water engineer in his native Northern Ireland. He had a great sense of humour and was a real character. One day Colin was meeting Mr Saed for the umpteenth time at the office. Yet again Mr Saed was unhappy. 'We are going on strike,' he told Colin with some determination.

'OK that's fine,' said Colin. 'But you do know what going on strike is all about, don't you?'

'No I don't really understand,' admitted Mr Saed through the interpreter, clearly puzzled.

'Well,' explained Colin, 'when you go on strike there are certain things you ask for. That is, you have to give the reasons why you are on strike. OK, so you say you want more money – but why? You say that you are going on strike but you are not giving me any more than that. You need to explain it more.'

Mr Saed was looking more and more baffled so Colin hit upon the brilliant idea of demonstrating to his guest what he meant. He picked up his chair and shuffled round to the other side of the table to take Mr Saed's place. 'OK, Mr Colin, I am Mr Saed,' said Colin. And he proceeded to give an entire speech about his grievances about negotiations and how to go on strike. As soon as he had finished, Colin shuffled around with his chair back to his side of the table and became himself again. 'Now, Mr Saed, what is it you wanted?' At this the oil boss recited almost exactly word for word what Colin had just said. And then just for good measure he added that they really were going to go on strike anyway.

Colin took this news in his stride. He explained to Mr Saed that it was his decision. But he had to understand that if his workers did stop work then Mr Andrew wouldn't pay then. 'So can you just make a formal note of when you are about to go on strike so that we can dock the wages from them, please?' asked Colin. Mr Saed was appalled. Up to that moment he had seemed very excited about his men downing tools. But the idea they wouldn't be paid came as a shock. Mr Saed went off for a quick huddle with senior officials. A few minutes later he came back with a determined look on his face.

'Mr Colin,' he announced, 'if we are not going to get paid while we are on strike then we are not going on strike!' And with that he and his team left the building as if they'd won the argument – which of course was part of Colin's skill. It didn't stop Mr Saed and his team trying it on again the following month. But at least this had bought us some respite.

In the middle of all this chaos we suddenly had another issue to deal with. Baghdad announced that the whole country was going to undergo a currency swap. This was an excellent idea. Now that Saddam had been toppled neither the people nor the coalition wanted his picture on Iraqi dinar notes any more. The aim was to remove all those old Saddam notes from the system and replace them with brand-new ones. This was to be done province by province though it was organised centrally by Baghdad.

Currency was a complicated issue in Iraq. Not only were there old dinars and soon to be new dinars, but there were US dollars too and also a special kind of super-valuable dinar known as the Swiss dinar. This had usually been paid to top officials and they weren't transferable. The notes were worth 150 times their face value. Then there was that old banking trick 'arbitrage' that has existed for a couple of hundred years or more, but which was now being used by Iraqi private banks to make large amounts of money. If a person went to a bank clutching a high-denomination note they wanted changed, the bank would only agree to do this for a small fee. In Iraq the private banks were making money out of people from changing their high-denomination dinar notes in this way.

With the currency swap the banks saw a chance to make even more money. There were few bank branches open at this time so instead people were storing money under their bed. Naturally, it was easier to do this with high-denomination notes, but the banks needed people to change these notes for smaller denominations if they were to make a profit. So the private banks sparked a rumour that all the old 10,000-dinar notes in circulation were counterfeits. As they expected this started a rush on 250-dinar notes as people hurriedly retrieved the 'counterfeit' 10,000-dinar notes from under their beds to change them. Pretty soon Basra had run out of 250-dinar notes and I was on the phone asking Baghdad for more. Baghdad eventually sent down 400 million Iraqi dinars in 250-dinar notes which went to the Central Bank. Immediately the private banks put pressure on the Central Bankers to exchange the money at face value with them – so that they could then change them with the public and take a commission. By now I realised what was going on and I refused. I insisted the money was needed to pay wages and stipends in those denominations. A day or so later I got an aggrieved phone call from David Oliver in Baghdad. 'Andrew, I have just had the governor of the Central Bank in Basra on the phone and he tells me you have stolen their four hundred million dinars.'

I just laughed.

'You do realise this is a very serious allegation?' said David.

'I'm sorry,' I explained to David. 'But I just can't take this allegation seriously! Do you know how much space 400 million dinars takes up?'

'No,' admitted David.

'Well you sent it to me in two hundred and fifty-dinar notes and that fills the equivalent of two forty-feet containers – where do you think I've hidden it? Under my bed?'

I could hear David's tone change. 'I guess you're right.'

'The reason they've said I've stolen is because I won't let them have it!' I then explained to David Oliver what I thought was going on, that the private banks were trying to get their hands on these 250-dinar notes so that they could make a fast buck on them from ordinary Iraqi people.

Overall the Iraqi Currency Exchange went remarkably smoothly. It was a triumph for the American team in Baghdad who organised it. The operation was vast and the volume of currency being moved around the country – both the old and the new – was so huge it was sometimes measured in tonnes not value. We had one or two early hiccups in the south. We had to find 38 banks across the southern regions able to take the cash. This wasn't easy especially in some of the more remote areas. We found that there were about 15 serviceable banks, and the rest had to be refurbished and made secure. Some of the bank branches that Baghdad wanted to send money to didn't actually exist. Officials would give us a grid reference for the place and we'd check it against our local maps. 'This place is in the middle of a desert,' we'd say to the authorities. 'But that's the grid reference we've been given,' would come the reply. Over the next month, however, the new Saddam-free notes came into circulation. Most Iraqis were themselves delighted to see the new currency – it symbolized a fresh start. One of the great sights was people pushing shopping trolleys literally stuffed with old notes to get changed into new ones.

On top of the currency exchange, progress was finally being made getting the money freed up for Colonel Tim's much-trumpeted Emergency Infrastructure Plan. Despite my early reservations I now saw that the plan was necessary. Iraqis had to see that something was being done to help retrieve southern Iraq from the mess it was in. However, the plan was held up by some unbelievable red tape. The money was coming from Whitehall, more used to giving money to sovereign governments than to temporary administrations run by the British after an invasion.

This meant the UK government treated the CPA as a foreign government. This led senior staff – including Sir Hilary – to wonder just what their legal liabilities might be if they signed an agreement for the money from Whitehall. Sir Hilary had bought into the Emergency Infrastructure Plan because he believed that it was important for Whitehall to be engaged. But as a diplomat, Sir Hilary was naturally wary about assuming responsibility for $100 million plus of UK taxpayers' money. Little did he know that downstairs we were happily handing out these sorts of amounts every month, with little regard for the legal position or the potential consequences. Eventually the matter was sorted out after a brief visit to Basra by Hilary Benn, DFID secretary of state, and his permanent secretary Suma Chakrabati, the department's top civil servant.

By now I was getting used to my new 'home' in the battered old CPA headquarters. There were four of us to a room. The furniture was sparse but functional. We had IKEA beds and a wardrobe and some of us were lucky enough to have metal lockers, made locally by craftsman, which we could padlock. This was where I could safely store my pistol. The bathroom facilities were even more modest. The water for the makeshift showers came from a tank on the roof and it got hot very quickly. In fact if you didn't have a shower by 9 am it was often simply too hot to use. The showers were a great leveller particularly since they didn't provide any great separation of the sexes. As projects manager Rosie Knight once said to me, it was quite hard looking at Sir Hilary in the same way in meetings when you'd just seen him in his dressing gown. When the US firm KBR finally arrived they built a proper shower area.

The eating conditions were also quite basic. The cookhouse was a trailer designed to cater for 30 but which now had to deal with 70 staff. Local carpenters built tables so we could eat outside – we used plastic cutlery to save on washing up. Our water was brought up in tankers from Kuwait – there was a concern that if we used local water it could be poisoned. After KBR took over the cuisine was very American – lots of burgers, though there were salads too. The social life, as one might expect, was limited. Since the early days we'd effectively been confined to quarters. The idea of going into town for a meal was now out of the question. Instead we had a small bar with a TV screen. Even so we were careful how we behaved and observed the 'two can' rule, mainly because of security. No one could be sure if and when the compound might face a major attack and people needed to have their wits about them. In any case drinking more than two cans of beer in such heat gave you a stinking headache the next morning.

At least I now had more room to work. The only good thing about the Japanese leaving was that it had freed up some office space. Pat and I had immediately looked at each other: 'Time to grab some real estate!' We made sure that we took over their office before anyone else moved in. Raneen joined us in our totally magnolia-walled office, with its two white-boards. On the ceiling were bare strip lights while the floor was covered in computer cables. In the background was the whirring sound of the primitive air conditioning system that reduced the temperature from 35 °C or 40 °C to about 25 °C; it was never cool but it was bearable. The room was so bare that a local Iraqi contractor took pity on us. 'Mr Andrew,' he told me, 'you cannot work in an office like this! Let me see what I can do for you.' Some time later he came back with a sizeable bundle. He had found a Persian carpet for us. It was large, red and blue and in quite good condition. It certainly made the place feel a little more human.

It was into this strange environment that I wanted to recruit my extra 37 advisers. Thanks largely to Sir Hilary's lobbying, Whitehall had finally given the green light to expand the team. Yet I also wanted to make sure we got the right people – having the wrong people on board would be worse than having no one at all. Whitehall was understandably keen that my new team members should represent the multi-national flavour of the coalition in the south of Iraq. Yet I was adamant they needed to speak good English.

On the other hand an international team could be a huge asset. Our work was enlivened by the arrival of a sizeable Italian contingent. The Italians had insisted they must have a senior figure in the CPA south since they had troops on the ground. And so Italian Ambassador Mario Maiolini was made Sir Hilary's deputy. Super Mario, as I privately dubbed him, was full of energy and enthusiasm. Every day he would call me or bombard me with a new name or CV to consider for my team. It was clear the Italians wanted to boost their representation in the CPA as much as possible. However, when I examined the Italian CVs in any detail it appeared that that most of the candidates were in their 60s and retired. I had nothing against experience. But the surroundings in Basra were challenging and I needed people who knew what to do but also with enough youth to be able to put their ideas into action. The last thing I needed was an Italian Dad's Army of advisers topping up their pension funds. Many of Super Mario's CVs ended up 'lost' in my in-tray.

5

NEW PREMISES, NEW BEGINNING

October 2003

Colonel David Amos, the deputy of the brigade who had encouraged me to follow my instincts and fly to meet David Oliver, had been a good ally and friend. However, like all military personnel, David was on a fixed tour and soon it would be time to for him to leave. Typically, he wanted to go in style and organised a farewell dinner in Baghdad. He invited me for the occasion and others came up from Basra too, including another TA officer Dominique Hope who had joined the trade and industry team. I jumped at the chance and scheduled a two-day trip to Baghdad.

David had chosen the old British Embassy for his farewell bash. It was being guarded by a detachment of the Light Dragoons, of whom David was the commanding officer. It's a fabulous old building that overlooks the Tigris, and was used in the early 1920s by the brilliant Gertrude Bell. This remarkable writer, political analyst and Middle Eastern expert was known as the 'Uncrowned Queen of Iraq' for her role in shaping the state and frontiers of modern Iraq. But it wasn't the history of the embassy that that first caught my attention. It was the fact that it wasn't located in the Green Zone. To get there Dom and I travelled in the back of a Land Rover through busy streets thronged with ordinary Iraqis going about their business. Outside the gates there was a mass of people eager to talk to the British soldiers. Nowhere else in Baghdad did they have such close contact with our troops.

Once inside we had a chance to look around. We were in a slightly decaying but charming colonial-style building with overgrown gardens and a sweeping driveway. It was like stepping back in time. The embassy had remained closed since the First Gulf War and the Iraqi caretaker had taken it upon himself to continue looking after the place. He had even removed the coat of arms from the front of the building to protect it. When British forces arrived in Baghdad they were greeted by the caretaker – who presented the coat of arms back to them. In what little free time they had the soldiers had since been busy restoring the old swimming pool. In the afternoon some of us went on a 'sightseeing' tour of the city in open top Land Rovers with a section of the Light Dragoons. This gave us a close view of the city and the people as we drove past. Many waved at us – Dominique was told that the Americans didn't get that kind of response. The tour included the monument to an unknown soldier, some of Saddam Hussein's palaces, his son Udeh's Palace and the impressive Baghdad Museum.

Dinner was to start at 7 pm. We all gathered on the embassy roof and stood there sipping champagne while the night sky was lit up with the tell-tale signs of tracer bullets. It was a surreal experience. The guest list was pretty impressive too, including the British Ambassador to Iraq, Sir Jeremy Greenstock, and the deputy commander of coalition forces in Iraq, General Freddy Viggers.

The meal was served in the embassy courtyard. The tables were laid formally with the regimental silver of the Light Dragoons. As Dominique remembered: 'We were entertained with British military music, gorgeous food, excellent conversation with two of the most powerful men in Iraq at that time – and in the background we could hear explosions and gun fire. It reminded me of the film *Carry on up the Khyber*, where at the end the British army officers all sit eating dinner as if nothing is happening whilst their garrison is being attacked.'

Later that evening David, Dominique and I sat on an upstairs balcony, on chairs overlooking the river. Below us was a public footpath, a reminder that we weren't in the safe Green Zone but the far more perilous Red Zone. Down on the path we could see ordinary Iraqis walking past chatting and occasionally we'd call out the greeting *'salaam aleikum'* in our basic Arabic. We heard one of them comment to a companion in English: 'That must be the British up there!' Sitting on that balcony overlooking the river, it felt as though we could have been anywhere in the world and for a moment life felt almost normal again.

Soon I was back to reality in Basra and the routine of 6 am starts and late-night finishes. Security had become a problem. Meetings would continue as AK 47 rounds crackled in the distance. Often they were 'happy rounds' but they were a reminder of how precarious we were in a poorly defended building. My old friend AJ and I once went for a quick break out the back of the building, he for a cigarette, me for a cup of tea. We stood there chatting when we heard a commotion. Looking up we saw a crutch coming over the wall at us. A group of invalided workers was staging a protest and this was their way of showing their anger. There was a comical element to it, of course – we'd come under attack from a flying crutch. But it brought home the fact that just one thin wall stood between us and the outside world. The military had closed off the access road to the building and put in HESCO barriers, tough structures made of steel and polypropylene. But the building was still vulnerable.

From his arrival Sir Hilary was adamant that we'd to move. If we were to act like an interim government then we needed to look like one. And though we worked happily enough together in our scruffy building, we were bursting at the seams. More people were starting to arrive and we had nowhere to house them, nor the means to feed them. We'd outgrown the building. Sir Hilary handed the task to John Dyson, a seasoned Foreign and Commonwealth Office veteran of countless overseas duties. John had a dry sense of humour and three other constants – he always wore shorts, was perpetually tanned and was seldom seen without a cigarette in his mouth. He was also an excellent project manager and in just ten weeks he converted our vague plans into the reality of a purpose-built office and camp complex with the capacity to house more than 300 people. We were set to move to a new home back at Basra palace.

The new venue made sense. The brigade was already based there and the palace was relatively well defended. But there was one drawback. The site was associated with the hated regime of Saddam Hussein. As Sir Hilary said in his typically understated way: 'I don't think that "The Palace" is a very good name for our new workplace – can anyone think of a better one?' People came up with a variety of suggestions, some frivolous some less so. They ranged from the racy 'The Casino' and 'The Phoenix' to the more prosaic 'Lakeside House'. In the end Sir Hilary went for Al-Sarraji, the name of a nearby river. The site had apparently borne this name before Saddam built his vast palace. The choice was run past Governor al-Latif and then became official.

There were so many of us at the CPA that the move had to take place over three nights. For security reasons it was also a secret. We weren't supposed to tell the Iraqi staff or our visitors although it soon became clear that they already knew. Sir Hilary, Allan Rosenberg and myself were the last of the management team to leave on the final night. I'd sent Jude and Pat ahead to set up operations at the other end. At Al-Sarraji we'd been given four large offices and our own small meeting room. In the final hour before we were due to depart, there was only one task left. I had to find our latest addition to the team – Oscar. Oscar was a feral kitten who had somehow found his way into the compound. He lived outside the front door of the building under the water barrel or skulking around the portakabin cookhouse in the hope that someone might feed him. With a good bath he would have been a beautiful white with a large grey patch across his back. Instead he was various shades of dusty grey with bright green eyes.

Despite his dusty appearance he was probably the luckiest cat in Basra. A common trait of security guards and soldiers is that most of them are smitten by small furry animals and children. Pretty soon, just about everyone loved Oscar. He had also become quite tame. Each evening at around 8 pm I'd come down from my office to sit in the chair next to the front door and see if I could persuade Oscar to come and join me for the sunset. After a few days he did, and soon it became a ritual, much to the amusement of the rest of the team. Of course we couldn't leave Oscar behind. But I also knew that he wouldn't willingly clamber into a box. So I pretended that nothing was amiss and settled down on my usual chair 15 minutes before we were due to move. I waited, but Oscar was nowhere to be seen. I sat anxiously as all around me people packed equipment into vehicles. Time was getting short and soon I'd have to leave – with Oscar or without. Finally I saw his familiar figure walking cautiously towards me. He knew something was up. Without giving him time to disappear again I scooped him up and deposited him in a box. This provoked a sudden explosion of wailing – but at least he was coming with us.

I'd been allocated my own vehicle to leave the CPA building. By now security staff from Control Risks Group were looking after us and the CRG team looked slightly perplexed when I appeared with a laptop bag and a large cardboard box. 'Are you carrying money again?' they asked.

'Something far more important.' I winked.

Some of the compound's officials, including some of the American administrators, were less than happy about having an animal roaming around the place. Indeed KBR, the US company running many of the services for the HQ – including the catering – were thought to be especially uneasy. Alarmed at the prospect of having our pet forcibly removed – or worse – there was only one course of action open to us. Oscar had to be protected by the full force of Her Majesty's Government. That was how a certain Oscar de la Shat Al-Arab came to be added to the diplomatic list in Basra, even though this new recruit never drew any salary. Oddly I don't think anyone ever questioned who this new 'person' was on the list. As well as demonstrating the British near-obsession with cuddly animals, Oscar did play a more serious role for us. Work was tough at the CPA and there were very few distractions from it. Oscar was a welcome topic of conversation away from the world of work. As Jude said: 'He gave us something else to talk about. He was great to have around and was good for morale. I think he was even given his own security pass in the end – they made a special one for him.'

Our new home was a vast improvement. My room had a proper bed, a desk, a wardrobe and I also had my own shower, hot-water tank, sink and WC. This was five-star accommodation compared to my previous bedroom. John Dyson had done a terrific job. I walked across the compound towards the lights of the main building. I was struck how liberating it felt just to have more open space and the possibility of walking around outside. I went into the new CPA building through large wooden doors, turned right and walked into one of our new department offices. It was cavernous. The walls were newly painted with crisp white paint, the floor was marble and the room was filled with large office desks – each with its own computer and flat-screen monitor.

Further on I walked through more ornate heavy double doors until I came to our second office, where there were three additional desks. Pat had already established himself. He greeted me with a smile as he leaned back in the large leather armchair each desk had been supplied with. 'Nice of you to show up,' he said. 'I thought you'd like the desk to the left' – the identical arrangement to our last office. I plonked my laptop onto the desk and my body armour on the floor and set about making myself at home. The first priority was a cup of tea, followed by the installation of my laptop and finally our carpet. Here was a place we could do business. It began to feel like a regional government.

The building seemed to have everything. We even had a small fridge. We also had two massive new safes in our office where Pat and I could keep up to $25 million at a time. However, the following morning I realised that we were missing one important service – local telephone access to the Iraqis. The engineers had installed a new telephone and satellite system that gave us communications with Baghdad and the outside world. But someone had completely overlooked the need to connect us to the local Basra phone network. I'd been used to speaking on a regular basis with the director generals by telephone. They also knew how to contact me. Now at a stroke my communications with the DGs had vanished. I spoke to the IT team. 'We have the US system and voice-over-internet protocol via a satellite on the roof,' the technician explained.

'Yes, I know, but we can't speak to anyone in Basra!' I said. Then Pat interrupted.

'What are you complaining about Andrew – we'll get lots more done.'

Another drawback was that our offices were a quarter of a mile walk from the front gate. And gradually our number of

Iraqi visitors diminished. We were all glad to be in new buildings with new facilities. But there was a danger that we would
begin to talk to ourselves.

Our old office equipment was handed over to the Iraqi
Ministry of Finance branch offices in Basra, as had been our
plan all along. And, as Jude found out, they needed it. Many of
the ministry's officials had now returned to their desks. They
took on more of the regular meetings with the director generals
– after all, the aim was to get the Iraqis back working the system
rather than us simply 'running' it. Instead we kept signatory
authority while Jude took charge of managing the relationship
with the ministry and its officials. 'They were occupying a shell
of a building in the centre of Basra. The hustle and bustle was
really bizarre, there were just so many people moving about,'
she remembered later. 'There were people sitting at desks
processing reams of paper and it all seemed chaotic. Everything
had to be referred to a supervisor – it reminded me of how it
used to be in Britain in banks in the days before computers.'

One problem we all faced was the bewildering number of
projects and different types of funds available. At the time we
were helping the Iraqi director generals rebuild schools, hospitals, power stations, roads and bridges, train staff, keep the
water flowing, pay wages and pensions, ensure food supplies
came through and that the oil workers were happy, among a
host of other projects. And the money to do this came from
various different sources. There was a fund called the Directors
Emergency Response Plan (DERP) and a parallel military
scheme called the Commanders' Emergency Response
Program (CERP). The Danish authorities also came up with
some funding of their own – around £2 million. On top of this
came the big money raised at the donor conference. These
huge sums were to be spent through an organisation called
the Program Management Office (PMO).

The PMO was to get $18 billion from the US. With other
donations the total figure to spend would come to around $33

billion. That was a colossal sum. Yet the way the PMO wanted to work was to crunch through big projects one at a time, not working through the existing economy and ministries but following a parallel path of its own. To be fair most of these ministries were still so dysfunctional that they probably couldn't have coped with such large sums. But the danger was that the projects got built without necessarily fitting in with what the ministries really wanted or needed. At the same time money was pouring into the pockets of contractors, causing massive inflation.

Another major problem was unemployment – especially among the young.

Early in September, a new jobs programme was announced in Baghdad. The idea was to employ 300,000 Iraqis across the country. Late one night I was in my office when the local governor Judge al-Latif and his chief of staff Hazim came to see me. Judge Abdul al-Latif had been nominated by councillors to act as the first Governor of Basra, after members of CPA South political section and Colonel David Amos had helped create a local city council. Judge al-Latif – who had been imprisoned under Saddam Hussein – was also on the national council in Baghdad so he was well connected at both ends.

'Hello, Your Excellency, hello Hazim,' I said, 'how can I help you?'

'Tell me,' said the governor, 'tomorrow I have to meet this American in Baghdad called Bremer, what should I ask for?' he asked.

'Well,' I said, 'he seems to be pushing this jobs programme at the moment ... maybe you could get some money and employ people to clean the streets.' Not only would it improve the condition of the city but he realised that it would increase his standing for the forthcoming council elections.

'OK I should ask for how many?' he asked.

'Whatever you wish, ' I replied.

'Can we ask for ten thousand?' asked Hazim.

'If that's what you want, then perhaps you might ask for more and then graciously accept when they don't give you the full amount.' I suggested.

'I like this plan,' said the Judge, 'I shall ask for twenty-five thousand jobs per month!' The next day he met Bremer in Baghdad and to his surprise the American was quick to grant the request.

Despite its relationship with al-Latif, the council had little formal power – all the money and thus all the influence of the centralised Iraqi system was channelled through the ministries based in Baghdad and their local branches in Basra. This was a problem because in the end the council would find money to run itself from elsewhere. And some of that money came from the leading and charismatic Shi'ite cleric called Muqtada al-Sadr.

By October 2003 it was already evident that al-Sadr was becoming a significant figure in Iraqi national politics and also a potential major focal point of opposition against the coalition authorities. He came from a prominent Shi'a family persecuted under Saddam Hussein and had shed no tears at the dictator's ousting. However, when he was asked in July 2003 whether he thanked the Americans for getting rid of the hated dictator, al-Sadr told a TV reporter: 'All credit for the removal of the regime goes only to almighty God,' and described himself as an enemy of the US. And though the cleric had been careful to say that he wasn't fighting the Americans, he set up a militia – known as the al-Mahdi army – to 'maintain peace and security in Iraq'. Al-Sadr was also trying to win the support of the councils by funding them – filling the financial gap that we'd left. What better way was there to buy influence? We were fairly sure that some of the money was coming via Iran. Al-Sadr publicly played down his links with the Sh'ite regime in Tehran but he'd visited it back in June.

A more unexpected problem in Basra was squatters, who had set up home in almost all of the government buildings.

Experience of the Balkans told us it would take a long time to evict them if there was any question over ownership. We had to find a new pensions office to handle pensioners and people on welfare payments. Sitting in our office in the CPA late one evening, long after the Iraqi staff had disappeared, we were struggling through various issues that had been raised that day. 'What are we going to do about the pensioners?' asked Pat. 'They were back in today and the DG wants to know about his office.'

'He hasn't got one.' I said.

' … but that doesn't mean he doesn't think he's entitled to one, along with the rest of the city.' Pat interrupted, laughing.

'We can't just give him an office because the whole of the rest of the city is filled either with squatters or these so-called new political parties that are springing up in any building that's unoccupied!' I complained.

'Why don't we give them the Ba'ath party headquarters, no one can claim that, since the Ba'ath party has been officially dissolved and the assets belong to the CPA?' said Pat. It was a good idea but it would take time to clear it of squatters and refurbish it. In the meantime, we needed to find a more immediate location to process pensions and welfare payments. We went to the central post office.

I spoke direct to Mr Abdullah, the telecom DG, telling him I wanted to see him. He had been one of my earliest Iraqi contacts and it was his engineers who for a small fee had dug the half-mile trench to connect us directly to the telephone exchange. They'd wanted a bigger payment but I'd gently pointed out that we were already paying all of his staff's salaries. 'Ah, yes. How had I forgotten this point?' he said, smiling.

Knowing that 'Mr Andrew' was coming to visit, Mr Abdullah insisted on a full tour of the facility. We saw their new telephone exchange and the improvements our recent project there had brought. Inside what looked from the exterior like a dilapidated building was a raised air-conditioned floor and bank after bank of modern digital telecom equipment. The post office section itself was complete except for the fact that there was no machinery, no staff and no parcels or letters! 'It is the afternoon, so the staff are at home and they're sleeping,' Mr Abdullah explained. Privately I wondered if many ever turned up for work except on pay day. 'We handle approximately three hundred letters per week,' he explained, 'it's not been the same since the war.' Looking at the facilities, I wondered which war he was referring to.

We went upstairs to the conference room. In front of us was a complete lamb lying on a large platter of yellow pilaf rice. 'Since you are our first British friend in Basra, you must have lunch with us,' said Mr Abdullah. The Iraqis are by nature very hospitable. Around the table were various other Iraqi staff, who spoke no English. So my interpreter Abdul translated my thanks and we sat down to eat using cardboard plates and our hands, with everything washed down with cans of Pepsi or bottled water.

I got down to business. 'Mr Abdullah,' I started, 'it's very kind of you to see us at such short notice. We actually have a request for you. We wondered if you would be prepared to make payments to the pensioners from your fine post office. You seem to have lots of space and it does not seem … *so* busy?'

'This is an interesting idea,' he said, 'we are often *very* busy, and these people are very many,' which I interpreted immediately as a 'no' but not a definitive no.

'Well, it might mean that there would be some overtime …' I added quickly before he had ruled out the idea completely. He paused, clearly thinking about the money.

'We will only be able to do this when the post office is not working … and only for a short time until they have their own office,' he said thoughtfully. Of course I now twigged that someone had tipped him off about why I was visiting, and he'd known all along what I'd ask for and how he would respond. The only secret seemed to be that there were no secrets when dealing with people in the Middle East.

The post office operated as the pensions outlet for a few months as work started on the creation of the new office in the former Ba'ath party headquarters, which was cleared peaceably after two months of occupation. But that wasn't the end of my headache. The refurbishment work was to be commissioned by US officials who had come down to Basra to oversee their laborious contracting procedures. I told one of their officials that I needed a social affairs office.

'OK, Andrew, so what exactly do you want in there?' came the reply.

'I just want some offices – it's that simple.' I said.

'I'm afraid you need to be more detailed than that,' said the official. 'We need to know how many windows, radiators, tables, desks, sockets and everything that you want and where,' he said.

'But I'm a financier, not a quantity surveyor!' I protested. But it was no use. Under the new rules the contracting officers needed a detailed plan if they were to get the work done. And as we didn't have such an expert surveyor on our books I had to do the work myself. So I found myself drawing up the plans.

From the start education was a priority for the CPA. It was felt that if we got the schools working that would help repair the fractured society. As Sir Hilary put it, this was a country where 'so many people have a hunger for learning and are desperate to re-connect to the wider world'. We started a programme of rebuilding. On average we spent about $50,000 on a school and because labour was relatively cheap that money went a long way. For that we'd clear out the sewage, repair the drains, clear up the debris, whitewash the walls, put in radiators, air conditioning and desks and chairs – all of which had been stolen. The next need was for text books and the British Council and other agencies helped supply some of these. There was also the 'school in a box' programme from UNESCO in which ready-to-use teaching kits were made available to schools.Our education specialist was Charles Monk, a Senior Master at Haileybury, the independent school in Hertford-shire. He had become the CPA South's education adviser in the early summer and was immediately plunged into some very difficult and politically charged issues. Under Saddam Hussein's rule the once high literacy rates in southern Iraq – up to 75 per cent, including for women – had tumbled. The schools and their equipment had been allowed to crumble while senior teachers were required to be members of the Ba'ath party. During the invasion, some of the schools were damaged in the fighting – for example the Technical College in Basra was the scene of a three-day battle and was hit by tank shells. Afterwards most schools were looted with equipment stolen and books destroyed. Only those with tough head teachers and security guards resisted this wide-scale destruction.

After the dust of the invasion had settled, one of the key dictates of the CPA in Baghdad was the need to rid Iraqi bureaucracy at all levels of senior Ba'ath party officials. It was thought this would help win public support for the coalition since many Iraqis loathed the nepotism and pervasive influ-ence of the Ba'ath party. The process, known as de-Ba'athification, was never carried through in many of the ministries in the south. This wasn't for political reasons – we simply didn't have the time. (In fact this turned out to be a blessing in disguise. They may have been Ba'ath party members but at least they were experienced in their jobs.) But unfortunately, the teaching profession had been targeted early on with the result that teachers who were party members had been removed from their posts. This was despite the fact that – as in communist countries – many of them had only joined the party because that was how you progressed in your career in Iraq.

Thousands of teachers lost their jobs as a result, many of them quite young. Others fled, some were even murdered. The US authorities gave the sacked teachers a right to appeal for reinstatement if they felt their dismissal was unjustified. But at the same time the Ministry of Education in Baghdad made it clear that there was no new money to pay any extra teachers – a complete payroll freeze was ordered. Unemployed teachers were furious and started demonstrating. Meanwhile director generals of education around the country started re-hiring sacked teachers without permission.

In Al-Basra province some 2,797 teachers demanded to be re-instated. And the local authorities claimed that all of them were needed to make the schools system work. It was utter chaos. As Charles said at the time: 'These people have had no income and have now had their hopes raised and then crushed.' Some were even so desperate that they travelled all the way to Baghdad themselves to protest. The situation wasn't helped by what one colleague described as the 'baleful' influence of the education director general. He was accused of intimidation, empire-building and corruption. Whether or not the allegations were correct, eventually, at the request of Governor al-Latif, he was sacked by the ministry in Baghdad.

Those teachers who were still employed – and there were around 12,000 of them in all – still needed paying. The cash came from the regular shipments of money that we'd flown down from Baghdad. But on one occasion the money was delayed and when their payday came round we still hadn't paid them what we owed them. I told Colin the situation and asked him if he would deliver the money himself. He agreed and took with him Stuart Hills, who was from the army's CIMIC group and who was also dealing with education matters. The pair jumped in their 4x4 car with two large black bin liners stuffed full of $6.5 million in cash. Unusually, Baghdad had sent us used dollar notes rather than brand-new ones. Nor was there time to arrange another vehicle to escort Colin and Stuart as was the usual practice. We had to pay the teachers quickly.

The pair drove off across Basra, both of them in military uniform, heading for their meeting with the Iraqi education officials. After a few minutes Stuart turned to Colin. 'Are you thinking what I'm thinking?'

Colin looked back at Stuart. 'I don't know, why, what are you thinking?'

After a brief hesitation Stuart uttered the unthinkable. 'I was just thinking that we've got $6.5 million in used notes in the back of the car ... what would stop us from turning left instead of right at the next roundabout and heading for Kuwait? It's only forty minutes away ... and we could split the money fifty-fifty,' concluded Stuart, who by now was looking anxiously at an impassive Colin, waiting for his response. Colin said nothing and just carried on driving. Stuart got more and more alarmed. Had he gone too far? Was Colin going to report him? They'd driven on for another 400 metres in silence when finally Stuart's patience snapped. 'For goodness sake, Colin,' he pleaded, 'tell me what you're thinking!'

Colin looked at Stuart and smiled. 'Actually I was just think-ing of shooting you!' The pair of them burst out laughing and needless to say they delivered the money safely.

By now, we were usually accompanied everywhere by our security team Control Risks Group. Many of their staff were ex-military or -police and were calm and experienced opera-tors in difficult situations. Every time we got into a vehicle with them they took us through the security drill, usually beginning with the words 'I know you may have heard this before but ... ' They drove us around in armoured vehicles which each had two fully armed men as well as full trauma medical packs. One of the new and increasingly common hazards were what are called in the jargon 'IEDs' – improvised explosive devices. These makeshift bombs were often left on the side of a road and detonated when coalition vehicles passed by.

Al-Sadr was increasingly making his presence felt, especially in Maysan and Dhi Qar provinces which were nearer to Baghdad than Basra. He and his al-Mahdi army used the classic IRA tactics of 'fight and negotiate' to extend his power. However, it wasn't always clear who was responsible for attacks. Local people always blamed 'foreigners', but it was a complex picture. Disputes and tensions often cut across simple Sh'ia and Sunni – or Iraqi and Iranian – lines and could simply be tribal in nature. The role and power of local tribal allegiances were very important in southern Iraq and very complex. And sometimes Iraqis themselves would gather together to fight militant groups. In the port city of Umm Qasr the coalition spent a lot of money getting the port working and brought relative prosperity to the area. When attackers tried to blow up the city's power supplies they were beaten off by a group of local people. It was the model that we all hoped would one day apply across Iraq – that local people would all feel they wanted to and could protect themselves as society prospered.

In general, however, it was the military who had to combat the frequent and increasingly sophisticated attacks on power supplies. The attackers knew that power stations themselves were easy to defend. But the pylons that stretched for miles across often remote terrain were far more vulnerable. They attached charges at the bottom of each tenth pylon, the master pylon that was stronger than the rest. By blowing these up they brought the whole line down. It became a lottery – could the attackers blow the pylons up faster than the military could replace them? The military were resourceful in their own counter-tactics, using reconnaissance assets to watch out for attacks and Chinook helicopters to lift up the pylons to be repaired.

Some of these attacks on the power cables were inspired by the age-old rivalries between Basra and Baghdad. Many in Basra felt resentful that, though much of the oil and power generation was in the south, a large amount of electricity was being directed to Baghdad. Though we couldn't prove it we suspected that the precise targeting of the right cables for destruction was being done with inside help. We thought it likely that someone at the ministry was being bribed or intimidated to hand over details of where to direct the bombs. They were literally destroying pylons on the edge of provincial borders to stop the power being sent up to the hated capital city. This was truly a power struggle in every sense.

The rivalry over electricity wasn't only between the Iraqis of Basra and Baghdad but between the British and US sectors too. The Americans were furious about the way that electricity was being prevented from reaching Baghdad. Our argument was that if Baghdad showed more interest in building new power stations in the south as well as around Baghdad then the attacks would diminish. Just as they sometimes accused us of being too Basra-centric we sometimes felt they were too fixated on Baghdad. As it was, overall power output hardly grew in the first few months. In May 2003 it was around 3,800 MW and by September it had crept up to about 4,100. The Iraqis took this slow progress as a sign that the coalition wasn't as interested in them as they claimed. Their view was: 'You are a superpower – if you really wanted electricity here you would just fly in generators in big containers, drop them and we'd have power!' Another frequently heard comment was: 'If the US could put a man on the moon, then they should be able to give us electricity.' Sadly power generation is not simple but one could sympathise with the

Iraqi frustration. Rather than power stations, there was a strange fixation on using diesel generators even though, because of a problem at refineries, Iraq was having to import diesel.

By now I was growing worried about the role of the Central Bank. All the money that was going to the ministries in Basra was channelled through this one institution. Pat and I wondered how efficient this was. It also invited corruption. We thought it was time to de-centralise the system and allow the different departments to open accounts at other banks. I asked various DGs what they thought and they were enthusiastic. They explained that such a system had existed before the Iran–Iraq war and Saddam Hussein had seized even greater central control over the economy. I summoned Mr Hareed, the area manager for Rafidain Bank, whose building we'd helped reconstruct. 'Mr Hareed, since we have repaired your bank, would you be prepared to take over the management of some of the operating budgets that are transferred from Baghdad each month?' I asked him. 'If we provide you with the details then perhaps the various DGs can open bank accounts at your bank, and you can use your account at the Central Bank.'

'Yes, of course,' he said, 'it will be an honour.' I thought to myself that this honour would also net them significant fees. However, since their bank was owned by the Iraqi government we were really just taking it out of one pocket and putting into another.

For the next few days it seemed our plan was working. Various organisations started opening bank accounts with Mr Hareed. Then one day he appeared at our offices looking crestfallen. He informed us he couldn't help us any more because he had been officially 'sanctioned'.

'Sanctioned?' I queried and Pat and I looked at each other, bemused.

'I have received this letter from my bank in Baghdad and it rebukes me for acting in a manner that is contrary to regulations.' To us this may have been just a letter. But to Mr Hareed it was a serious matter – he had lost face in front of his superiors.

'How do they know about this?' I asked, exasperated at yet more bureaucratic interference.

Mr Hareed was reluctant to say. But finally he admitted: 'I think the Central Bank must have told them.' It was time to speak to the Central Bank.

Mr Raffaq came to my office the next day. It was clear he knew why we wanted to see him. 'Mr Raffaq, we discussed this change to the system last week and you agreed this with me. Why do I find that you are trying to prevent it from happening?' I wanted to know.

'It is against regulations,' he offered lamely, shuffling his feet and avoiding eye contact.

'But we are the interim government,' I said simply. 'We'll carry out an audit on your accounts and I hope they're in order. If they're not, then you'll know why we want to do this!' I added angrily, although I knew that admonishing him would have little effect.

That same evening I received an email from one of the young finance team in Baghdad demanding to know what we were doing opening new bank accounts. I was so astonished I immediately picked up the telephone and called the adviser's office in Baghdad and asked to speak to the young man who had emailed me. 'Speaking,' he said.

'This is Andrew down in Basra. I've just seen your mail and we need to speak about bank accounts.' I launched straight in. 'We're opening bank accounts here because we want the money to start moving and for the various departments to begin taking some financial responsibility.'

'You aren't authorised to open bank accounts, it's is illegal. We're operating using one Central Bank account, it makes it easier to audit,' he replied. I couldn't believe my ears!

'What kind of financial system are you trying to create?' I demanded.

'We're using the treasury model. They only use one bank account,' he explained.

'For the whole government?' I asked incredulously. 'Are you telling me that you think you can run Iraq on one bank account, and the model they use in the UK and the US?' I waited, knowing what would follow.

'Yes,' came the reply.

'Are you seriously trying to suggest that a hospital in Southampton has the same bank account as the Bank of England in London?' I asked.

'Yes – and you're not authorised to open bank accounts,' he said although there was now a note of doubt in his voice.

'Well, it's too late, I've opened them, and the system was working quite well until you intervened in Baghdad.'

'But that means that to do an audit that we'll have to look at thousands of bank accounts,' he replied.

'Yes, theoretically it would, if you were trying to audit a country!' I replied sarcastically.

'We'll have to think about what we say to the Central Bank here in Baghdad,' he said. I rang off.

I turned to Pat in the office and said, 'I do wonder if those guys have any idea what they're doing!'

'You're a quick learner,' said Pat. As ever his humour eased my frustration. We had to laugh at the nonsense of the whole situation.

The following day Pat began an audit of the books for the Central Bank, covering the past three months. After two weeks of checking he gave me the answer I feared. 'We're only $7 million adrift,' he said, 'but the good news is that they seem to write everything down.' I wondered what the bad news could be. 'The bad news is that they don't appear to understand basic double-entry bookkeeping,' said Pat.

'I think we have to change the Central Bank manager,' I said.

'Actually I think he wants to retire – the stress of my audit seems to have been too much for him,' said Pat. 'And he was due to go in six weeks anyway.'

After two more weeks we gradually reduced the deficit in the audit. Most of the missing funds were to be found in an additional ledger where all the money had been carefully annotated and accounted. We asked why they hadn't included this ledger when we carried out the original audit.

'You didn't ask for this ledger,' came the reply.

Meanwhile I offered Mr Raffaq early retirement on very good terms. He beamed with pleasure when I broke the news to him. 'Thank you, Mr Andrew, I am very happy!' If I'd known it would be so straightforward I would probably have got rid of him earlier. Mr Raffaq was replaced by one of his deputies, a Mr Ali. He was a breath of fresh air as he was professional, focussed and a team player. In particular he formed a good working relationship with Jude and another key member of the finance team, Tony Bennett.

By late October my team was beginning to grow in numbers and expertise. I already had Pat as the senior accountant, and Jude Dunn and Tony Bennett on the way. Another financial specialist, Katharina Pfitzner, was also due to start work soon. I was sometimes criticised for being too finance-centred but I firmly believed that the effectiveness of the CPA's work began and ended with money and its effective use and control. And that applied just as much to the governorate teams as to us in Basra.

As well as the finance advisers we also had Dominique Hope, who had transferred from military duties to business development, Michael Whitehead in health, Brian McCarthy in waste management, Peter Bingham covering the ports, Ed Lock for electricity transmission, Colin McBride for sewage – he would become the head of utilities – Kevin Thomas for fuels and Bjorn Brandtzaeg for trade and industry.

I knew that these expert advisers were vital if we were to make a real difference. From the outset the CPA had suffered from a lack of expertise. The Foreign Office had its Arabists but it wasn't used to running countries – the old days of the colonies had long gone. As for the military they'd fought in the Gulf War back in 1991 but that had been a 'fighting' war and they hadn't occupied land afterwards. Meanwhile, those civil servants sent to take charge of reconstruction on the British side weren't used to working in the Middle East. The developing world and especially Africa was their area of speciality. It was true that many of the NGOs, our own military and our civil servants had worked in post-conflict zones such as Kosovo and Sierra Leone. But they were very different areas of operation. Indeed most of us who came to work in southern Iraq had little or no experience of the region. I'd never been to the Middle East and spoke no Arabic. We were all unprepared when it came to running southern Iraq. General Graham Lamb summed it up well when he said we hadn't planned for 'cataclysmic success' in the military operation. The coalition had conquered Baghdad in a third of the expected time. When we found ourselves with a country to run we were ill-equipped to do it.

In the early days none of this seemed to matter so much. There was such a feeling of optimism and the fact that few of us knew the language or culture – and religion – didn't appear to be critical. Yet as the goodwill dissolved the need for experts who could make a real and swift difference grew. We wanted to help the Iraqis to help themselves and not become dependent on aid packages. Sir Hilary summed it up when he said: 'We cannot do everything and nor should we strive for perfection. We must concentrate on capacity building and try to discourage a dependency culture according to which the coalition becomes a sort of benign Saddam.'

Despite the many problems we faced I felt strangely optimistic at the time. There was just one small cloud on the horizon. At this point I still hadn't been offered a contract to stay on in Iraq. I was still technically part of the military operation but my tour of duty was due to finish at the end of October. From then on I'd be a free agent. Whitehall, however, seemed to be blissfully unaware of this. I even heard on the grapevine that Hilary Benn had contacted Sir Hilary to congratulate him on 'keeping the services of your merchant banker'. Yet I hadn't even discussed terms with anyone. I rang my contact at the Crown Agents in London who was in charge of recruiting my new team with help from other agencies. 'How are things going, Andrew?' he asked.

'Fine thanks,' I replied. 'Oh, and by the way, I'm leaving on Saturday.'

'OK,' he said. 'Maybe we can speak on Monday and catch up on things.'

'No I mean I'm *leaving* … I'm flying to Hong Kong to look for a job.'

'But why?'

'Because it's the end of my tour and I need to find a job.' There was a slight pause.

'But we assumed you would be going back to Iraq,' he said finally.

'That's great but no one's discussed that with me!' Naturally I'd hoped and indeed expected I would be offered a contract. But I wanted the best possible terms. I'd been on a major's wages for four months doing a very tough job and I felt that now was payback time financially. More importantly I needed a fall-back position in case I wasn't offered a contract or we couldn't reach an agreement. I couldn't afford to find myself suddenly leaving Iraq with no job to go to. My contact said that he was sure that a contract could be sorted out quickly.

'OK, let's discuss figures,' I said.

'I'm sorry I can't discuss figures with you, Andrew,' he said.

'Why not?'

'Because it would be inappropriate, I need to speak to your boss.'

'Well there's only one person more senior here and that's Sir Hilary and he has no idea what I should be earning.' I said. So we briefly discussed some figures and then he went off to make some phone calls.

Half an hour later Sir Hilary came to my office with a smile on his face. 'You owe me dinner!' he said.

'Great!' I replied, realising he'd sorted out my contract.

Then he looked at me and shook his head slowly. 'I knew I'd made a mistake,' said Sir Hilary. 'I should have retired and come back as a consultant.' I later received an email from London confirming that Whitehall had indeed given the green light on my contract. It had been a productive day.

6

GATHERING MOMENTUM

November–December 2003

Though my contract was now resolved I still decided to take some leave. I was ending my army tour and being re-hired as a civilian. That meant bringing out all my military kit – including my pistol – most of which had lain unpacked and unused in my locker. Before flying off to Hong Kong I met a Japanese friend in London. He comes from a very powerful and influential Japanese family which owned some major business interests. Over coffee we talked about what I was doing in Iraq. 'Why don't you come over to Japan?' said my friend, who was very well connected in government circles. 'There are people there who would be very interested in hearing about your job.' I decided to take up his offer.

In Tokyo I was introduced to a senior vice-minister in the Japanese Ministry of Foreign Affairs. He greeted me warmly in his office and we chatted as we drank tea. The minister was keen to learn about what was really going on in Iraq. After discussing the security situation I explained the significance of southern Iraq and especially of Samawah, where the Japanese troops were stationed. Half an hour later I was being ushered downstairs to meet an official in their Iraq programme and his staff. In a large conference room I met representatives from all the Japanese development agencies as well as foreign ministry staff. I was grateful for my investment banking connections.

'We are pleased to welcome you to Tokyo,' said the official, 'As you know, it is very difficult for the Japanese government to visit Iraq and we wish to thank you for coming to meet us. You are the first person to come from Iraq to Tokyo.' I was embarrassed at this praise but he went on. 'Please can you tell us about the security situation and also your thoughts about reconstruction in Iraq, and especially southern Iraq. As you know, the Japanese government has pledged five billion dollars to Iraq and we are interested in what you wish to say.'

After expressing my sorrow at the murder of two Japanese diplomats in Iraq a few weeks earlier I outlined the huge task ahead in the country. I'd brought maps with me of the southern cities and I laid these out on the floor while the Japanese asked me questions. They were keen to know about the condition of the basic utilities such as electricity and water, hospitals and schools. I tried to impress on them that the layers of bureaucracy in Baghdad might prevent money getting through quickly to the south, including Samawah. My aim was to encourage them to deal with us directly in Basra. US spending seemed to be almost entirely focussed in and around Baghdad. Many of us in the south thought that the economy needed to be fixed first in the north and the south of the country and that the centre – around Baghdad – should be last because it was such a tough nut to crack.

The official told me they'd set aside $30 million for 'emergency grant aid for Basra and southern Iraq' to be used for refuse trucks. It was a start but I knew in the long term the region would need a lot more. I handed over a $1 billion 'shopping list' of potential projects for the south – a list pulled together by my team. At the end of the meeting my host walked me to the entrance of the building to say goodbye and promised to stay in touch by email. It was a useful first step. I hadn't gone there on behalf of the British government – Whitehall didn't even know I was there. But this was a golden opportunity to influence where the Japanese spent their money and was too good to miss.

Back in Basra we were now ready to welcome the four new regional governorate teams in Al-Basra, Dhi Qar, Maysan and Al-Muthanna. Each team reported directly to Paul Bremer. Our job was to support them over finance and help them with strategic issues such as oil, water and power. At last I felt we were moving from mere fire-fighting to proper regional strategic government.

We also spent money on some less official but equally important projects. This was thanks to another interpreter who had joined my team. Ahmed was a computer programmer and was a very bright and ingenious man. In fact it was his restless mind that brought him to us from his work as an interpreter for the military. An officer at brigade HQ said to me: 'Andrew can you take this man off our hands for us please – he's too intelligent and he's driving us nuts!' It was their loss and our gain. Ahmed was born and bred in Basra and knew the city inside out. Soon, I learnt to trust his judgement on what was really going on in the city. 'You are my eyes and ears,' I often told Ahmed, something of which he was proud.

One day I was worrying about the local fertiliser plant, a key industry in the region that helped the local farmers and employed 12,000 people. We'd been paying the staff's salaries for several months but I'd heard that many of them weren't actually going to work. Often they would just go to the plant to collect their wages. Then Mr Naheed the plant's wily DG came to see me. 'Mr Andrew, I want one hundred million dollars!' What on earth for, I wanted to know? 'We need our own power plant,' he replied. I could see what he meant. The factory used a lot of energy and the electricity supplies were still not very reliable. He had also heard about the billions of dollars that were being promised to rebuild the country. So I guess he figured, what's $100 million against all that? I promised to look into it.

First of all we sent our power expert Robert Apsley out to the power plant to report on the situation. 'They don't need a new power station,' said Robert after his fact-finding mission. 'We could put in a standby generator and string up some new cables to connect it to the grid.'

'How much would all that cost? I wanted to know.

'About five million dollars I think,' replied Robert. Meanwhile I'd gone to Ahmed, given him a $20 note for taxis, and told him to go out and find out what he could. He went off and spoke to people in the workforce, people who knew what was really going on and the kind of people we didn't get to speak to.

'The DG is OK, but does not really know what is going on. And half the workforce is not even at work,' explained Ahmed, who then gave me lots more inside information about the company. This was invaluable. It meant the next time I met Mr Naheed I was able to negotiate with him on a basis of real knowledge. He then agreed simply to have a standby generator put in.

Ahmed wasn't content just with being told what to do. He came up with his own ideas too. One day he said: 'Mr Andrew, you need to buy consent in the area.'

'What do you mean, Ahmed?' I asked

'I mean that if you look after the neighbourhood they will look after you.' He was talking about security, making sure those nearest to us wouldn't become a danger to us. It seemed like an obvious idea.

'OK so what do you have in mind?' I asked. 'And how much will it cost?'

'We don't need to spend very much money, Mr Andrew, and certainly not millions,' he replied. 'It is *how* we spend the money that matters.' And so Ahmed drew up his small shopping list of what we could do to help win over our neighbours.

In one case we simply bought electric fans for the local mosques to give to people when the heat became close to unbearable. These were very gratefully received and we got some wonderful thank-you letters. Then Ahmed suggested that he buy some computers and also some sewing machines for local girls' schools.

'Sewing machines, Ahmed? Are you sure?' I asked.

'Yes, Mr Andrew, just a few machines will make all the difference.' Once again he was right and they were very well received. It may not have been very politically correct but this was a traditional area and sewing machines for the girls was what they wanted. We were delighted with the outcome and so was Ahmed. As he proudly told me later: 'CPA gave me thirty thousand dollars and with this money I opened ten computer centres in ten secondary schools, ten sewing machine centres in ten secondary schools for girls, gave more than over three hundreds [sic] blankets to the poor and the same number of oil heaters – and over five hundreds [sic] fans to the needy.'

Ahmed was also ingenious when it came to solving problems in the CPA compound: he translated all the Iraqi financial information into English, and also helped with problems we had over local visitors. The Al-Sarraji HQ was a large complex and the rule was that Iraqi visitors had to wait at the gates until their contact inside had personally trekked down there to collect them. I don't think we ever fully appreciated just how much danger we were putting our visitors in. First they had to come through the crowds always at our gate, then they were seen coming into the compound, then they had to wait. And so Ahmed, using his programming skills, created a whole computerised booking system that hugely streamlined the process and meant our visitors spent less time waiting around outside, becoming potential targets.

Most of the time I was either in Basra or Baghdad. But sometimes I got the chance to see more of southern Iraq. On a couple of occasions I drove to the vast largely desert province of Al-Muthanna, whose capital is Samawah. The first time I went with Charles Monk. I wanted to speak to the outgoing US CIMIC team based there and see how it was handling economic issues. Charles wanted to visit the Technical Institute and understand the requirements for the education directorate. We were allowed to go with just one vehicle because we were heading out into the desert, effectively bypassing population centres, and travelling to one of Iraq's westernmost and most remote areas. However, we were each armed with pistols, and had two clips each totalling forty rounds of ammunition, flak jackets and helmets, as well as small rucksacks with sleeping bags and wash-kit.

We got up at dawn and drove off in a land cruiser. It was only then that I began to understand truly how vast and desolate parts of Iraq could be. We drove for mile after mile surrounded by nothing but desert. We eventually passed by Ur, said to be the birthplace of Abraham. Nearby there is also a monument to the ancient Sumerian sun god and an ancient royal tomb. It's an impressive place. However, for most of the time there was little to see except sand. Occasionally we'd glimpse the figure of a woman, dressed completely in black, walking on her own. Where she'd come from and where she was heading in this wilderness we had no idea. In other places we'd see row upon row of plastic sheets used to capture moisture on the ground that might gather during the coolness of the night. Field boundaries were made not with fences or hedges but with mounds of earth. Passing through one village, I was struck by the unchanged house-building methods, the mud bricks and thatched roofs made from reeds from a nearby oasis. This was a world far removed from the industrial centres of Baghdad and Basra. This was subsistence living in one of the harshest environments on the planet. On the outward journey the temperature gauge in the car recorded 65 °C or 149 °F, the highest I'd ever seen.

The roads were amazing too. Saddam Hussein had spent vast sums of money to build these routes crossing the desert and in many places they were still in very good condition; there was no frost and very little traffic to damage them. They were mini-motorways with two lanes in either direction, though there was no longer a central reservation as the metal barriers had long since been looted. Only the studs in the ground remained. All the road signs had also been stolen, which added to the eeriness of driving through the desert. How could you be sure you were going the right way? And despite the lack of traffic the roads could be dangerous. The few Iraqis that came this way didn't pay much attention to which lane or even which side of the road they were on. Whenever we suddenly saw another vehicle speeding towards us in the same lane our tactic was to stay in the our proper lane and flash our headlights furiously. In the end the other car would get the message and swerve to avoid us. 'What's wrong with your side of the road?' I'd mutter impotently as they whizzed past.

Another hazard were road bridges. Some of them had collapsed and traffic would be reduced to a single file around the obstructions. This was especially tricky at night time. Suddenly great lumps of stone would loom up at us from the middle of the carriageway and we'd have to slam on our brakes and swerve. Bridges that were still intact were scarcely less alarming. There were stories of people dropping hand grenades from them upon unsuspecting drivers passing underneath.

The aim of my second trip was to take a look at the infrastructure – or lack of it – in the area. The large but mostly empty expanse of Al-Muthanna had a population of about 300,000 and had never had a regular electricity supply. Electricity in Iraq tended to be moved northwards, only coming south to this area bordering Saudi Arabia if there was any spare capacity in the grid. This rarely, if ever, happened. It was literally the end of the line. The people had to rely instead on generators. We saw here a clear chance to do something tangible. Al-Muthanna had two industries, cement and brick-making, both carried out by the same factory. Now without a proper power supply it lay idle. Robert had concluded that it would be possible to build a power station there, since there was already a gas pipeline that passed not 5 km from the main town which could supply fuel.

In Samawah town hall we walked through a columned covered walkway from one side of the building to the other, where we were ushered into the governor's temporary office. Mr Hassani welcomed us and then pleaded his case: 'The people of Samawah need your help. We have a cement factory where we make cement and also bricks but we need electricity and we need fresh water. Please can you help us?' Looking around at this desolate area it was hard to refuse.

'Thank you for your hospitality. I'm returning to Basra and I'll tell the Ambassador that this is the priority for the people of Samawah and we will work hard to see what we can do.' I was careful not to make any rash promises we couldn't keep.

When this was translated, he smiled and thanked us in Arabic, '*Shukran, shukran.*'

To signal that the meeting was over he invited us to sit down and offered us mint tea. Two minutes later an aide appeared with four glasses filled with black tea, with mint leaves on the saucers. I hesitated and the governor must have noticed because he rattled a question at his interpreter. I was concerned that I might have offended him. So I was relieved when the interpreter asked: 'This is the first time that you have had mint tea in the Arabic way?' It was.

'*Nam,*' I said hesitantly. He nodded and, picking up the leaf, dropped it into the glass of hot sugared tea. Following his lead I did likewise and took a sip. To my surprise it was quite delicious, the sugar and mint banishing the taste of tannin. We sat and drank tea for a few minutes, no one saying anything. Once we'd finished we stood up and said goodbye to Mr Hassani. It had been a successful meeting.

My decision not to make any quick promises to the governor proved a wise one, however. With our brigadier I flew to Baghdad to tell the programme review board that we needed $30 million for the project. We explained to US officials that it was supported by the local people and would make a real difference. But we met a lot of resistance. Some officials feared that using the gas from the pipeline that ran though Al-Muthanna would divert supplies from elsewhere. However, we'd already spoken to Mr Waleed from South Oil and he'd explained to us that there was plenty of gas to meet both needs. Eventually the board agreed to the plan – but only on condition that the Ministry of Electricity signed it off.

The ministry, however, refused. 'We have been told that there is not enough gas,' an official explained when I questioned their decision. By now I was stumbling from one office to another in Baghdad's Green Zone trying to get the issue sorted.

'Who told you that?' I asked.

'The Ministry of Oil,' the official told me. I was beginning to lose patience.

'But the Ministry of Oil hasn't even been down to the area,' I exclaimed. 'And Mr Waleed has – and he says there's enough gas.' In fairness Mr Waleed had also said the pipelines might need to be repaired. But if they gave him the money to do that then he was confident there would be enough gas. The truth was that the Ministry of Electricity wanted to keep all the gas for themselves and not share it with Al-Muthanna. So I asked Mr Waleed to write a letter confirming directly that there was indeed enough gas for everyone. In the end the project was approved and Robert began work on it. The process would turn out to be a long and arduous one lasting several years but eventually Al-Muthanna would get its power station.

By now I was spending more and more time in Baghdad. It was where the money was and where the Project Management Office was based. The PMO was set up to oversee the spending of the $18 billion dollars that the United States had already pledged to help rebuild Iraq. The problem for us was that southern Iraq wasn't on their radar screen. We were a multi-national group of Britons, Italians, Australians, Danes, Czechs, Romanians, Poles and others and the PMO, like other US-centred groups, didn't really know much about us – they only listened to other Americans. To Baghdad we weren't CPA South but CPA-who? 'Do we *have* a CPA office in Basra?' more than one American official in Baghdad asked me. Somehow we needed to make sure that the PMO would commit some of the vast sums they had to spend on the huge infrastructure problems we had in the south. Our attempts to impress the Madrid donors conference hadn't gone well, because we'd had so little time to prepare for it. Now it was time to get the PMO to sit up and notice us.

Rear Admiral David J. Nash was director of the PMO and ran the operation from small nondescript offices next to the main palace complex in Baghdad. His naval background was in engineering, procurement and project management, so in many ways he was ideally suited for the job. He was also immensely charismatic and I liked him immediately. 'Who are you?' he asked in a friendly voice as I was introduced to him in his office.

'I'm Andrew Alderson, I work in Basra.'

His deputy, with whom I'd already made contact, turned to Dave at this point. 'He's the David Oliver of the south.' This made Dave smile. He obviously knew who David Oliver was and what he did and this comment told him all he needed to know.

From chatting to Dave I quickly realised that here was a man who could cut through a lot of the red tape that inevitably seemed to surround any dealings with Baghdad. The capital was often guilty of what is called 'stove-pipe planning'. Individual ministries went about their own work but did not necessarily communicate well – or sometimes at all – with other ministries whose business might cross over with theirs. The result was a chronic lack of co-ordination. At least in Dave I'd found someone with whom I could discuss the bigger picture. For example he told me that he would have at his disposal around $2.5 billion to spend on electricity generation and distribution across the whole of the country. As the south made up a fifth of that, I made a pitch for a share of that money. 'By my reckoning that means the south should get about $500 million!' I said, with a smile. Dave of course wasn't about to make any rash promises. But now at least we had someone to speak to about it.

I could share my exasperation at dealing with some of the ministries with him. I told him about the problems with the Ministry of Oil and how they were trying to make decisions about the south without even visiting it. 'It sometimes feels as if I'm banging my head against a brick wall dealing with them,' I complained. It was now that Dave gave me one of the most amusing and wisest pieces of advice that I was to receive during my time in the Middle East.

'You know, Andrew,' he said, leaning towards me, 'in Iraq I work on one principle – and that is to proceed until apprehended!'

Another crucial ally in Baghdad was my old friend Tash Coxen, the UK liaison officer who reported to Andy Bearpark. Tash helped co-ordinate visits but more importantly she prowled the corridors of Baghdad and knew where the levers of power were. If some officials were dragging their heels over an issue in the capital you could email Tash and she would go and bang heads together. She was brilliant at her job and had the knack of knowing exactly the right person to see. She was also always overworked and not someone to get on the wrong side of – as well as a sharp mind she had a sharp tongue.

Tash gave me valuable insights into how the relationship between Baghdad and Basra worked – or didn't work. She was later fairly scathing about the way the US-dominated capital viewed the rest of Iraq. 'I got the impression that for the US CPA in Baghdad, life in Iraq outside the capital didn't really exist. The place was like an enormous self-licking lollipop, and very little attention paid to the millions of Iraqis trying to get on with daily life across the rest of the country. In terms of the media message … as long as the *Washington Post* and *New York Times* were getting it right they didn't give a shit about anyone else.

'The Iraqis were very much an afterthought from what I saw. That's not so say there weren't some dedicated people in Baghdad. But as an organisational whole … it wasn't there for altruistic Iraqi advancement.' One of the problems, she said, was that there had been so little advance planning that much of the organisation's time and focus was taken up simply trying to make itself work. The plans came later. 'Months after the CPA came into existence the strategic planning department finally produced this coloured graph with triangles, circles and squares and various time lines,' said Tash. 'They said "Hey look here's the strategic plan for how we're going to do it." Everyone just laughed.'

'The regions were regarded by the people in the centre of Baghdad as fairly unimportant. As long as there wasn't a big problem they could be ignored,' she said. The south in particular was regarded as a 'problem child' by Baghdad. 'I often felt I was in a no-win situation – both ends, Baghdad and Basra, would each accuse me of being "on the other's side". And trust me, it often really felt like the two elements of the CPA were at war – the Iraqis didn't appear to come into the equation.'

If it was sometimes hard to get Basra's voice heard in Baghdad, there was at least one subject that usually helped to get their attention – oil. Oil was and is the lifeblood of the Iraqi economy and, contrary to popular belief, its sale to the international markets, both under Saddam Hussein and after the conflict, was vital to secure much-needed revenue for the Iraqi economy. In general Baghdad insisted on dealing with most issues concerning oil, including paying oil workers. However, after several months, all kinds of problems were beginning to emerge. At the local level, groups of oil workers we barely knew about weren't being paid, and their local staff visited us to complain. One group of workers going on strike would only provoke others to follow suit. It struck me that this new-found freedom was one thing, but their ability to go on strike every month was ruining any plans we had to manage the economy.

Then one day I was approached by a British army captain. He was working with the US oil task force stationed out at Basra airport. 'Can I have a word?' he asked as I took a coffee break outside my office.

'Sure. How can I help?' I said.

'I'm told that you have the money, and you might be able to help us.' I was immediately on my guard. Whilst we had several million dollars to allocate in projects, I was sure that anything to do with the oil sector would quickly devour our budget. He explained that he had experience working in the oil sector and that there was a company called the Oil Drilling Company outside Basra which was financed from Baghdad, but which lacked new oil-drilling rigs.

'OK,' I said, my interest picking up at the mention of the drilling company, 'How can I help?'

'I want to show you a graph and an Excel spreadsheet of what production can be achieved by either repairing old drilling wells or drilling new ones, then I'll let you decide.' He went on to explain that the Iraqis were more than capable of drilling their own wells – they'd been doing so for 15 years. And each new drilling rig could add potentially hundreds of million of dollars in revenue from every new well it could drill – on average one every 45 days. Indeed for less than $5 million, the young captain was confident that we could bring almost half a billion into the coffers of the Iraqi exchequer.

'The numbers look compelling,' I agreed. 'So why aren't we doing this?'

Then I remembered a conversation I'd had with South Oil's Mr Waleed who was baffled at the US contractors KBR being used to drill wells and not them. 'Their cost is around one million dollars per well. If you would give us the equipment, we can do it for less than one hundred thousand dollars,' he had told me in his usual forthright way. His argument had made sense but this was the politics of oil and these were decisions that were being taken far above my head, most likely in Washington. For once my instincts told me we should back away from a full-on fight.

'We're already questioning their whole strategy in the electricity sector, I'm not sure we can go after them in the oil sector too,' I told the captain. But I promised that on my next trip to Baghdad I'd make some enquiries.

In Baghdad I called in at the Oil Ministry offices where I met a jovial Welshman called Bob Morgan, an experienced senior ex-BP executive who was part of the team responsible for giving the Iraqis strategic advice on the industry. I was shocked to learn that the proposed strategy was leaning towards nationalisation. This was yet another example of centralist thinking. Bob then said to me, 'But what I'm really concerned about is the condition of their oil reservoirs.' I asked him to explain. 'Well, they need to protect the reservoirs because the lack of investment over the years is taking its toll. If they aren't careful there's a real risk that they may damage the reservoirs irreparably. Many of the wells have all kinds of equipment sunk thousands of feet below the surface, and they haven't maintained the reservoirs and oil sands at all well. This is a major concern. Basically their infrastructure is a mess.' Ultimately there was a danger that they wouldn't be able to extract all the oil.

A huge volume of email traffic greeted me the next day when I got back to Basra. On top of meeting requests from local Iraqis, I'd received more than 150 urgent emails from the governorate teams, my own team in Basra, the management team upstairs, from Baghdad and even London. I complained to Colin about how we were swamped with requests for information or action. 'What I find,' Colin said mysteriously, 'is that though there are so many alligators snapping at the edge of the boat, the fact there are so many of them means that the ones at the back just seem to get stuck, jammed together, and they die. Meanwhile the really nasty ones though still make it to the boat – and by then they are really big so you have to deal with them,' he continued.

I looked at him questioningly. 'Yes,' I said, 'but who's looking out for where the boat is going?' I asked.

'That's your job.' He replied smiling.

There were yet other headaches associated with oil. At the time petrol was heavily subsidised and cost just five cents a litre. But the refineries were either broken or didn't have enough capacity to produce enough petrol and diesel. This meant that Iraq was at the time importing about $250 million worth of fuel for the country's vehicles every month, or $3 billion a year. On top of this about $5 billion a year was going on subsidising cheap food rations for the Iraqi people. Yet oil exports were only bringing in $15 billion a year and with no one paying any tax, this was the country's entire income. So about half of the total income was going into fuel and food subsidies.

But as the state got poorer, some enterprising Iraqis started to get very rich. They were buying the subsided fuel in Iraq at 5 cents a litre then driving it across the border into Kuwait. Here they sold it for a fat profit. The Kuwaitis didn't mind, however, because they were then able to sell the same fuel back to the Iraqi state at the full market rate – around 20 cents per litre. It was a classic piece of 'arbitrage'.

We first experienced this business first hand when our fuel expert Kevin Thomas bought 14 new fuel tankers for $3.5 million. The idea was to use the tankers to transport petrol around quickly in the event of a fuel shortage. Colin went down to oversee the moving of the 14 tankers from Shaibah, south-west of Basra, further north to Al-Amara. Each one was laden with 5,000 litres of fuel so Colin had some armed soldiers with him. However, as Colin made the arrangements for the convoy to start he noticed something odd. Although Kevin had bought 14 tankers there were now 15 of them standing ready to leave. Which one was the extra tanker? And why had it joined the convoy? None of the local drivers seemed willing to divulge which was the odd one out. So Colin gathered everyone together and announced that each lorry was to have a soldier riding in its cab for protection. And he pointedly told the soldiers: 'If any driver deviates a yard from his course then shoot him and drive the lorry yourself.' Colin was joking. But the Iraqis, who were listening through an interpreter, didn't know that. As a result all 14 tankers plus the extra one made it safely to their destination. The plan had been simple. The rogue driver had joined the convoy and loaded up on cheap Iraqi fuel. At a set moment in the journey he planned to veer off across the desert and make his way to Kuwait, to sell his valuable cargo. Fortunately Colin had been too alert to be caught out like that.

The issue of oil was such an important one that I wrote a discussion paper on the subject and distributed it to interested parties. A copy of it must have floated its way to Whitehall because a few days later I had a call from a woman at the Foreign Office. I can't recall her name but she was very brisk and to the point. She said: 'I'm from the Iraqi policy unit and I want to know who you think you are producing policy documents on Iraq's fuel?' My telephone number linked through Baghdad and I had an 'American' number in Iraq – so perhaps she thought I was in the Iraqi capital. I explained to her that I was director of the economic planning and development department in Basra and that 70 per cent of the country's oil came from the south.

'I'm also responsible for the finances in southern Iraq so actually I think I'm quite well qualified to talk about it,' I told

The military HQ at Basra Palace

Basra Palace complex,
aerial view

The state of Basra's
sewage and refuse

Basra's Central Bank vaults

The Central Bank's
temporary offices
– in a container

Regional HQ bank records

Money arriving from the Central Bank for safekeeping

Major Frances Castle leaning against July 2003's delivery of $48m

Another money delivery in August

Payment in the form of a cheque

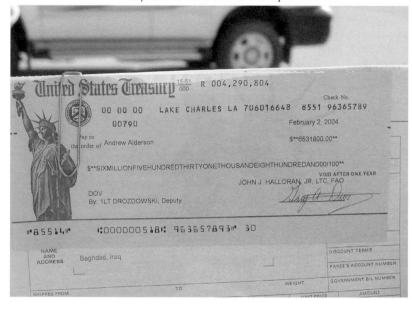

Riots in Basra

Car bombs in Basra

A car bomb in Baghdad

Pat McLoughlin in our new
office after our land grab

Our new accommodation
from October 2003

Iraq's shipping industry – one of the 240 vessels that is either partially
submerged or sunk along the Shat Al-Arab waterway

RAF repairing pylons

New technical college for Basra's education department

My team

Tony Blair meets
team member
Colin McBride

HRH Prince Charles
meets my team

her. 'And by the way, since we're on the subject – who are you?'

The announcement on 14 December 2003 that Saddam Hussein had finally been captured by the Americans after eight months in hiding caused jubilation across Iraq. In Basra we too felt a sense of cautious optimism and many of us gathered for drinks that evening in the Oasis Bar.The outside bar that we used in the evenings was just about our only focal point for socialising and occasionally it got a little too exuberant. For example during the Muslim holy month of Ramadan the bar had to be moved inside because people had been making too much noise into the night, well past the scheduled 11pm closing time. The CPA chief of staff Colonel Peter Duklis told us: 'This is out of respect for our neighbours during their holy month of Ramadan. The noise can be heard over the walls and through-out Al-Sarraji – last night's session was quite vociferous and went on well past the closing hours.' He even threatened to close the bar permanently if people didn't obey the rules.

However, on the evening of Saddam's arrest just about all the staff went to the bar for a drink to mark this milestone in Iraqi history. It was quite a sight – 100 civilians standing around at the bar sipping drinks, all wearing helmets. We feared the same explosion of 'happy rounds' that had greeted the deaths of Saddam's sons back in the summer, when up to 57 people had died around the country and countless cars had been dented by bullets falling back to earth. In fact the reaction, though jubilant, was far more restrained. The army had spoken to the mullahs about the risks of 'happy rounds' and the mullahs had spoken to the people on loud hailers. 'Save your bullets for when he is executed – don't shoot now he is only arrested,' they told the people. The fact that this instruction was almost universally obeyed showed the power of the clerics over the people.

Before the end of the year I had to deal with a few prob-lems among the staff at the CPA. Most of the new arrivals had turned out to be as good as or even better than we'd hoped. However, there was a slight problem with one Italian – he spoke hardly a word of English. 'Angelo' was as far as I could tell a delightful man but unfortunately we needed rather more than that. He seemed to spend much of his time drifting around chatting and writing reports in Italian about the transport system. I would sometimes ask him 'Angelo, what are you doing?' He would reply: 'I'm sorry my English is not very good, I don't understand.' I'm sure that he was very capable in his specialist area of roads. But he just didn't justify his place as far as I was concerned. There was another Italian and two Britons who failed to fit in. The problem with one of these wasn't so much his work but his overbearing manner. Some of his colleagues came to me and said: 'If this guy doesn't go we're off!' Tensions are of course inevitable in any team and on the whole you just get on with it. But we had little time to spend on personnel issues and it was easier to let some people go. So the Italians and the Brits were thanked and told their services would no longer be required after Christmas.

The next day I was summoned to see Sir Hilary. The Italian ambassador Mario Maiolini had steamed in to see him about me 'sacking' the two Italians and to complain about this abrupt reduction in the ratio of Italian representation. 'I think you've just created a diplomatic incident,' said Sir Hilary coolly, as I entered his office.

I looked at him. 'Ah,' was all I could think of saying.

'I think you know exactly what I'm talking about,' continued Sir Hilary.

'Yes,' I said as he fixed me with his steely gaze.

'Were you going to ask me?' I was just about to stammer an answer when the ambassador cut in. 'No, don't answer that. I know what you'll say, that if you'd asked me I wouldn't have let you do it and you wanted to do it anyway. Is that right?'

'Er, yeah,' I admitted.

'I see,' said Sir Hilary thoughtfully, 'that would have been difficult … '

'Anyway it's OK, Sir Hilary,' I added brightly, 'because the ratio of Italians is still the same as it was.'

'Why's that?' he asked.

'Because two Brits have gone as well,' I replied.

Sir Hilary laughed. 'OK, well I'm glad you told me,' he said. And that was the end of the matter as far as I was concerned. From the start I'd insisted that if I wasn't happy with a member of the team I should have the right to let them go. It was written into their contract. I also knew that Mario's objections weren't about the quality of the two Italians' contribution, but about his country's representation. Sir Hilary now had something to mollify him with.

There were some less serious moments as the year came to an end. Oscar the cat had become such a hit in some quarters that his name was now being raised in staff meetings. Sir Hilary's wife had started sending the animal food parcels containing Kit-e-Kat through the BFPO postal service. 'What's really annoying,' said Sir Hilary in his dry way, 'is that I think the cat gets more stuff than I do!' On another occasion Oscar, who always behaved as if he owned the place, had taken a sudden dislike to one of Sir Hilary's jackets and decided to sharpen his claws on it. 'That cat of yours has just ripped the shoulder of one of my best Hackett jackets!' he told me in the corridor. I felt like suggesting that Sir Hilary shouldn't have left his jacket on a chair in temptation's way but thought better of it. In any case Oscar seemed to be in an unassailable position if the ambassador's wife had adopted him as a long-distance pet.

The highlight of the end of the year for many in the CPA who hadn't managed to get away on leave was Christmas Day. Mario Maiolini had pre-lunch drinks for some of us at his portakabin where the Italian ambassador produced bottles of red wine, Parma ham and some parmesan cheese. It never ceased to amaze me how he could produce such items, which came in the diplomatic bag I think. Later there was a Christmas lunch with turkey and Christmas pudding though no alcohol. Rosie Knight also helped organise some festive events, which included a treasure hunt and a fancy-dress party. It was a fun day though I spent much of it sleeping or reading a book, grateful for a chance to unwind for a few hours. I and many in the CPA felt reasonably happy about what we'd done and cautiously optimistic about the coming year. We believed we'd stabilised the south and there was also a sense that we in the British sector had got things right – unlike in Baghdad. And though there had been a few worrying signs of an increase in violence in Maysan on the whole the security situation was more or less under control. Or so we thought.

7

SPEND, SPEND, SPEND

January–February 2004

The New Year started with a high-profile visit from Prime Minister Tony Blair. Much of the publicity inevitably focussed on the PM's meetings with the British military. We had become used to the fact that it was always the soldiers who made the headlines while our work in the CPA rarely made the news. However, Judge al-Latif had a private meeting with Mr Blair in which the governor praised the work of the CPA and said that while unemployment was still a problem, water and power provision had improved. As for the prime minister, he spoke about the need to finish the job of re-building the country that we'd started. He announced: 'As far as we're concerned … we will stay with this to get it done. The task is not to get half-started and then not finished. It's got to be finished, because it is important to this country and indeed to the whole world.' These were fine words and I'm sure he meant them at the time, but they were to ring a little hollow to us as events unfolded later that year.

I wasn't in Basra to meet the PM, having flown to Baghdad that morning on another money run. In any case I was confident that our team was sufficiently outspoken about the challenges that we were facing to make the right points. Colin McBride and Robert Apsley, for example, were concerned that instead of building new gas-fired power stations the US were trying to keep going ancient ramshackle installations that should have been scrapped. 'Bonkers' was Robert's view. They were also unhappy that the UK military was still fixated on small diesel power stations when Iraq was chronically short of diesel. I was sure they'd make their voices heard.

The next day I returned with yet another heavy suitcase of cash, $1.6 milion this time. I was amused to see various photos of team members meeting a grinning Tony Blair with captions next to them. 'We need more power,' had been Colin's simple comment delivered in his broad Belfast accent.

'So do you think he got the message?' I asked Colin.

'Well if he didn't get the short version from me, Robert gave him both barrels and the long technical version, ' Colin said with a grin. I could just imagine. Robert was passionate and extremely knowledgeable about his subject. And he was extremely critical of the current energy policy – or, as he preferred to put it, the complete lack of one.

The PM's visit was generally judged a success and Iraqi local staff in particular were delighted that Mr Blair was happy to be photographed with them. Even so there were one or two small hiccups that seemed symbolic even then. For example, though the visit made headlines in the UK, the local Iraqi media weren't present. Why they weren't included I was never sure. But it meant that Mr Blair's visit had limited impact in the country itself. Then when Judge al-Latif publicly praised our work at the CPA in front of the TV cameras some of his words were drowned out by the noise of a military helicopter and gunfire coming from the streets of Basra. This was a sign of what was to come; how the growing violence and deteriorating security in the country gradually overshadowed what we were trying to achieve.

Our relations with the Iraqi people were also beginning to suffer because of the unrealistic claims that many – and especially the US media through their administration – were starting to make. From the start of the year there was a string of announce-ment of 'successes' that bore little relation to reality. For example in Nasariyah the US organisation Restore Iraqi Electricity – or RIE – had announced that they would soon have on line a new power station providing 250 MW of power. This was made up of two 125 MW units that were to be installed into the existing power plant. Yet Robert Apsley had already visited the site and found out that the units wouldn't fit in the plant as planned. So as far as he was concerned they'd have to be re-engineered.

Coincidentally an American colonel from the RIE team came to Basra for a meeting to discuss the ongoing emergency infrastructure plan. The American officer said that the new power station in Nasariyah 'would be on line in March' – just eight weeks away – and said how 'exciting' the project was. Sir Hilary, who was chairing the meeting, sat listening in stony silence and let the officer have his say. Finally Sir Hilary spoke.

'Have these units been installed yet?' he asked the officer.

'No,' came the reply.

'But my advisers tell me that if you haven't even broken ground yet then there is no way you will have the generators online in eight weeks … '

The American colonel paused. 'No, that's true,' he admitted.

It was the first and only time I saw Sir Hilary really lose it. He was absolutely furious that the colonel was making prom-ises that couldn't be kept. 'Is this the presentation that is going to Paul Bremer?' demanded Sir Hilary, who himself reported directly to the American head of the CPA in Baghdad. 'Is this the information that is being passed back to Washington?'

'Yes,' admitted the hapless colonel, utterly crestfallen.

'But this is fabrication, isn't it? This is not reality, is it?' raged Sir Hilary.

'No Sir, that's true,' conceded the colonel. It was a chilling example of the kind of 'disconnect' that was occurring. Who could blame the Iraqis if they felt increasingly bewildered about the difference between what people were saying and what was really happening?

It wasn't hard to see why the Americans were keen to develop a 'good news culture'. After the optimism of the early weeks of occupation, events had begun to unravel. The US feared getting bogged down in the country. The spectre of the years they spent in Vietnam worried some. So they talked up the achievements. This also explained why Paul Bremer and the US leadership were so keen to hand over power to the Iraqis. Initially we'd been led to believe that the CPA would exist until December 2004, giving us some time to make real progress in reconstruction. But in November 2003 the US had made it clear that they wanted to hand over at the end of June. Since no one knew what our roles would be after the hand-over this might leave us with us just six months to complete our work.

The sheer scale of the work still needed to rebuild Iraq was mind-boggling. Though there was enough oil money to pay wages and fund smaller scale projects the really big work was going to require vast sums of cash. Lack of investment in past decades, neglect and, more recently, looting meant that to restore Iraq's shattered infrastructure to reasonable working order would cost around $80 billion. In reality only a quarter of any projects would be likely to be completed by June. And this assumed that the security situation wouldn't deteriorate. So as security did get worse, more and more of the cash was used up simply keeping people safe.

The vital sweet-water canal near Basra was a victim of this funding problem. During the past few months, many surveys had been completed, firstly by Bechtel, then by the military, then by CPA South specialists, then by CPA-allocated person-nel from Baghdad, then by the PMO engineers. Everyone agreed that it was a problem, but it was so large that no one could agree how it should be tackled. The whole canal was in such poor repair that while you fixed one part it would simply put even more pressure on another part. It was a project where work and costs were liable to spiral out of control. Yet it delivered two million litres of water a day to the people of Basra so it was of critical importance to us.

We called together the Iraqis from the water company, the team from Bechtel, the engineering branch from the military and our own specialists to have our very own water summit. The groups met in the CPA upstairs boardroom, a tiled room that had been a bathroom in another life. All 12 seats around the table were filled. I asked our water expert Wally Weeks to kick off the meeting and explain the scale of the problem – he was respected by everyone and was always diplomatic, which he needed to be because there were such tensions over this vital issue. We knew the Iraqis were critical of Bechtel because they felt that they were being ignored by them. The US firms meanwhile felt the problem was too large to be addressed and were concerned that funding didn't yet exist for the project. Both sides had a point but the bottom line was that we couldn't afford to have the canal breached, and for Basra to run out of water.

The Iraqi contingent were adamant that we should repair large sections of the canal – they felt we owed it to them. But when they saw everyone shaking their heads they began to realise that this wasn't a realistic outcome. We seemed to be at an impasse. Then Wally put forward a compromise. 'Maybe Bechtel could provide equipment and some supplies for the Iraqi ministry team to work with – with Bechtel just overseeing the project?' It was an elegant solution that would mean at least some of the vital work would be carried out, even if there wasn't enough cash to carry out all that was really needed. It would also save face all round. It reduced the costs because we were paying the Iraqi staff wages in any case and Bechtel already had much of the plant and machinery nearby. Moreover the military would also be able to offer some limited engineering support. The strategy was agreed. It would be a genuine team effort but it had only been agreed at the eleventh hour.

As I returned to my office I told Pat of my frustration. 'Why does it take a crisis like this to bring everyone around the same table to establish a common way forward?'

'The left hand isn't speaking to the right hand,' he said. It was a common problem across the country.

At the time many contractors – especially American ones – were doing extremely well out of the cash that was sloshing around in Iraq. Some of them were being awarded what are known as 'cost plus' contracts. This means that the profit margin that the company will make on the deal is agreed in advance. So whatever work the company carries out they are guaranteed to make a good profit, no matter what expenses they incur. In other words, they are fantastic contracts.

In addition, the irony was that as the main finance man for the CPA in the south I had absolutely no say in spending at the CPA itself. For example KBR – the contactor at our site – announced they were building us a soccer pitch and a volleyball court from fine sand. Up to then we'd been quite happy to have a kick around in the dirt or throw frisbees. But they built them anyway and the final bill would have been sent to the US. Later on Whitehall would use these kinds of costs to argue that we were too expensive. But that was simply because we had no control over them.

Yet even though contractors, my team and the governorate teams were spending money as fast as we could, it seemed this wasn't fast enough. We were told this at one of the weekly heads of department meetings held in the compound's Iftar tent. Iftar is the meal the Muslims have after sunset at the end of their day of fasting during Ramadan and this tent was where we used to invite local dignitaries. On this occasion, with the rain pouring down outside, we sat attentively on plastic chairs while Sir Hilary told us what the latest instructions were from Baghdad. Sir Hilary had just returned from the capital where Bremer had complained about the lack of spending in the south. The aim now was to 'buy consent' from the Iraqi people. And this was to be achieved by accelerating the programme of projects. In simple terms this meant spend, spend, spend.

By this time CPA South was already spending something like $2.5 million a week on projects. This was now to increase to $5 million. The main source of this money was called the Developmental Fund for Iraq (DFI). This was Iraq's own oil money being circulated back into the economy and given to the CPA regions via a programme which was called the Regional Rapid Response Program (R3P). This fund was similar in concept to the Commanders' Emergency Response Programme (CERP) which came from the same source of Iraqi oil funds. One of the Dutch military officers in Al-Muthanna was pretty cynical about all the different funding rules and names. 'By the end of this, I expect Andrew will have a speedboat called CERP and a yacht called DERP, and no-one except us here will understand why' he joked.

However, there was a serious limitation on the use of these DFI funds. The Iraqi oil funds weren't allowed to be used for the reparation of war damage, incurred during either the 1991 Gulf War or the 2003 invasion. This meant that key infrastructure projects, such as the repair of a road bridge or a key utility or a government building, couldn't be undertaken because the use of DFI funding would have been vetoed – the project would be classified as the repair of war damage. So we found ourselves in the crazy situation where international law prevented us from helping repair some of Iraq's most visible infrastructure. The US's own contracting rules were a real burden too. The contracting office in Baghdad became a bottleneck where important projects could get held up for weeks. The results could be significant. For example, the water team had predicted that flooding could be a major problem in cities in the south in January. They drew up a project to buy special equipment to help tackle this problem. But because of delays in the contracting and procurement process these didn't arrive till the end of February – by when most of the floodwaters had gone down.

We also had to coordinate with the military who had their own projects, funded directly by the UK Treasury. At the start there was a real lack of coordination between what we were trying to do and what the military were doing. However, having people such as Brigadier Peter Williams on board was a real help. He was the deputy divisional commander, head of Operations Support and the CPA's military adviser. His presence meant we could start to reduce the conflicts between projects and even pool resources. Gradually the military in southern Iraq began to change their view of the CPA. The divisional commander visited us in February and met with various advisers in the main conference room. The talk ranged from electricity, water, oil and gas, through agriculture and aqua culture to trade, finance and healthcare. The meeting overran because he was so interested in the discussions and wanted to hear more. Eventually it finished and the commander told me: 'I wish I'd visited this headquarters sooner, you really seem to understand how all this works.' I made no comment and simply hoped that we might be taken more seriously by the military in the future.

However, I now felt that the new 'spend, spend, spend' policy threatened to undermine our work. It was the only time that I had a serious disagreement with Sir Hilary.

'Just for the record, Sir Hilary, I think this is a mistake,' I said in his office.

'Why's that?' he asked.

'Because I'm concerned that it'll mean I'll have to pull my teams out from the ministries where they are really getting to grips with them,' I replied.

'But you have a big team and they can do more projects,' he replied firmly.

'I'm also worried that we're going to be trying to push too much money too quickly into an economy that simply can't absorb it,' I said. 'It will push up inflation and lead to corruption.'

However, Sir Hilary was adamant that this was the new policy and of course I had to accept that. Though we didn't have a row, it was clear we were fundamentally at odds on this. I was worried that what we were being ordered to do was a knee-jerk reaction.

I wasn't alone in feeling that politics lay behind this. The US presidential election campaign was getting under way and we seemed to be rushing head first towards the handover date throwing money around as we went – without proper thought about longer-term consequences. Brigadier Williams summed it up well when he said that we were now being asked to focus on 'an end date not an end state'. I was worried that if my finance team had to concentrate on projects rather than keeping a close eye on the running of the finance ministry and Central Bank it might start to fall apart. I felt it was as import-ant to work to help the Iraqis get the ministries working as it was to throw yet more money at extra projects – many of which scarcely involved the Iraqis at all. But some ministries had been so damaged that they weren't yet able to function properly. I recalled the words of TE Lawrence – Lawrence of Arabia – who probably knew this part of the world as well as any westerner ever had. 'Better to let them do it imperfectly than to do it perfectly yourself, for it is their country, their way, and your time is short.'

Meanwhile yet another source of funding was set up – the Local Governance Fund – $1 million was to be given to each of the 18 governorates. It was a good idea in principle but within eight weeks Pat and I became aware of payment discrepancies and allegations of fraud. And because payments came in small tranches – $10,000–15,000 on average – this meant that there were at least 75–100 separate bureaucratic contracting actions. All this extra paperwork had to be co-ordinated with the Iraqis. It was massively labour-intensive and we'd warned anyone who would listen that it would lead to problems later. During one such conversation with Baghdad, Pat was told: 'It's only eighteen million dollars and the Iraqis need practice with budgeting ...'

The great irony for me was that what we were being asked to do was to perform like any old-style command economy. The United States of America, the great champion of free-market economics, was telling us to focus on how much we spent rather than the how well it was spent. So, for example, we spent several million dollars on provision of a small fleet of shiny new fire engines for a petrochemical factory in the south, yet there was no allocation for maintenance of the fleet. The Iraqis in the ministry responsible certainly had no such budget available and we were rapidly using up all our money. The result? As far as I know the fire engines were run into the ground for lack of money in the kitty to keep them running properly.

And this was happening all over Iraq. I heard a story of a US army captain who had overseen the refurbishment of a broken-down sewage plant near Baghdad. He was rightly proud of the achievement. A year or so later he returned to Iraq – he was a reservist on a second tour – and went to inspect the plant. He was horrified. 'It was as if we'd never done anything to it at all,' he said sadly. 'It had been run until it broke.' The reason was simple. The coalition had rebuilt the plant but the Iraqis had no operations or maintenance budget to keep it running in a proper condition.

On another occasion, we'd carefully installed some water pumps at strategic locations around Basra to provide pumped washing water from the Shat Al-Arab. Electricity was also needed to operate them and so we provided standby generators. One morning a very agitated Colin McBride came into my office. 'I cannot bloody believe it, we've installed brand-new pumps finally, and what do the Iraqis do?'

'Humour us,' I said, looking up from my desk expectantly, knowing the reply would be good.

'They have their brand-new pumps but know that a power failure might damage them. So the DG has simply switched them off. He thinks they may run out of diesel for the generator.'

'You can't fault his logic.' I smiled.

'Why couldn't the bloody man come and ask for more money for diesel, instead of just switching the pumps off?' said Colin, who was quite exasperated.

The problem became progressively worse as the months rolled on and more and more projects came on line. Instead of maintaining the equipment we were promoting a culture of obsolescence. Several weeks after a vehicle broke down the Iraqis would simply request another one, and perhaps later use the original for spares. It was probably not how the original reconstruction project was designed. My view was that it would have been better to have handpicked a handful of really big important projects and get them up and running and properly funded for the future.

Rosie Knight, who was in charge of projects for the Al-Basra governorate team, was at the sharp end when it came to this acceleration of spending. She oversaw 260 projects costing around $27 million. These ranged from rebuilding blood banks and bank vaults to providing computers for the town councils, women's education and training and sanitation projects. 'I think we even helped fund a poetry festival at one time,' she said later. The problem was that she had little time to focus on any of them. 'That was one of the saddest things, it was difficult to engage with a particular project. The pressures were so great. You were just working from six am to one am every day.'

At one time Rosie went on leave for two weeks – to celebrate her birthday – but later deeply regretted going away. 'When I got back I came the nearest I have ever come to suffering a nervous breakdown,' she admitted later. 'I was being told that this hadn't happened or that hadn't happened. I decided then I wouldn't go on leave again until the work was finished in June. It was just not worth it.' I also remember Rosie's reaction one day when she was informed that she might be able to spend another sum of money from a new source. 'Not more money, not more paperwork,' she wailed. 'I can't spend the money I've already got!'

The race to spend money quickly worried some of us for other reasons too. We were by now committed to funnelling about $180 million on projects in the south. But it was being spent so fast, who was keeping a proper eye on the proper procedures? Pat McLoughlin had become the fund custodian as he was a chartered accountant. But even before the new 'spend, spend' order came down from Baghdad he was concerned about pushing money fast through governorate teams, some of whom had little or no financial training. Inevitably that would mean that not all the rules would be followed correctly.

The situation hadn't been made any easier when early in January the new finance officers in Maysan and Dhi Qar left and weren't immediately replaced. 'And guess what?' Pat told me one day. 'I'm the one who's going to be accountable in the end. This is going to come back and bite us,' he said, the anxiety clear in his voice. We already knew that that the auditors in Baghdad were beginning to move in and examine how all the money was being used. So we were being squeezed at both ends. Baghdad wanted us to spend money as fast as we could. But we also had to follow the Byzantine US rules on spending to get past the auditors. Sometimes we were accused of being too tight. But we were just being cautious – we knew that ultimately the responsibility for how the money was spent would lie with us.

In one governorate one senior official cheerfully admitted that he had 'completely ignored' the rules on spending. I spoke to one of the finance staff at another governorate – not one under my control – and and asked him: 'How on earth are you spending all this money with such tight rules?' I'll never forget his reply.

'Well Andrew,' he drawled, 'it's like this. There are some rules you can bend – and some rules you can just get around.' What he was telling me was that their paperwork appeared on the surface in perfect order, even if at a later date it might not stand up to very close scrutiny.

The pressure that many of the staff felt at this period was summed up by Rosie. The ambassador had been allocated a big tough US marine – no one was quite sure where he came from – and so Sir Hilary decided to make him his project instigator. 'And this gave him *carte blanche* to use US military-style bullying tactics on the four projects officers,' said Rosie. 'And of course who was the easiest one for him to reach? Me, because I was in the same compound in Basra. So he just came and stood over my desk and shouted at me. "Why has this not been done?" he would demand to know. And of course he wouldn't wait for an answer but instead bawled at me again. "I don't want excuses – I want it DONE!" Needless to say, though I usually loved Sir Hilary, he wasn't my favourite person on such occasions,' she conceded. 'Eventually the marine did get kicked out, I think after I'd flipped slightly and said to Sir Hilary that the soldier wasn't helping! I'm sure he was really a nice guy, the marine – but how do you squeeze blood out of a stone that has no blood left in it? I wasn't alone in how I felt – there was no more left to give.'

At the time there were rumours circulating in London about what would replace the CPA once the handover of power took place at the end of June. Obviously the CPA itself was to vanish, but equally obviously – or so I thought – a lot of us would be needed to stay on and help the Iraqi ministries in their work. Yet a well-briefed contact of mine in London told me of Whitehall's planning for the British presence post-handover. This seemed to amount to a consulate office and a tiny number of advisers. I fired off an angry email to my source at the time. 'As for the UK's effort – what a crock of ****!' I wrote. 'This will be like a pimple on a bear's arse compared to a US embassy of 3,000 people. And they expect to have some "influence"? We've been trying to get a grip of the Ministry of Finance for over a year and we're still trying.' At the same time a senior civil servant I knew described Whitehall's thinking as 'soggy'. Yet though I was exasperated by the rumours, I was still not unduly worried. June was still some months away and I felt there was still plenty of time for Whitehall to come to their senses and see that we had a major role to play after 30 June.

Just as the pressure mounted to get projects finished, so did tension over the security system. It was true that in Basra we'd always been able to hear gunfire somewhere in the city. But we increasingly felt that we were becoming the target. Once again the man in the front line was Ian McClymont. He'd continued to stand outside with his brave interpreters, to talk to the protestors. It was noticeable to him and to the rest of us that hostility was growing not just towards us but towards the Iraqis who worked for us, and particularly the women. One day a woman in her 30s – a single mother called Falak – came to the compound looking for a job as one of Ian's interpreters. Just as she arrived an angry crowd arrived at the gates. 'So I turned to her and said, "OK this is your baptism of fire – let's see how you react to this!" I stepped outside and Falak, who was of course wearing a headscarf, came with me and stood behind me to translate what was being said to me.

'As usual the crowd were all men and some of them started shouting. They were saying very hurtful things aimed at Falak – that she was a slut and so on. I could see she was very upset as she translated this to me but she stood her ground and I admired that. But I then realised that one man in particular was being very aggressive. I asked Falak what he was shouting at her but she didn't want to tell me. I looked back at him again and I could tell from his body language and from my experience that he was threatening her. I asked Falak if this was so and she said yes,' recalled Ian.

'This was too much. So I walked quickly into the crowd right up to this man and stood literally nose to nose with him. I made very clear in English what would happen to him if he didn't immediately desist from his actions – that he would be disappeared by the SAS, or that if need be I'd do it myself. He didn't like this one little bit – he clearly understood what I was saying. I'd discovered that when protestors are in a crowd they can be very brave and shout, but when you single someone out they don't like it. Here in Iraq everyone else would stop what they were doing and just watch. And here he was with me standing nose to nose to him. So he slunk off. I think some of the others in the crowd actually approved of what I'd done – that guy had really been out of order. And Falak got the job.'

In general, Ian won the respect of many of the protestors at the CPA gates. He made a policy of never lying to anyone. He would always try to find out for them what was going on. But if he didn't know he would tell them so. Even during the very hottest of days – it would sometimes reach 60° C in the sun – Ian stood outside. On one occasion some demonstrators were wilting in the heat and asked if there was any shelter. Ian told them with a smile: 'If I can stand here with a bald head, then so can you!' Many in the city referred to him as '*haji*' a term of respect usually reserved for Muslims who have been on the pilgrimage or '*haj*' to Mecca.

However, in January one demonstration turned especially nasty at the Al-Sarraji HQ. Many of us were away at the time, attending the Rebuild Iraq conference in Kuwait, a chance to persuade investors from around the globe to help in reconstructing the country. One morning a large crowd began to gather in the city and moved menacingly towards the Al-Sarraji compound. About 2,000 people, led by the head of a local Islamic council, stopped about 400 metres from the entrance. The US soldiers in the compound and the CIA guys stood at the gates, armed to the teeth, to watch what would happen next. The Islamic council leader stood in the middle of the crowd armed with a microphone connected to two large speakers supported on sticks held by aides. The cleric was in full flow when Ian and his interpreter Sadiq left the compound gates and walked, unarmed, towards the crowd. 'We walked the four hundred metres to the crowd and when we got there it just parted in front of us,' recalled Ian. 'Then it closed behind us as we carried on walking. Soon I was face to face with the head of the Islamic council. He was a fat well-fed man who then began to harangue me, with Sadiq interpreting. He was complaining that the youth were unhappy, that there were no jobs, that the city was filthy and not being cleaned properly – a number of complaints. Then as soon as he had stopped speaking he opened his hand and the microphone disappeared across his shoulder, not to be seen again. He clearly didn't want to give me the right to reply or let the crowd hear to anything I might have to say,' said Ian.

'But I started talking anyway and told him that I understood his point of view and that I would pass on his views to the ambassador, and thanked him for coming. But I also went on to say that I wanted him to know that all the top players in the CPA were at that moment at a conference in Kuwait trying to persuade companies to come to Basra and Iraq in general. These companies, I said, would provide trade and create jobs and make his people prosperous and help keep the youth off the streets. Then I said to him: "Now you can play your part in this by stopping the bombs going off. Because the companies won't come if there are bombs going off. And you have the ability and you know you have the ability to stop that. So please do that and we'll all be happy." The cleric wasn't a happy man, I could see. Anyway, with that Sadiq and I turned on our heels and started to walk away. It was then that I saw that there had been a local TV crew filming the incident and their mike had picked up what I said.

'Thankfully the crowd parted once more as we walked back and in a few minutes we were back inside the compound. When we got back to the gate one of the CIA guys looked at me. "Hey buddy I wouldn't have gone out there like you did." I looked straight back at him. "Nor would I if I'd had your accent!" I replied.

'The next day one of my interpreters came to me. He said "Haji, we saw you on the TV last night. It was great!" He then explained how Iraqi television had shown three scenes from the previous day involving crowds and coalition troops. In the first they'd shown heavily armed American soldiers talking to the crowds in Baghdad where the US spokesman wore a helmet, dark glasses and had his pistol drawn. Next they cut to a scene of Italian soldiers doing basically the same thing elsewhere in Iraq. Finally they showed a clip of me, a lone British soldier and his interpreter standing unarmed and at the mercy of a large crowd. What I only found out later was that someone in the CPA had recorded the scene and Sir Hilary later saw it. And he was kind enough to put me forward for a QCVS – queen's commendation for valuable service.'

In the middle of such tense situations I had a more mundane battle on my hand. Many of us working at the CPA in the south were Territorial Army officers or NCOs. We'd come with the TA but had transferred to work as civilians for the CPA after the end of our military 'tour'. In the TA members get a tax-free lump sum each year known as a 'bounty'. However, to get your bounty a TA member has to meet certain conditions, one of which is to do 12 days of in-camp training – or MTDs – with the organisation. However, as we'd been in Iraq for months, very few of us had had the chance to do any training. I'd raised this issue with Brigadier John Thomson who was in charge of the TA in the UK. He was sure that a solution could be reached and that those of us in the TA would still get our bounty. However, when in February I emailed to check with the adjutant of my TA regiment I received a shock. It read:

Andrew
I hope you are having fun out in the sunny wastelands, very jealous of you back here.

You will probably not get your bounty. You are required to do 12 MTD's outside your deployment ... As you are in Iraq it is unlikely you will get those days in.

I could hardly believe it. We were risking life and limb in Iraq on behalf of a British Government that had chosen to invade the country, yet we were being told we wouldn't qualify for our modest bounties. I wrote again to Brigadier Thomson and was supported by Brigadier Williams who weighed in on our behalf. It seemed the rules couldn't be changed. And so I lost my £900 tax-free bonus for the time I served in Iraq as a TA officer as did other colleagues. It wasn't so much the money that was at issue but the principle.

Sometimes it felt as if our lives were entirely hamstrung by bureaucracy. At other times the CPA's rules at Al-Sarraji seemed over-zealous. The ever-inventive Ahmed had decided to open a small gift shop within the compound selling local items ranging from ornaments and clothes to rugs. It was intended to give civilian staff a small taste of what Iraqi culture could offer. It was also a chance for Ahmed to show a little private enterprise and make some extra money. Pat had helped to fund it. However, there was a worried response from the CPA chief of staff Colonel Peter Duklis.

'Who said this could open?' he wanted to know. 'The agreement was only on Fridays. Who's running it? Please, let me know ASAP.' It wasn't meant unkindly and the gift shop was allowed to stay open. But it felt once more that bureaucracy wanted a hand in everything. I had similar problems when I was tempted to open a coffee shop in the camp. We could never get a really good cup of coffee in the compound and my idea was to import the wherewithal from a coffee store in Edinburgh where my brother is in the catering equipment business. The authorities, however, were bitterly opposed.

Another contentious issue was the dining facility or 'DFAC'. As well as CPA personnel, visitors could also eat at the DFAC as long as we got them a meal ticket. However, we were supposed to give 24 hours' notice if we wanted to bring someone for lunch and we were discouraged from arranging meetings based around a lunch. Yet inevitably among a group of people from many different nations and with many different backgrounds, these rules were more honoured in the breach than in the observance. So bureaucracy fought back. Colonel Duklis informed us all that because the meal-ticket policy rules had been ignored he was to suspend them indefinitely. 'The DFAC is designed to be for CPA staff only,' he said. 'If people do not have a badge or a visitor's badge to include meals, they will not be permitted into the DFAC to eat.' And he pointed out that from September to December the DFAC had been half a million dollars or more over budget.

But things got worse, however, over the *colour* of these badges. A blue badge enabled a person to eat at the DFAC, and that was the badge that we wore. But the local Iraqi staff were allocated yellow badges – which didn't allow them to use the dining facilities. However, Ahmed, who had been allocated his badge in the early days, had somehow acquired a coveted blue badge. This didn't go down well with everyone. One of the Italian advisers spotted Ahmed's badge and wrote in dismay to Peter Duklis asking: 'Could you let me know if Iraqi blue collar workers can eat at Dining Facilities?' It was I think an extremely petty and small-minded request, because the Italian knew quite well what the answer was and what the result would be. Peter Duklis was obliged to follow the procedure for getting Ahmed a yellow badge instead of a blue one. Those were of course the rules.

These may have been minor issues as far but they were major issues as far as the local Iraqi staff were concerned. I believe Pete Duklis was concerned that food was being taken from the dining facility to feed various Iraqi families. It was declared that the local Iraqi staff technically 'lived out' and therefore they'd have to provide for their own meals. This was an unpopular decision, and it introduced a concept of 'us and them' which Sir Hilary and I, in particular, had worked hard to avoid. Of course, Raneen, Ahmed and Abdul took it well when I explained the rules but they'd lost face. And from my perspective I found it inexcusable and unnecessary.

It had already been a difficult start to the year. Then we received some more bad news – Sir Hilary was leaving. Perhaps it shouldn't have come as such a surprise. He had delayed his retirement to take up the post and had been here for nearly six months. The ambassador made the announcement himself in typically low-key fashion at a regular Friday meeting of heads of department, just a week before he was due to depart. His private secretary later told me Sir Hilary had kept the news to the last minute because he had feared it could be a blow to morale. And it was. He was someone who had really believed in the multi-national outfit that we'd become, one that was immeasurably more efficient and effective than it was when he'd taken it over. His departure felt like the end of something. The Foreign Secretary Jack Straw said some kind words about Sir Hilary and praised his 'truly remarkable achievement'. Those of us who worked in the CPA agreed. Perhaps one of the reasons why Sir Hilary had been so effective was that he was about to retire and therefore probably didn't worry about treading on anyone's toes. He did and said what he had to do to get things done. We had a chance to say goodbye to Sir Hilary over a curry buffet dinner held in the Iftar tent, followed by a farewell party with beer and wine. Sir Hilary spoke of how proud he was to have worked with us and the way we'd 'helped to stabilise Iraq'. The following morning he was gone. His successor Patrick Nixon arrived soon afterwards.

Patrick was 59 at the time spoke fluent Arabic and had just finished a stint as British Ambassador to the United Arab Emirates. He was a very different kind of person from Sir Hilary, much quieter and less charismatic. I always felt he was very much Whitehall's man, with instructions to steer a safe course through to the handover at the end of June without rocking the boat. Perhaps inevitably he never made as big an impression in Iraq as Sir Hilary had. I was told by a friend in Baghdad that a couple of months after his arrival Patrick sent an email to the Ministry of Transport in Baghdad. One of the advisers had queried this with my friend. 'Patrick *who*?' he had asked. Certainly he and I didn't get off to the best of starts when a jet-lagged Patrick fell asleep during a meeting with me. 'I think we'd better continue this another time,' he said to me.

By now I too was pretty exhausted. Apart from two seven-day breaks I'd had little respite from our gruelling 24/7 schedule in the last eight months. Raneen and Pat persuaded me I needed a holiday. I had the offer of a couple of weeks skiing in Champéry in the Alps and I jumped at the chance. However, first I wanted to go back to Japan to check on the progress of the Iraq aid. This time the Crown Agents in London agreed to pick up the bill on behalf of the British Government. I'd spoken about my plans to Sir Hilary just before he left and had had a meeting in which we were joined by Brigadier Peter Williams and Rod Matthews, the senior civil servant who was head of the reconstruction programme.

I'd been surprised by Rod's reaction to my proposed Japanese trip. 'As the Head of Reconstruction here in Basra, *I* should be responsible for communication with the Japanese government on matters of reconstruction,' he insisted.

Sir Hilary was very tactful. 'It is as a result of Andrew's initiative that we are able to speak to them directly at all,' he reminded Rod. 'He's been speaking to them for the past three months. Whilst I'm mindful of the need to inform London, I'm also aware of the expediency of being able to shortcut the bureaucracy and influence an outcome that is favourable for us here in southern Iraq. Andrew has the connections, and he is planning to fly to Tokyo. I am happy that he should go; he will make contact and involve you when he arrives there.'

Just before flying off I had some trouble getting $5 million in cash from Baghdad. Usually I just flew up to the capital and collected the cash myself and brought it back. It's what I'd done from the start. But on this occasion there was a security lock-down in Baghdad and they were nervous about handing it over. So they decided to write out a cheque instead. The first somehow got lost. So I flew to Baghdad to pick up a second. This was a US treasury cheque for $5.8 million and was made out to me personally. It was as good as having cash in my pocket.

I flew back to Basra from where Pat and I were to drive to Kuwait to cash the cheque. I'd phoned ahead to the US base in southern Kuwait – Camp Arifjan – to say I was on my way. We had to go in with a military escort for security as Control Risks had no visas for Kuwait. So two young soldiers, a corporal and a private, took us all the way to Camp Arifjan.

'This is certainly an experience,' said Pat when we arrived.

'It's fun,' I said, 'when did you last get a cheque for five-point-eight million dollars made out to you personally?'

The finance office was tucked away behind a nondescript door. Pat and I entered to find a US staff sergeant waiting like a quartermaster behind his desk. Behind him were several large black plastic carrying cases, the kind normally used for shipping documents.

'Are you the guy that called us?' he enquired.

'Yes. I have a Treasury cheque for five-point-eight million dollars,' I explained.

'Can I see it?'

'Of course.'

'Please sign the back of it and sign that you have received the funds.'

'OK,' I said and signed my name.

The sergeant now lifted $100,000 'bricks' of 100-dollar bills from the containers and counted out 58 of them. This was almost too easy. We smiled, carefully stacked up the cash and turned to leave. 'Nice doing business with you,' said Pat as we walked out the door.

We put the cash into two large black holdalls and returned heavily laden to the vehicle in the car park.

'Where to, boss?' asked the corporal. 'Back the way we came,' I said.

We left the camp and drove north. On the way I turned to Pat and said: 'We can save time if you just drop me at the airport. My flight to Tokyo is tonight and I can work at the airport for a couple of hours.'

The two soldiers in the front seat exchanged terrified glances. This detour wasn't part of their briefing and we now had all that money in the back of the car. Pat and I looked at each other and smiled – they were convinced that I was going to abscond with the money. Arriving at the drop-off area to the airport, we opened the back of the car and I carefully lifted out my own bag.

'It's OK,' I explained to the soldiers. 'Pat has the cash and he will see it gets back to Basra. Did you seriously think that I would get on a plane with five-point-eight million dollars in cash?' I asked.

'Sir, we did wonder.' said the corporal visibly relieved.

∗

My first meeting in Tokyo was on Friday 13 with another of the senior vice-ministers within the Japanese Ministry of Foreign Affairs. I spoke about security and the situation on the ground and then touched on what Japan's priorities might be. His analysis took me aback. 'The problem with Iraq now is that there is a mismatch of expectations. You are busy on the ground trying to bring electricity and water to maintain peace, but there is no infrastructure.' He was speaking in short staccato sentences and leaving little room for disagreement. 'There is no government with whom we can negotiate. You speak passionately about electricity. Iraq has no energy policy, and so they will not have electricity for at least another five years,' he said, concluding: 'We cannot commit to any strategic projects unless we complete the necessary studies, which will take one to two years. Please meet my colleague to discuss our priorities. The information that you can provide us may help us.'

I was crestfallen. I tried to explain our concerns that focussing on the ministries in Baghdad would most likely result in little or no aid getting through to the people on the ground because of the continuing lack of Iraqi administration and the levels of corruption at most levels of Iraqi officialdom. But I made little headway. I was learning fast about the bureaucracy of central government and this was a setback. But I couldn't give up that easily.

That evening I had dinner with an old friend, very influential behind the scenes within the Japanese administration. We met at a very expensive restaurant, a far cry from the food in Basra. I told him my concern over the lack of strategic thinking about the long-term future within the CPA administration. My friend meanwhile apologised for Japanese bureaucracy, explaining that all spending decisions for the Iraq reconstruction effort were being taken at Cabinet level and that the process was rather long-winded and frustrating. He said the Japanese had feared criticism for sending only money and that was why this time they'd sent troops as well. However, this had been a political risk for Prime Minister Koizumi and any significant casualties would result in his automatic resignation. It struck me how much that differed from the situation in London and Washington. My companion also explained that he was meeting the Prime Minister the following day and would brief him about our discussions. Late that evening I retuned to my hotel, feeling that perhaps all was not lost. But I also knew we wouldn't see any significant funds from Japan in Iraq in the coming months.

The next day I arrived at the ministry offices for the follow-up meeting. Officials from various Japanese agencies were also there. As agreed I'd arranged to have Rod and several of our specialists on a conference call with Basra. 'Well, hello. How's Tokyo?' asked Pat when he answered the telephone.

'Good, but a long way away. How's Basra?'

'Getting warmer,' said Pat, 'at least the flooding has stopped. I'll put you on to the gang here.' He switched the phone across to conference mode. Rod, Colin, Robert and Wally were sitting around the small circular meeting table in the middle of my office.

'This is Rod Matthews calling on behalf of the British government,' he began. 'We are making initial contact with Tokyo,' he said formally. Although Rod's introduction was absolutely correct, I wondered if there were a few raised eyebrows among the Japanese as they tried to work out who they were now talking to – as, after all, we'd been speaking for the past three months. So I moved it along quickly and introduced the rest of my team in Basra. We discussed a number of detailed questions about a small aid donation of $40 million in equipment they might be able to provide direct for us from Tokyo. Perhaps my trip hadn't been wasted after all.

8

FIGHT AGAINST TIME

March 2004

The contrast could hardly have been stronger. Within the space of a couple of days I'd swapped the dust, heat and chaos of southern Iraq for the well-ordered and calm atmosphere of the Swiss ski resort of Champéry. Here on the mountains, nestled between Mont Blanc in nearby France and Lake Geneva, I was for the first time in nearly eight months thrust back into 'normal' life. I was on a skiing holiday with five friends, people who worked in the City and had no connection with my life in Iraq. Instead, like everyone else in the resort, they were intent on having a good time.

Though I knew I needed this break I found it hard to fit in. I felt an enormous weight of responsibility upon me. And try as I might I found it just about impossible to discuss my life in Iraq with my friends. Even arriving back in Britain had been strange. It was the oddest feeling walking down the streets of south-west London and realising that I didn't need a flak jacket or personal security. I looked people straight in the eye, as you did in Basra – if someone meant you harm, it was generally believed that you could see it in their eyes first. Here the pedestrians must have thought I'd just left an asylum as I fixed them with a penetrating gaze.

Mishaps seemed to follow me around too. One day I was out skiing off piste with my friend Dan when he took a wrong turn and ended up flying over the top of a small ravine. I could see him lying in a crumpled heap, his skis bent at an odd and disturbing angle. Both his ski poles had been rammed under his rib cage and he was now gasping for breath. I feared that he'd punctured a lung and called the rescue services on my mobile phone. Within a few minutes a helicopter arrived and Dan was airlifted to hospital. He was lucky: he had been very badly winded but had otherwise escaped serious injury. But I felt dogged by dramas.

Despite my feeling of isolation, the holiday was still enjoyable and I'd needed the change of scene. All too soon I was back in London to collect my 'uniform' of polo shirts and chinos before flying back to Basra via Kuwait. I'd kept in touch with the office via email, so I knew before I drove into Basra that there had been some tensions in my absence. However, I was unprepared for the atmosphere I now found.

Walking back into my office I was struck by the lack of enthusiasm from Pat and several others.

'So what's up?' I asked.

'Well, we have a new Ambassador ... '

'So what's it been like?'

'He's not like Sir Hilary, that's all I'm saying,' came the rather circumspect reply.

I climbed out of my office window – my usual exit route – and toured the department's various offices. I was shocked by the lack of buzz I found. I returned to the main building and headed upstairs. It was around 8.30 pm and I was surprised to see that the ambassador's door was closed and the lights were off. However, Brigadier Peter Williams was at his desk, and he smiled and looked up at me: 'So the wanderer returns.' After a few minutes of banter and a general catch-up, I asked him if we could speak in private.

'Of course,' he said and I closed the door.

'What the hell's going on Peter?' I asked. 'I've been back less than an hour but the whole place feels flat. The energy that we had at the end of January seems to have disappeared.'

He looked me in the eye and said, 'It's your department, and it's your job to get them back on track.'

The change in mood hadn't come as a total surprise. Patrick Nixon and I hadn't worked well together even before I went on holiday. An obvious sign had been the regular 6 pm heads of department meetings. Gone was the central role that Sir Hilary had given me. Instead for most of the hour I'd sit and listen to the other sections talking about their issues, many of them administrative ones about our compound. Often I felt there was little time left for what, given my position, I considered to be more important issues – namely, the economy. Although Patrick had been told by Whitehall not to rock the boat, I felt I was being frozen out. In the previous months I had felt that there had been a very strong collegiate spirit; everyone mucked in together to get things done. Suddenly it seemed the CPA had other priorities. I felt that something or someone had poisoned Patrick against my agenda, my plans, though I had no idea what or who.

I asked Peter Williams about Patrick's reaction to me. Peter looked at me for a moment. 'Well, if you want to know, Patrick thinks you're a prima donna.' I could hardly believe what I was hearing. Where was this coming from?

'What do you mean?' I said incredulously.

'Well, he thinks that you want all the attention,' continued Peter. 'Don't take it the wrong way,' he added helpfully. But how the hell was I supposed to take such news? Here I was doing what I thought was an OK job in extremely difficult circumstances, leading an excellent team who were making a real difference in southern Iraq. Yet Whitehall's main representative in Basra apparently just thought I was on an ego trip!

I was devastated. For a while I carried out a kind of silent protest. I skipped the directors meetings and instead let senior members of my team attend instead. I know it was childish but I never stopped carrying out my job working with the Iraqis. Colin covered for me beautifully and, on more than one occasion, I met one of my fellow directors at breakfast who said to me, bemused: 'I thought you were in Baghdad?'

'No,' I'd reply innocently, 'whatever gave you that idea?'

This meant I had some spare time on my hands. So I joined the expanding group of 'Ultimate Frisbee' players at the opposite end of the camp. With two cones for goals at either end of the pitch, two teams of five or six players would run around and battle it out. It's a non-contact sport and the player holding the frisbee can't move. Goals are scored by passing the frisbee to a colleague running through the goal mouth. Whilst it's an exhilarating sport, and was popular among both men and women alike, it was extremely tiring – especially when played in 30 °C degrees of heat. And after two weeks I returned to the evening meetings. I hoped I'd made a point. But in any case I knew our work was far more important than my clash of personality with the new ambassador. I also recalled my last meeting with Sir Hilary when he'd turned to me and said: 'Andrew, be gentle with Patrick – he might need your help.'

I continued to play frisbee but stopped before 6 pm and raced to get showered before the evening meetings. I knew by now I needed the exercise. I'd been invited to go running by my friend Aran Maree. As we set off on a three-mile hike around the vast palace compound I soon realised how unfit I'd become in just a few months of desk work. 'You've been eating too much KBR food,' said Aran, who's a cardiologist. 'It's all laced with sugar. You need to get out and run more.'

'I just don't seem to have the time,' I gasped, trying to keep up. It was sort of true. I had a morning meeting at 8.00 am and various commitments right through the day, followed by the evening meeting and then supper – last orders were at 7.20 pm. I knew that I could make the time if I really wanted to, but there was so much to do. And then there was the heat.

'I'll come and drag you off at five pm from time to time,' said Aran, who irritatingly was scarcely out of breath. I reluctantly agreed.

After one run, I arrived at the evening meeting quite flushed. 'What have you been up to?' one of my fellow directors enquired.

'Isn't that dangerous?' queried another when I explained.

'That's why Andrew takes his personal consultant cardiologist with them!' joked another and the room collapsed into laughter. I may have had my initial differences with Patrick but there was usually a good team spirit among the heads of departments despite our different backgrounds.

My team's morale took some time to restore but we got there. The mood in Basra itself, however, grew far more serious. While I was skiing I'd been told about a tragedy that had struck two members of the Iraqi staff who worked at the Al-Sarraji compound. Shaimaa Falih and Likaa Falih were sisters aged 16 and 18, who worked in the CPA laundry. Both spoke excellent English and worked 12-hour shifts uncomplainingly in the tiny laundry-room area for about $350 a month. Both of them were warm and friendly girls and they'd smile and chat with us when we dropped off our laundry.

One evening after work they were being taken home by taxi as usual when the vehicle was confronted by four masked gunmen in a street just a few hundred yards from the girls' home. One of the gunmen fired a bullet to stop the taxi while another tried to pull one of the sisters out of the car. She resisted and was shot in the head. When the other sister got out of the car she was also shot. The men then drove off in a getaway car. It was clear that Shaimaa and Likaa were murdered simply because they'd been working for foreigners. A few days later anonymous leaflets were left in the city denouncing the 'traitorous' and 'immoral' actions of the sisters for working with the CPA. They also threatened more attacks on Iraqi staff.

It was an appalling, senseless killing that deeply shocked everyone at the CPA. The other Iraqi staff were especially disturbed. At least one quit immediately for fear that he too would be targeted. And it emerged that threats had been made in the past against local staff. Raneen's family was trying to put pressure on her to leave the CPA in case she became a victim. I spoke with her about the situation soon after my return.

'I'm sure that Pat will have told you we don't want to lose you,' I told Raneen. 'But nothing that's taking place here is worth the loss of another life needlessly. So please if you ever feel threatened in any way, you must tell us.'

'Thank you.' She replied. 'It's becoming much more dangerous for us in Basra. Now, for the first time I have to wear the hijab to cover myself when I'm walking around town. These religious people are making things very difficult for us.' Raneen had taken to coming to work with her western clothes hidden under a traditional outfit that she took off once she was safely in the compound.

The sombre mood of the discussion was broken when Ahmed walked in. It was the first time I'd seen him since my return. 'How are you, Sir?' he asked cheerfully. 'How was your holiday? Have you found a wife yet? Did you bring me a present?' As ever he was bombarding me for information.

'In answer to your questions, Yes it was a good holiday. No I haven't found a wife. And if you're nice to me, maybe I have brought you a present.'

'Oh good,' he said, with a broad smile, 'then there is still time for me to find you a good traditional Iraqi girl. So what have you brought me?' he demanded, hopping impatiently from foot to foot in front of my desk like a bird.

I was aware of the Arab custom of gifts, so made sure that I returned with something for each of my Iraqi staff. I leaned down and dug into my bag and produced two small packages, one for Raneen and one for Ahmed. Ahmed eagerly tore open his package. He beamed with delight when he read the label. 'These are seeds for English roses that I asked you for – you remembered!' he said. Ahmed had a thing about English roses and I'd promised I would try to help him get some. For Raneen I'd bought a Hermès scarf I'd seen during my short stop in Geneva.

'Where's mine?' asked Pat cheekily.

And then Katrina called out from her desk. 'And mine?'

'Don't you two start – it took me long enough to find the right roses. I knew if I didn't find them he'd never stop complaining,' I replied, pointing at Ahmed and grinning. Despite the many difficulties it felt good to be back with my adopted family.

However, the murder of the two sisters and my talk with Raneen made me more worried than ever about the mood on the streets. It was clear that a stricter interpretation of Islamic rules on dress code and behaviour was emerging. Soon after the invasion a few shops selling alcohol had opened in the city, a symbol of how some Iraqis were embracing their new freedoms. By now, however, those alcohol stores that hadn't already been forced to close were being firebombed.

One reason for this growth in religious intolerance was that two of the most important figures in Iraqi society at the time were both hard-line religious leaders. Grand Ayatollah Ali Sistani was the most senior Sh'ia figure in Iraq. A conservative, quiet, almost reclusive figure he nonetheless had enormous influence over the majority Shi'ia population. From the early days of the occupation he had been regarded by the coalition as one of the key players in Iraq. Muqtada al-Sadr was different. A much younger man, the podgy-faced al-Sadr was the son of a Shi'a cleric who had been killed in 1999, almost certainly by Saddam Hussein's security agents. Though little known outside the country, the son had used his father's reputation and his own charisma to build up a network of charities around the country to provide a power base – especially among the poorer and more radical Sh'ia. At the start we weren't really aware of al-Sadr as a potential problem. And by the time he had made his presence felt – partly through his al-Mahdi army – it was hard to take action because the 'reason' for the coalition's presence in Iraq seemed to have changed.

One of the principal justifications given for the 2003 invasion was to destroy Saddam's supposed stockpile of weapons of mass destruction. After the invasion the hunt was on to find them but the trail soon ran cold. In Basra we had a visit from one of the specialist US teams whose thankless task it was to search for WMD. You could sense that deep down these guys no longer really believed in their mission but they were professionals and kept on going to the bitter end. I had a chat with one of the square-jawed sergeants on the team.

'We've been to a lot of facilities and found nothing, but perhaps our reports might be of some use to you?' he said to me. 'And perhaps in return you might have some information of interest to us?' I agreed to help and had a chat with Abdul and Ahmed in case they'd heard anything about weapons being hidden. Both were fairly dismissive of the claims that there had been WMD. Abdul did have one thought.

'I remember someone digging up a patch of land somewhere just before the invasion,' he said. The US team went to the area he'd mentioned but found nothing and their fruitless search continued.

This failure to find any weapons meant that we had to find a new reason for being in Iraq. We were no longer hunting WMD. Instead we were bringing democracy to the Middle East. But if we were encouraging people to take part in society and build political parties it was then less easy to try to attack people like al-Sadr. To say 'We want you to have a democratic voice for the first time in decades and be free to express yourselves – but on the other hand don't go too far' was a difficult message to get across. So although al-Sadr and his followers were now being flagged as a serious security risk, the coalition was reluctant to take action against him.

The rivalry between followers of al-Sadr and Sistani showed that there were conflicts within the Shi'a as well as between them and the Sunnis. Tribal loyalties and differences also played a key role in local politics, complicating the picture still further. Nonetheless the gulf between Sunnis and Shi'as was very real. Colin and Robert, both from Northern Ireland, found this when they visited the southern dispatch centre, where the electricity is directed around the grid from the various power stations. Sending power to Baghdad was always unpopular. At one point the CPA electricity team in Baghdad had even suggested that in order to supply Baghdad, Basra would have to be 'equalised' and receive around eight hours of power per day, a reduction of approximately ten hours a day from current levels. Colin and Robert had gone to investigate. After a brief welcome, the Iraqi DG explained that this was a difficult job for him because he was a Sunni and he was operating in a Shi'a area. Colin looked across and pointed at Robert, 'We're both Irish. One of us is Catholic and the other is Protestant. So the question is, are you a Protestant Sunni or a Catholic Sunni?' His question was greeted by much laughter.

Meanwhile the security situation in the 'safe' south began to get worse. One of the worst affected areas was Maysan province. This was where Iraq's Marsh Arabs lived, known to some as 'Ali Babas' after the old Middle Eastern story. On one occasion soldiers from the 1st Battalion The Light Infantry came under fire from machine guns and rocket-propelled grenades as they carried out a patrol in the village of Qalat Salih, in Maysan province. They were eventually rescued but not before seven of them were wounded. The governorate HQ in Al-Amarah, meanwhile, came under regular mortar fire.

Even in Basra, where security had been much better than in most of the country, the situation started to deteriorate. Iraqi director generals became concerned for our safety. 'Please, Mr Andrew, it is better that I come to see you – it is safer that way,' a DG told me one day as news of more attacks and explosions filtered through. At the compound itself we were given protection in our 'hooches' as our cabins were known. Sandbags were placed around the head space of our beds to shield us in case of a mortar blast. The mortar rounds often arrived around 11 pm at night, in particular after Friday prayers, or sometimes on Saturday after morning prayers. The timing was so regular that you could almost set your watch by them. The attackers knew that our military had become very good at tracking where the mortars were fired from, so they'd fire three or four in quick succession then vanish. The soldiers would just find the base plates. And as the attackers gained more experience with using mortars, guns and IEDs so they got better at it. On one occasion an explosive device was hidden under a dead dog by the side of the road. An engineer from Mott MacDonald was badly hurt in a roadside bomb blast, losing part of his hand, while others lost their hearing for several days from the effects of the blast.

The growing anti-coalition mood was clear during the debate over the Transitional Administrative Law or TAL, which was eventually signed by Iraqi leaders in March 2004. This document set in place the interim constitution under which Iraqis would draft their full constitution and have full elections. Critics both inside and outside Iraq saw the TAL as 'neo-colonial'. They claimed it was designed by the Americans, who were fearful that the country would fall under the dominance of the Sh'ia majority and become a quasi-Islamic state like Iran. The disquiet that many in Shi'ite Basra felt about the TAL chimed with a leaflet that had been handed out in the town earlier in the year. Part of it read:

Iraq is passing through circumstances which may not be apparent to some because they have been woven together by the crafty minds of foreigners who do not wish the best for Iraq; and in order to prevent Iraq from falling into a colonial future and in order to defend the interests of the Iraqi people, the supreme religious authority Ayatollah Sistani, with the support of all the principle religious authorities, is of the view that a stand should be taken against the occupation forces by [the people] making clear that it is their view that they should choose their government and their transitional law.

We call upon all those who love their country and the faith and who care for their people and their nation, of whatever religion, sect or political orientation to confirm their Iraqi identity in this process.

This is not only an invitation; it is a religious and national duty.

Such growing dissent inevitably increased our own fears and the burden of responsibility weighed on me ever more heavily. It was part of my job to make sure the advisers working for me were safe. One day, James Sharp, our telecom expert came to see me. 'What's your view about me going out for a meeting today, Andrew?' he asked. The security situation had been tight in recent days so it was an understandable question. I looked across to Raneen to see what she thought – the invaluable Iraqi staff always knew what the real mood was on the streets.

'What's your view?' I asked her.

'I think it will be OK today,' she said and so Jim went off to his meeting and returned unharmed. On another occasion, though, he wasn't so lucky. He and the telecom director general Mr Abdullah were travelling south when their vehicles came under attack. Jim emerged unscathed but Mr Abdullah took a couple of rounds in the leg when the bullets pierced the soft unprotected exterior of his car. 'I had a bit of a close shave today,' was Jim's deadpan comment later.

It was at such times I understood the loneliness of command. I felt a bit like the BBC journalist Brian Hanrahan who famously 'counted them all out and counted them all in' as he reported on British aircraft movement during the Falklands War. Every night I used to pray that none of my team would get hurt and that they'd make it safely through the following day. I also made sure they checked their movements in with the Foreign Office man in charge of security for the CPA staff, and that they followed the security instructions while out in their vehicles. I was very aware that many of my team were civilians with no military background or training – they'd come to Iraq to help rebuild the country not to shoot people. If I was involved in an ambush and one of our Control Risks guys was hit then I could at least pick up the rifle and fire back. That wasn't true of everyone.

The Control Risks Group staff were very professional. One of the key instructions was not to run off if the convoy came under attack. 'If one of the vehicles is hit, then the other will come to recover it,' they said. However, when it came to rocket-propelled grenades, RPGs, we knew such advice would count for little. As we often noted with grim humour: 'If one of those hits us we *will* be exiting the vehicle – through the roof at three hundred mph!'

Raneen didn't just advise me on the safety of my team members but on my own too. One morning I was due to go to a meeting at the Central Bank offices when she came up to me, evidently very worried. 'Please, Mr Andrew, you mustn't go to the Central Bank today,' she said.

'Why not, what's the matter?' I asked.

'They know you are coming,' she said, referring to potential attackers. 'Just don't go.'

'How do you know?' I questioned. Raneen told me that she had heard it from someone who worked in the bank. 'They are loyal and they know I work for you so they contacted me to warn you not to come,' Raneen said. By now I'd learnt to trust my staff implicitly so I re-arranged the meeting for another day. Though I was probably no more at risk that anyone else in the CPA, I was aware that my prominent role in finance I could be a tempting target. So I'd always kept a low profile. For most people I was just a name – they didn't know what I looked like and I preferred it that way. They knew my name was 'Mr Andrew' and that my signature was important, but that was about all.

Amid the gloom and tension, I was reminded that many Iraqis still supported what the CPA was trying to do for them. Abdul told me: 'Mr Andrew, we're still very happy to see you in our country. But we just want you to do more.'

A conversation with a senior Iraqi education official put a rather different slant on things. We were discussing the the splits between the various communities such – Kurds, Shi'ia and Sunnis. Mr Sanah was very erudite and well-educated. As he leaned back in his chair in my office he told me: 'Mr Andrew, you have to remember that this is history and that history repeats itself. We had a strong leader and he suppressed the differences. Now he has gone we will have factions and splits and maybe we will divide into three different areas, the same country, but three different areas. But then a strong leader will come and unite us once more as a strong country. History repeats itself,' he said. It was a remarkably fatalistic view.

Like many educated Iraqis of his generation Mr Sanah, who was in his 40s, had been to a British university. Cardiff and Liverpool seem to have been popular universities for Iraqis, so they knew quite a lot about British people and the British way of life. Yet they said that, though they thought they knew Britain and its people, they were nonetheless puzzled as to why we'd chosen to invade their country. 'Why is your Tony Blair doing this?' I was asked more than once. At other times they'd say: 'We know this is not your fault, Mr Andrew, it is the politicians. But we have always been your friends so why is your country fighting us? The problem is not with us but over there …' With that they'd indicate the direction of the Iranian border. Though people in southern Iraq may be Sh'ias, in common with the vast majority of Iranians, this does not mean that Iran is universally loved in the south. Many southern Iraqis perished in the long attritional war with their neighbour.

Iraqi frustration at the slow progress of rebuilding the country was becoming more apparent. Ahmed came to work one morning in floods of tears. He had just met a local man who was carrying his daughter in his arms. 'She was half dead,' Ahmed told me, explaining that the girl had a bullet lodged in her skull when a so-called 'happy round' had fallen back to the ground. 'The local hospital refused to admit her on the grounds that it would be better for her to die at home.' In other words they'd said they were unable to help her. 'This man was hoping that the CPA could do something, hoping for a miracle,' said Ahmed, who was now crying like a baby. Without waiting to hear exactly what was wrong with the child, I organised a whip-round and between us Pat and I had soon raised $500. Ahmed took this to the girl's father who took his daughter to a private clinic where she was treated. She survived. 'From time to time I see this small girl running about the streets,' a delighted Ahmed told me later.

However, after he had helped getting the girl into the clinic, I told Ahmed to take the rest of the day off to find out why the public hospital had felt unable to treat her. It turned out that they had no money because their budget was frozen in a dispute between two senior officials up at the ministry in Baghdad. In any case it was common knowledge that the state-supply organisation, which used to supply drugs and other vital material for hospitals, was deeply corrupt. Drugs were being brought to Baghdad but then were being sold by corrupt officials on the black market into Syria and Iran – many of them never reached hospitals in Iraq at all.

Jane Wilshaw, a member of our health team who arrived in March, worked closely with the Iraqis and the British military to help solve some of these problems. 'The problem was that the lorries were just getting hijacked,' she said later, 'and of course it was the ordinary Iraqis who suffered. In fact if a hospital wanted drugs it was actually easier for them to take some money and go down to the local market to buy the drugs there – there was an extraordinary black market, painkillers, everything.' The situation improved when the military helped build safe pharmacy store rooms at two hospitals and trained staff to keep drugs secure. The military also helped bring in some convoys of drugs to the city.

Drugs weren't the only items that went missing. My cardiologist friend and head of our social services team Dr Aran Maree, who had worked for the pharmaceutical company Merck in Australia, had arranged for the purchase of a new X-ray machine. This was bought in Kuwait and taken to its new home, a hospital in Nasariyah. Unfortunately within a short time of its arrival the machine had vanished. Aran, an old friend of mine I'd personally recruited, came to see me. 'What should we do, Andrew?' he wanted to know. 'I think they're going to sell it!'

I thought for a moment. 'The only way we're going to get this back is to shame them into it,' I said. So we asked the head of public affairs at the CPA to tell the director general of health that there was going to be a press conference. This would announce the great news that the X-ray machine had finally arrived at the hospital.

A few days later, Aran came back to see me. 'It's funny,' he said. 'We've had the press conference and the X-ray machine has mysteriously re-appeared!'

Had it not been returned, the X-ray machine would have undoubtedly ended up for sale at the market with other looted equipment. 'You could buy anything in the market,' said Jane. 'The hospitals had been stripped bare after the invasion and people had taken all the equipment home with them. There were people with heart monitors in their homes – what were *they* going to do with them?' One of her colleagues was Spanish and much of the new equipment that arrived for hospitals came from Spanish-speaking parts of the world. 'Unfortunately this sometimes meant that the Iraqis were unable to use it – instructions were in the wrong language and no one could read them.' The Iraqis might have been better off with less high-tech equipment rather than the ultra-modern state-of-the-art kit they were getting from overseas. 'They had been used to simpler equipment that they could make function rather than the all-singing all-dancing stuff that ended up not really working.' She once visited a hospital where the CPA was helping to refurbish the burns unit with new equipment. 'I was shown into a room and it was stacked high full of unopened boxes. "What's going on?" I asked. "We don't know how to set it up and we don't know how to use it," I was told. "We need help." Though we had already shown them plans of how the unit rooms should look and how the equipment should be set up, I think they were just overwhelmed,' said Jane. 'So we brought in the military to help unpack it and got it sorted out and worked on it with them. It wasn't always about a lack of resources – it was about making things work.'

Despite setbacks Jane and the health team were in fact able to achieve a lot working with the Iraqi health ministry. Since the early days the CPA had been lucky to have had the services of a string of expert volunteers on loan from the Department of Health. That was one of the patterns of the CPA – inevitably expert advisers came and went. Most of them had full-time jobs back at home and had volunteered their services for a few months in Iraq before returning to their day jobs. Their courage and dedication never ceased to amaze me.

Jane was typical of many of the volunteers who gave their time and labour to help in Iraq. A former nurse, she had been director of nursing and public and patient involvement on the Isle of Wight and then acting deputy chief executive. She was due to revert to her old job when the department sent out a circular asking for volunteers to work in southern Iraq. 'I was reluctant to go back to my original role and was keen to do something different,' she explained. 'And I saw this as a real opportunity. Yes I felt nervous – I had a husband and grown-up children I was leaving behind – but sometimes you have to do something a bit different don't you?'

Like all the advisers sent to Iraq, Jane first had to go on a 'hostile environment course' to learn, among others things, what to do in the case of a kidnap attempt. So in the Brecon Beacons Jane and other volunteers had to act out different abduction scenarios. 'It was scary but useful,' she said. 'You are taught always to stay at eye level with the kidnappers if you can. So I just told my "abductors" that I was too old and had bad knees so couldn't kneel down as they asked!' Afterwards Jane embarked on the gruelling 30-hour journey via Kuwait and Baghdad before finally arrived in Basra late one evening. 'After thirty hours' travelling I was quite surprised to learn that I was expected in the office at oh-eight-thirty hours the following morning,' she said. 'The days were long and although the local Iraqis had a Friday off, we didn't.'

At the beginning she was struck by the woeful state of the health service in the south. 'It was shocking. It had been run down over the last thirty-five years because Saddam didn't recognise anywhere other than Baghdad,' Jane said. 'The mental health care system was almost non-existent, there were no drugs and the primary health care system wasn't working because people didn't dare to go to the clinics. They were in the middle of towns and cities where the environment was too hostile. And even if the centres had received drugs, they would have all have been taken.

'The state of the hospitals was also appalling. The best one was the university hospital in Basra where there was a really good director who was to prove a great help in training staff. But even there you walked through this concrete building with no paint, where the operating theatres were dirty and the loos and showers were filthy – it was dreadful.' In the kitchens, for example, there were holes in the floor and the tiles were chipped. The patients' lunch was kept in a big pot sitting on that very dirty floor, waiting to be ladled out. 'The director proudly told me that he always made sure he tasted it before it went to the patients,' said Jane. 'I thought "How could you?" I wouldn't even want to go near it!' Before the invasion the hospital had been cleaner but it had suffered like everything else when the power and water supplies and the sewage system were affected in the fighting. People were starting then to get things back together but it was a very bleak picture.

Yet thanks to the work of advisers such as Jane and the dedication of local Iraqi staff the situation steadily improved. As she later reported: 'We'd got infection-control teams and cleaning teams in and had new equipment and new primary care centres. We built new emergency units and trained people, then trained trainers. I had to write and deliver an emergency-care training programme myself with the help of a lieutenant colonel in the military. Because of the security situation we couldn't get trainers in so we did it ourselves.'

Though Jane's main brief was to look after the general running and training of the health service, she also paid particular attention to the local nursing situation. This was pretty dire at the beginning. The profession was so run down that there were only about 300 fully qualified nurses in the whole of Iraq and about 20 in Al-Basra province. 'About thirty-five years ago it had been one of the best health systems in the Middle East,' said Jane. 'Women nurses were well respected. But it had fallen to the bottom of the scale and many families no longer let their daughters join the profession. Most of the nurses were men and the perception was that they were the ones who had been rejected from the army, the police or the prison services. I'm not sure how true that was, but that was the perception. As for the women who were still nurses, it was sad to hear the ways they were talked about. One of the names they were called was "whore" – it was shocking.'

The head of nursing was an Iraqi woman called Nawar in her late 40s. Never married, she lived with her family and though there was something about her that suggested a past secret sadness involving someone, now she was married to her job. Nawar was highly qualified for her role – she was very intelligent and had a master's degree. However, she had been unable to get her voice heard in the health system because nursing had been so marginalized. Jane became friendly with her and gradually helped her to improve the image of nursing and encouraged the male-dominated health system to take nursing more seriously. 'You could gradually see her coming out of her shell.' said Jane. 'I think that was one of my biggest achievements, personally – by working with Nawar and the nursing team we managed to raise its profile. By the time I left she had developed a really good working relationship with the director general and was actually invited by him to meetings. That had never happened before. She was pragmatic but also passionate about getting better representation for her nurses.'

One of the projects that Jane pushed hard for was to take a group of Iraqi health professionals to London for a leadership training course. She had to network and lobby hard to get the money for the scheme – as she admits herself she was a complete pain in the neck about it. But her persistence paid off and they took 54 Iraqis to London where they were trained under the auspices of the leading health experts the King's Fund. 'It was not about telling them how to run their health service,' said Jane. 'It was about showing them how ours worked so they could take any bits they liked from it and apply it back in Iraq. It was something they really wanted to do – they were desperate to have this kind of information.'

One of the interesting points about the trip was that the group included 14 nurses, something that would have been unthinkable before the invasion. 'I told them that I wouldn't take a hospital director if he didn't take his chief nurse,' said Jane. 'They took it OK – they knew me well enough by then! One of the women in London delivering the programme was a nurse – and also a chief executive – and I think this helped them realise the value of working with their nurses.' The gulf in the backgrounds between the doctors and the nurses was still apparent on the trip, however. Most of the doctors spoke English – many had trained abroad or learnt their medicine in English. Most of the nurses just spoke Arabic.

One of my main concerns at this time was the fate of Basra airport. This had been built 20 years before with the help of German engineers, and was an impressive place. It had been designed as an international airport though it hadn't yet operated as one. From the start the CPA in the south realised that opening the airport would be a major boost for the region's economy, bringing in goods and potentially passengers too. As early as May 2003 a Virgin Atlantic jet had landed with a cargo of first-aid relief at the airport. And by August six airlines had been lined up in a tender process that would have seen one or more of them operating a freight service.

However, the August 2003 riots in Basra had made Whitehall nervous about opening up the airport to civilian traffic. They argued that the risk of a civilian aircraft being shot down was too great – and that it would be the British government, rather than the Iraqis, who would be liable. At the time Sir Hilary and I'd argued that a deal could be struck with an airline and some kind of 'comfort letter' drawn up to reduce our government's risk. In an email to London we also pointed out that some civilian aeroplanes had already started landing at Baghdad airport and as part of the coalition Britain would be just as liable as the US if a plane were shot down there. Basra, in contrast, was a far safer option. However, Whitehall were adamant that the airport remain closed. I was frustrated but also baffled. We also heard in another email that Whitehall were worried about health and safety in the airport itself – someone was concerned that passengers could slip and injure themselves on the marble floors and might then sue the UK government.

I called Baghdad and spoke to Tash Coxen about the strange legal hold-up in Whitehall. 'It's not that simple,' Tash explained. 'The message from Bremer's office seems to be that on no account will Basra airport open for full commercial operations ahead of Baghdad.'

'Why not?' I asked

'Because it will look bad for the US internationally,' she said. This was unbelievable.

'But Basra is benign and we have an opportunity to have a major success for the coalition on our hands. How can we redevelop the economy and promote inward investment if no-one can get here?' I asked. Tash agreed it made little sense but there was little either of us could do. This debate was taking place well above our pay grade. The frustrating part was that Basra airport was actually functioning and receiving more than 45 military and humanitarian flights each week.

The debate over which airport would open first as a civilian operation – Erbil in the north was another candidate – was then settled beyond all doubt by US paymasters. The US-dominated CPA transport team in Baghdad allocated all available funding for airport development exclusively to Baghdad. And they then announced that no additional funding was available for either Erbil or Basra. It was a major blow. But I didn't give up all hope – I'd seen this happen before. One week the US comptrollers would announce that the budgets were tight, the next they'd mysteriously find hundreds of millions of extra dollars. We had to wait and develop our own plans in readiness.

I decided to discuss the issue with the RAF which was responsible for the airfield and drove out to meet John Maas, the impressive RAF group captain responsible for the Basra air station. He ran through the advanced modern technology required for running an airport and handling aircraft, as well as the complexity of international regulations. He thought it would be three years before the Iraqis were well enough trained to handle their own air operations. My own concern was that military divisional HQ was still based in the airport terminal. As long as they stayed in the building there was zero chance of opening as a civilian operation. However, I was told that they were planning to move soon. I was relieved.

My relief didn't last long, however. Colonel Tim Grimshaw had indeed decided that the division would move its HQ. Unfortunately his new choice of venue was the airport hotel just 150 yards across the road. I couldn't believe it – this meant the military would still be slap in the middle of Basra airport. I immediately rang Major Susie Holmes, who was my point of contact at the airport.

'Susie, I hear that the division is moving from the airport terminal?' I said.

'Yes. This will allow the airport to re-open.' she replied optimistically.

'But you are only moving one hundred and fifty yards across the road. Can you tell me where in the world there exists a civilian airport with a military division located in the middle of it?' I was seriously annoyed. For perhaps the first time the objectives of the civilian CPA and the UK military were gravely at odds with each other.

'We *need* to open the airport for commercial use,' I continued, 'and the security implications of having a military HQ
mixed up in the middle of it mean that it will just not
happen.'

Susie said I'd have to speak to the engineers about that. 'The
MOD has already spent more than a million dollars renovating the hotel,' she pointed out.

'Excellent – that's a great start for getting the airport re-
opened. It needs a hotel,' I said sarcastically.

'Nice try,' said Susie. 'I don't think that they'll move that
easily.'

By chance there was a high-level meeting at the airport a
few days later. This involved the RAF's Basra Airport Working
Group which we'd recently joined, plus the deputy minister
of transport Mr Attah from Baghdad, and the Iraqi director
general responsible for air operations. John Maas saw this as
an ideal chance to show off the military's latest plans for the
airport – which would be for dual civilian/military use. But
privately I hoped the Iraqis would show their impatience at
not getting their airport back.

The meeting took place in the VIP lounge that had been
converted into the divisional commander's conference room.
Sandwiches and coffee were laid on for lunch, and John introduced the team. The group captain then started with a
PowerPoint presentation about the challenges and the opportunities. He put up a map of the airport buildings showing
how much was presently occupied by the military – the UK
division and the RAF together. This amounted to almost 100
per cent. He put up the next slide which showed their new
plan. Under this about 25 per cent would be re-allocated to
the Iraqis. John had just moved on to the next slide when Mr
Attah stood up and waved for him to go back to the previous
one. The deputy minister then walked across to the wall and
pointed to a large expanse of open ground to the north-east of
the airport, where there were no buildings at all.

'Why can't you go over here?' he wanted to know. 'Then we can resume commercial air traffic. We want our airport back,' he said emphatically.

This was a sign of how the Iraqis were beginning to assert themselves. It was clear that after the handover of power in June the coalition military would stay on to provide security, but as yet there was no agreement as to the precise terms of their role. There was no 'Status of Forces Agreement' or SOFA, as it was affectionately known. Even though the Iraqis were beginning to exert greater influence, the situation at Basra airport reached an impasse. The division moved out of the terminal into the hotel, which was a small step in the right direction. But after John Maas and his excellent team left at the end of their tour of duty little progress was made in finding a solution.

In February and March we had another go at cracking the problem. We got together a team of our experts including Nigel Forrest, my head of finance and economics, Jon Walden, a logistics specialist from Crown Agents, and Allan Williams, who had consultancy experience building the new Hong Kong airport. We soon realised the potential for the airport. The railway line from Umm Qasr and Khor Az Zubayr ports ran within a kilometre of the edge of the airfield, and then on to Baghdad. With some investment, it would be possible to create a cargo operation at the airport that would be linked both to the ports and Baghdad to turn it into a hub airport similar to the one at Dubai. It was an ambitious idea but it was feasible if we could get the money to do it. One source of funding might be the $18 billion pledged by the US. Little or none of this had been spent in Iraq at this point. The PMO was in charge of spending this cash. So I went to see Dave Nash in Baghdad. I knew that the PMO would need a logistical base in the south for its projects and explained to Dave that we had two major ports and an airport. If developed they could be of enormous value to his work.

'Yes,' he agreed, 'those ports of yours are Iraq's crown jewels. Everything of any significant size in terms of construction equipment has to come through there.' I seemed to be pushing at an open door.

'Great,' I said, 'we have a plan to link the airport and the port, and we wondered if, as part of your logistics plan, we might persuade you to invest a couple of million dollars into the infrastructure?'

'You know,' said Dave, 'there is nothing that I'd like to do more – everything you say makes complete sense.' But there was a snag. The money the PMO had at its disposal had already been earmarked for specific projects. And they had no money to spend on making their own operation more efficient. 'There's no funding available to finance our own logistics chain and its infrastructure.' Dave said ruefully. It was another blow to our airport plans and another victory for bureaucracy.

Back at Al-Sarraji there was more minor bureaucratic irritation over the dining room. New visitors' badges had been made, emblazoned with the words 'No Meals Authorised'. Abdul in particular was unhappy about the badge, which was given to people even when they didn't arrive at meal times. He pointed out that the recipients of this distinctly unfriendly message included director generals, members of leading NGOs, politicians and local sheikhs. 'Iraqis find it insulting because they say "well we didn't ask for your food anyway" and because they are always very hospitable when they entertain visitors,' Abdul said. 'And other visitors just find it very strange and very rude! Are we going to have a sign next summer saying "No Water Authorised" as well?' he demanded.

This kind of incident highlighted the potential awkwardness between the Iraqis and ourselves, the foreign 'invaders' – even though many were still glad we were there trying to help. This tension was summed up by a joke doing the rounds at the time and which was told beautifully by Pat McLoughlin. An American, a Brit and an Iraqi were in a bar one night having a beer. The Yankee gulped down his beer, threw the glass in the air, pulled out a gun and shot it to pieces. He looked at his companions and explained: 'In the US our glasses are so cheap that we don't need to drink from the same one twice.' The British guy was impressed, so he swallowed his own beer, tossed the glass into the air and shot it to pieces. He boasted: 'In Britain we have so much sand to make glasses that we don't need to drink out of the same glass twice either.' Their Iraqi companion paused for a moment, picked up his beer, drank it, threw the glass into the air – then pulled out his gun and shot the American and the Brit dead. 'In Baghdad we have so many Americans and Brits that we don't need to drink with the same ones twice,' he said.

9

A SENSE OF HOPELESSNESS
AND BETRAYAL

April 2004

Sir Hilary had always said he hoped we'd be able to do 'just enough' to help rebuild the south for the Iraqis. There were only a few months to go before handover and still no one knew what our role would be afterwards. But I was starting to feel more confident that we could reach Sir Hilary's goal. Some of the projects were having a real impact. One of the best was an idea from our head of water and sewerage team, Wally Weeks. In January, Wally and other members of the team had arranged to see the city's director general for water. There was growing pressure to get the problems of water shortages sorted out before the summer heat arrived – we'd learnt from the previous year how deadly the combination of soaring temperatures and water shortages could be.

As Wally later remembered: 'The problem was that there were a lot of different agendas about what to do – but not really an Iraqi agenda, so I asked the director general what he wanted to happen about the water. He looked at me in total astonishment. He was in his late fifties or early sixties and was of the old school. I knew this was a top-down society where no one took the initiative – everyone always waited for instructions, to be told what to do. "What do you mean, what do I want, Mr Wally?" he asked me, still looking genuinely surprised to be consulted. "Here's a map of Basra – you mark the ten worst places for water shortages in the city and we will supply water to them," I told him.

The DG gathered his advisers together in a huddle and talked for about two hours. They were clearly trying to agree exactly where the main problems were – they'd never been put on the spot like this before. Eventually the DG came back, took the felt-tip pen and circled ten areas on the map. 'OK, we will run ten pipes straight from the water plant to those areas,' said Wally. There were already pipes through Basra but under Saddam there had been no money for maintenance and the whole place was just like a colander. Now that the DG had identified the worst sections, the aim was to bring new pipes straight down to those areas. 'It was something of an agricultural solution but we needed to get water through in a few months,' Wally explained.

A few months went by as the contractors prepared themselves. But finally the full scale of Wally's plan became apparent. The idea was that thousands of Iraqi workmen would be employed to dig the trenches for the new pipes – by hand. 'Apart from providing water to areas that needed it we also wanted to employ as many people as possible to do the job,' said Wally. 'They used machines to dig through the concrete but otherwise it was all done by hand. It was an enormous task – like digging a trench across London.' Wally and his team kept a close eye on the project but it was supervised on the ground by local contractors. 'It was a great sight. The contractors would mark chalk on the road where the pipes had to go. The following morning the labourers were lined up every 20 feet or so and in the course of the day they had to dig towards the next man to join up the trench. They used pickaxes, shovels and wheelbarrows – it was like building the pyramids.'

Wally's team was using blue polyethylene pipes, the first time they'd been used in the city, and the workers had to be trained how to lay and join them. The sight of so many people digging up the roads also caused something of a stir in the neighbourhoods. But even though the security situation had generally got worse in the city, there was no attempt to disrupt the work. 'The local communities were fascinated by the work,' said Wally. 'And we had no problems with mischief or people trying to sabotage the work because the communities saw that it was a project that would benefit them. They protected us.' Overnight the landscape changed and soon the whole of Basra was one giant set of road works. Mile after mile of trenches were dug well before the large blue plastic pipes were delivered. Knowing the Iraqis as we did, we were fairly sure that some enterprising individuals were digging trenches of their own to alter the course of the water main in their favour.

The first part of the project involved the laying of 48 km of trenches and pipes. It was finished in just ten weeks. 'I think it was about as quick as if we'd done it with diggers,' said Wally. 'They laid an astonishing amount of pipe in such a short period of time.' The project was so successful that the idea was later rolled out to other places in the south, including Nasariyah. Much of its success was down to the hard work and ingenuity of Wally and his team who became known as the 'dirty dozen'. He explained: 'We all came from very different backgrounds and none of us knew each other before we got there. But after a while we really clicked, the chemistry was right and we became the best we could be – we all found our roles. It was very exciting being part of something that was delivering results.'

Another success story – of a very different type – came from Dominique Hope, in the trade and industry team. By now it was too late to hope that many new large-scale projects be finished by the end of June. 'I want to do something that is practical and also beneficial for the whole region,' she said as we discussed possible ideas. I believed the best way to safeguard Iraq from extremism in the long run was to open the country up to the west.

'We need to make sure that people have a stake in their community, that there's freedom of information they can access from around the globe via the internet so that they can make up their own minds,' I said. 'And we need to get foreign investors to invest in the country to help start this process,' I added. We'd been getting lots of queries about how foreign companies could work in Iraq – not just ones looking for large government contracts but private enterprises that wanted to forge long-term links with the region.

It wasn't easy for such firms. At the time Iraq still had no investment law. And with no investment law, no rule of law in general, and no respect for property rights it would be hard to encourage inward investment. In Basra we had no power to change all of that. But we could tell outside businesses how they could still get involved. I said to Dom: 'I want you to imagine that you're sitting at your desk in a business in the UK and that your boss has set you the task of finding out how the firm could invest in Iraq. You'd need to know how to move money, people and goods from London to and from an office in Iraq.' I told her to write something that would answer all those questions. And so she set off. Dom was a real dynamo with a great blend of civilian and military skills – if you set her a challenge she goes out and does it.

What she came up with was incredible. Her Iraq business handbook was 150 pages long and described in detail where the crossing points in the country were, the banking rules, the rules of ownership of companies and property. The point was that unless firms knew how they *could* do business in Iraq there was no chance at all that they *would* do business there. One of Dom's colleagues, Pradeep Mittal, a research analyst from India, contributed some investment case studies to show companies what could be achieved. Many people I spoke to said that these documents were some of the best things that came out of the CPA – they were still being used a couple of years later.

In fact the Iraqi business handbook was so successful that Dom organised a conference on the back of it. Originally the idea was to hold a trade fair in Basra, but security concerns ruled that out. Instead we opted for Kuwait. The response was amazing. More than 300 foreign representatives from companies and organisations across the petrochemical, steel, construction material and food industries were keen to attend. Most importantly the Iraqis themselves were committed to the idea and the new Minister for Industry announced that he wanted to go and speak at the conference. There was just one problem to overcome – getting the Iraqi delegates into Kuwait. Abdul, who was now working for the trade team, worked hard to get visas for the Iraqi delegates. 'Nothing was finalised until the last minute and right up to arrival at the Kuwaiti border we weren't sure whether they would get in,' said Dom. The minister, meanwhile, was on a direct flight from Baghdad and again there were doubts about whether he would be able to fly to Kuwait. However, the Kuwaitis welcomed the delegates and the minister with open arms. 'They declared that they would give him a proper official diplomatic welcome with armed escort and that they would host the whole Iraqi delegation while they were in the country,' she said. 'It was fantastic. I discovered that this would be the first Iraqi official to visit Kuwait since the first Gulf conflict – a momentous occasion.' The Iraqis rightfully stole the show and the conference was declared a success.

Our trade and industry team typified the multinational character of the CPA in Basra. A key member of the team was an Italian Daniela Fiori, a specialist in the small and medium enterprises (SMEs) sector. This was an area we were keen to develop in a country which until then had known only soviet-style centralised industries. The head of the team was Bjorn Brandtzaeg, a Norwegian economist, and included Paul Attenborough, our industrial and heavy-industry consultant, and Pradeep Mittal. I'd also asked Abdul to join their team as an assistant.

I believed passionately that trade and industry, frequently overlooked by the development agencies, was a key area. If we made progress here we could improve the situation for ordinary people in southern Iraq. We met resistance in Baghdad when we proposed funding the rebuilding of the many rundown state owned organisations (SOEs) in the south. The view in the capital seemed to be that they should be allowed to wither and die. One US adviser at the Ministry of Industry in Baghdad told me: 'We have a policy to privatise these organisations so we can sell them off to the international private sector. We will not support them with reconstruction funds.' I thought this was hopelessly unrealistic and took little account of the reality on the ground. The idea that foreign investors would be queuing up to buy companies in Iraq that had no audited accounts and uncertain business models struck me as absurd. It also ignored the fact that these firms were still major local employers of labour. And we knew that unemployment was a significant cause of discontent on the streets.

I raised my concerns with Tash Coxen, who was plugged in to the latest thinking in Baghdad. 'The best description I have heard of their private-sector development strategy is that it's like a group of 20-something MBA students on an away-study weekend in Iraq, for whom this is all a rather interesting intellectual case study.' she told me.

'But how can they starve these institutions of funding when they belong to the Iraqi government?' I asked. 'Surely these are no different to the schools, clinics and hospitals? In fact aren't they more important because potentially they derive an income for the Iraqi government rather than merely acting as a cost centre?'

Despite Baghdad's attitude Bjorn, Paul and Pradeep carried out a detailed study of 40 such companies in the south and their financial track records. The Iraqis cooperated fully once they realised that my team knew what they were doing. Soon we'd drawn up extremely detailed and practical plans for many of the facilities. Some of the facilities needed a level of funding that was way beyond our scope at CPA South. But with others we could really have an impact. For example, we spent around $1 million to re-equip a heavy engineering plant, which had in the past built bridges, onshore and offshore oil facilities and oil-storage tanks. This was very different from the policy in Baghdad. Their view was that much of this work should be undertaken by US contractors – who would make their own arrangements with Iraqi private sub-contractors. But since the pool of Iraqi private contractors was relatively small this approach pushed up costs and fuelled inflation.

It wasn't easy handling a talented but diverse and multi-national team. They naturally wanted to do things their own way. They could – and occasionally did – turn round to me and say: 'Andrew, I'm not working for you – you don't pay my bills.' One member of my team disappeared one day to Baghdad and returned to announce: 'Basra isn't important – all the big decisions are being taken in Baghdad. So I'm going to work for the ministries there.' As tempting as it was to move to Baghdad permanently, and many of the team were approached to work there on more than one occasion, the issue was that we were contracted to undertake a difficult job in the southern region. Often the job was made more difficult by decisions coming from Baghdad, but the south remained our responsibility. So I decided not to renew his contract when it expired at the end of April. In the end that was my only real sanction – to send someone home. Managing my team, I sometimes concluded, was a bit like trying to herd cats.

We had a restricted social life in Basra and made the most of any opportunities for amusement when they came along. 'Today life is good in Basra,' I wrote to a friend, 'although I have a headache and missed breakfast as a result of drinking wine with the Italian Ambassador last night. He had some delightful parmesan and prosciutto to accompany it, which made a wonderful break from the normal food that we're

served by KBR. We almost forgot we were in the CPA compound here in Basra, especially because it has been raining,
which always feels strange in the desert.'

But it wasn't just the wine that was giving me headaches.
The unseemly rush to complete projects across the whole of
southern Iraq was starting to add to the chaos and lack of
coordination. Different parts of the CPA began to fight over
resources, with the governorate teams in the four provinces
asking the capital for more money to get projects off the
ground before 30 June. The danger was that they wouldn't be
able to cope with more resources and would get swamped.
It's one thing to get approval for extra cash. But that's just the
first of about 20 steps you need to take to get the projects completed. They were all willing and competent people – but most
of them were simply not specialists. Meanwhile our advisers
– who *were* specialists – weren't always able to get the money
they needed to carry through vital strategic projects since
Baghdad was funnelling it all through the governorate teams.
Inevitably there were tensions between us and the GTs.
Though they reported to Ambassador Bremer we kept control
of some of the purse strings. Projects over a certain cash limit
had to be referred by the GTs to us for sanction, funding and
approval. If the project exceeded our own limit then we sent it
to the programme review board in Baghdad for their approval.
Although theoretically it was possible for the GTs to bypass
us, in practice there were few projects that we were unable to
finance from our resources. The GTs were also hampered by
their lack of manpower. In effect we operated a bit like a bank,
controlling the flow of credit to the GTs. And when it came to
financial controls we had a real expert.

Katharina Pfitzner is a German national, qualified in
accounting and budgeting. Her methodical and uncompromising approach to her work was all the more effective because
she was both pretty and determined. I remember one of the
poor project officers being addressed by her. 'You *will* bring

me the receipts,' she told the hapless individual in her excellent but accented English. 'When I have the receipts I shall give you more money, but not until then. These are the rules.' Pat and I would exchange quiet smiles whenever Katharina confronted an offending project officer for receipts and correctly completed paperwork.

Despite the tensions we tried to be sensitive to the needs of the governorate teams who were often working in exceptionally difficult circumstances. And we tried to avoid situations where – through our contacts with the Iraqi ministries – we might inadvertently leave the provinces out of the loop. From our own dealings with Baghdad we knew how irritating that could be. But there were differences of opinion. The trade and industry team, for example, had a plan to refurbish the paper mill at Al-Amarah, which had been heavily looted. One of its important by-products had been water production, and we reasoned that by kitting them out with a working reverse-osmosis plant they could at least produce water – and bring in some money for their company at the same time. Unfortunately the local governorate head disagreed. She took the Washington view that such state-owned enterprises weren't to be supported. Instead she wanted the funding to go towards a $1 million jobs programme. We finally went along with this – after all, they were the team on the ground.

However, one of the biggest rows over funding wasn't between us and the provinces – but within CPA South itself. I was in Baghdad dealing with another issue when I found myself outside the adviser's office at the Ministry of Finance. Inside there was a meeting going on and from the people who were present I could work out what was being discussed. The US comptroller was clearly reporting on the funds available for Iraq – which depended on international oil sales. I knew there had been a recent surge in oil prices so I suspected that suddenly there was more of this so-called DFI money to spend. As the comptroller left I greeted him and asked if I could come and see him about our project funding for the south. 'I hope you'll still have enough left for our existing programmes?' I said light-heartedly, gently fishing for his reaction.

'There's plenty of money at the moment,' he let slip, then quickly realised he shouldn't have said anything. 'Come and see me, when you're ready,' he said hurrying off to his office. I had the inside information I needed.

I went immediately to Tash's office and borrowed her phone to call Pat in Basra. 'Hello my friend,' I said quietly to avoid being overheard, 'can you go up to Patrick Nixon's office and speak to him urgently. I reckon there are several hundred million dollars of windfall DFI funds in the account this month, and grabbing some of it could really solve some of our project-funding issues.'

'Okey, dokey,' he replied, 'What sort of amount do you want us to ask for?'

'I think there's at least one hundred and fifty to two hundred and fifty million available so we could make a claim to twenty-five million. What do you think?'

'Sounds good to me,' said Pat. 'It'll stop the project officers complaining.'

'OK, but ask Patrick to ask for thirty to thirty-five million,' I told Pat. 'I'm sure they'll haircut our request, and then we should probably land up with the twenty-five million we want.'

Later in the day, I went back to the same Ministry of Finance office. This time I met George Wolfe, the senior adviser. 'Hello,' he said, 'I've just received a request from your ambassador in CPA South for twenty-five million dollars of funding. Is this a co-incidence?' He was clearly – and correctly – suspicious that I'd heard something about extra oil revenue.

'Should it be?' I replied innocently. I tried to cover my tracks by explaining why we'd asked for the money now. 'We're getting up to full speed with project spending as per Ambassador Bremer's instructions. We could use the cash.' It was vital to drop Ambassador Bremer's name into this kind of conversation if you wanted results. The CPA Baghdad administration was heavily dependent on his personal authority.

'We do have some surplus DFI funds, so your timing is good,' said George. 'I can't grant you the full amount, because the other regions may complain, but I can probably get you sixteen million.'

'Great,' I said and hastily withdrew in case he got more suspicious and started asking questions. I was delighted with the outcome but at the same time I was wondering why Patrick hadn't asked for $30 million as I'd recommended. Later Pat told me that Patrick had thought the demand was too high and that we wouldn't be able to deploy that amount of cash in the time available. According to Pat he may also have believed that he would get exactly what he asked for because he was the regional co-ordinator.

I returned to Basra where Patrick had announced that he'd secured the new funding. He now asked for my advisers at CPA South and the governorate teams to submit a list of projects that could benefit from the extra money. The Project Review Board would then decided which projects would get the go-ahead.

'I have a bad feeling about this,' I told Pat and Katrina, 'they'll slice this into lots of projects, without any regard to an overall strategy.' I didn't believe that the governorate teams would be physically able to start, fund and complete any new projects in the short time remaining. We already had evidence that the teams had so far only been able to spend a third of the money they'd been allocated on many of the existing projects. Now they'd be swamped with yet more cash they couldn't deal with.

'We have specialists screaming for funds for bigger projects and we also have the ability to manage these projects better from here,' I complained. 'Doesn't the board see that the effect will be the same whoever does these projects? It's not as if the projects are going to take place anywhere other than the four southern governorates. We aren't another governorate – we should not be competing for this funding.'

I went to see the board but got nowhere. I was asked to submit our proposed projects in order of perceived priority.

'I cannot prioritise the funding requirements of my team without any knowledge of the other projects that are out there,' I argued. 'We're working alongside and for the governorate teams.' I also pointed out that the whole reason for the closed-door programme review board each week was to decide what could and could not be done and to work out overall strategy. But although I was annoyed I held back from pointing out why we'd received this extra funding in the first place.

Soon afterwards there was a meeting with the governorate heads and the board announced that the GTs would get around $14 million of the $16 million available. Our own specialists, who had worked out detailed plans that had been waiting for weeks to get approved, got just $1.5 million to spend. I made little attempt to hide my anger. 'Andrew, you seem agitated,' said Patrick.

'Yes, you're right. I am annoyed,' I told him. 'Every time we receive funding, we start running round like kids in a sweet shop without pausing to work through the practicalities of how these funds should be best allocated and deployed. 'You've just allocated fourteen million dollars to approximately sixteen members of staff across four governorates, to be spent in the next thirteen weeks against projects that I suspect are barely more than a line on a piece of paper. And you've chosen to disregard projects that have been designed by experts for those very same provinces. Generalists are dictating policy in economic re-development ahead of highly skilled consultants.'

'This is our decision,' he said again. I stood up and walked out of the meeting.

'How did it go?' asked Pat when I stormed back to my office. I just glowered at him.

'That well, then. Look on the bright side, we won't have anything to do for the next few months – administering that lot would have been a real headache. Instead I just get to write out four forms, hand over the cash and they can manage it all. I might as well go home.'

'Don't you believe it,' I replied, 'we'll be picking up the fallout from this decision for the next three months. They won't be able to spend the money and in a few weeks' time, there will be funds being sent back to us unspent.'

'Then they'll be asking us to implement our projects in double-quick time!' said Pat, laughing. Once again Pat's humour pulled me out of my black mood and I smiled and got on with my work.

At the next evening meeting when Patrick turned to me for my report I replied, 'Nothing to report from my department, although I think the governorate teams are quite busy.'

I found the lack of effective co-ordination and joined-up strategic thinking in Baghdad and national capitals very frustrating. There seemed almost to be a feeling of reticence within the CPA about its role in Iraq. People seemed embarrassed by the fact that to all intents and purposes we'd been running the country for the last ten months. Yet that's precisely what had been necessary since the Iraq government had vanished after the invasion. During one trip to Amman I was forcibly reminded by the British ambassador to Jordan, Christopher Prentice, that it wasn't the role of Her Majesty's Government to take charge in Iraq. 'Andrew you need to remember that that the colonial days are long gone and we're not meant to be running the country,' he told me.

'But Mr Ambassador, we *are* running the country!' I said.

The ambassador looked at me doubtfully. 'Well that wouldn't be appropriate,' he observed.

It was true of course that the old Colonial Office – which had run large parts of the globe – had vanished and no one wanted to see its return. Instead a new breed of 'post-conflict' nation-building specialists had developed across various Whitehall departments as well as in NGOs and the United Nations. Their aim was to help existing government institutions to take charge of their own countries. The problem in Iraq was that there were no functioning institutions left to take charge. In an ideal world the Iraqi ministries would have co-ordinated the reconstruction work they needed, aided by advice and money from us. But the ministries were still far too weak, even a year after the invasion. Something or someone had to step into that power vacuum.

Schemes like Wally's showed that by working closely with the Iraqis we could both make an impact on the ground *and* help re-build the country's shattered government at the same time. The problem was that there were other agendas. One was the pressure of international politics – Britain and especially the US had to be seen to be handing full sovereignty back to the Iraqis as soon as possible. And that meant 30 June. Another problem was that the lead British government department in Iraq, DFID, had their own way of tackling a country's problems. And helping to run it was most certainly not on their agenda.

From my first dealings with DFID I could see that they had a very different world view from me. I shall always treasure a discussion I had with Jim Drummond, a senior civil servant who was head of the DFID Iraq directorate in London. He proudly showed me a document that proclaimed that the department's mission was to 'eradicate poverty'. He said to me: 'What do you think, Andrew?'

I replied: 'Do you really want me to say what I think?' He nodded. I said: 'Poverty is relative – someone is always going to be poor in relation to someone else. By definition your aim is never achievable. So why have you chosen it as your mission statement?'

Jim of course didn't agree. 'Your problem is that you're too commercial, Andrew.' It was true that I come from a commercial background, and it was also true that I enjoyed teasing DFID in this way. But there was a serious point behind what I said. DFID struggled to get to grips with what Iraq needed because it wasn't the kind of country they were used to dealing with. It was not a developing country but a major oil producer.

Wally Weeks, who had himself spent years working in the developing world, said that DFID had felt more comfortable with their role immediately after the invasion. 'There were a lot of people who needed assistance,' observed Wally. 'So it fitted with DFID's approach. But as the year rolled on, the nature of the problem changed and it fitted less well with their view of the world. Their main focus is on developing countries. They see Malawi as a poor country that needs help. But they look at Iraq and see it sitting on the world's second largest oil field and they don't then see it as being worthy of so much attention – and that became apparent in 2004.'

The difference in DFID's approach compared with that of other organisations was rammed home to me by some of their priorities over staffing and funding. For example just a couple of months after the dangerous riots of August 2003 the department sent out a woman to report on and work with 'gender issues' in southern Iraq. Addressing the way women are treated in a conservative Muslim society such as Iraq is obviously very important. No one doubted that. And the woman they sent out to Basra, an equality development officer with East Renfrewshire Council in Scotland, did some good work. This included arranging a high-profile conference of women from the region. But I wasn't alone in wondering whether it was really a priority issue in terms of money and personnel, at a time of crippling economic problems and a worsening security situation, when we were struggling to recruit staff for health, education, water, power and finance. Similarly, DFID sent someone to report on environmental issues. Dominique, Kevin Thomas and I had just been discussing the issue of Basra's oil refinery and how it should be developed. It was after all one of the most strategic assets in the south of the country. The DFID envoy said that she'd just visited the site. 'I'm very concerned about the environmental impact that this particular plant has,' she said. 'There is funding available via DFID's environmental fund in London to complete an environmental impact study.' Of course I didn't object to taking the environment into account, but it needed to be done in the context of a wider look at the role of the refinery in the country's economy.

'At the moment Iraq is importing a lot of its daily requirement for refined fuels and therefore paying for products that it should produce itself,' I explained. 'This refinery is one of only two refineries in Iraq, and responsible for approximately six hundred thousand barrels output of refined product.'

As Jane Wilshaw from the health team later said: 'Gender and the environment are important but you have to have the infrastructure first.' She had her own experiences with DFID after June when she worked directly for them in Iraq. 'They seemed to have their own way of doing things,' she recalled. 'They asked me to do things that I had no background in – for example they wanted me to do some research into HIV when actually what was needed were more practical things and the projects that we were already doing.'

The work of these officials – who often worked independently of us – also gave London a curious picture of what was going on in Iraq. While Patrick Nixon was sending his reports back through the filter of the Foreign Office or Baghdad, DFID were getting direct reports on the environment and gender – parts of the jigsaw, certainly, but only parts of a very much bigger picture. So different parts of Whitehall ended up focussing on a range of widely different issues. As one senior official at the CPA in Basra told me: 'The trouble with Whitehall is that they're looking through the wrong end of the binoculars.' Inevitably there was a clash of cultures. I believed the key thing was to develop the infrastructure and get the economy working, encouraging both foreign and, ultimately,

Iraqi private companies wherever possible to boost it. Whitehall seemed to think that concentrating on elections and politics as well as working on 'softer' issues would set the conditions for everyone to be happy – and the private sector would look after itself.

However, I still assumed that the expertise that we'd developed in the CPA in water, power, finance, transport and other areas wouldn't be lost. I felt certain that our reservoir of knowledge and personal contacts with the Iraqis would still be needed after the handover in June. That wasn't just our view or the view of most local Iraqi officials. I'd got to know Daniel Ruiz from the United Nations in the early days of the CPA, when CPA South had been struggling to get its act together. Now Daniel returned on a visit and he was astonished at the transformation. 'Andrew, this is amazing,' he said as we strolled around the compound. 'It's working isn't it?' Then he added: 'You can't dismantle all of this, can you?'

'Absolutely not,' I agreed. At the time I think both of us hoped that the UN could step in to play a bigger role after the handover and that much of the work we were doing could carry on through them. And I felt sure that despite the rumours that Whitehall were planning to keep only a tiny team after the handover, this wouldn't be the ultimate outcome. Yes, they might want to cut and trim our team a bit after the CPA vanished on 30 June. But in my naivety I thought they'd say 'This is brilliant, it works, we need to keep it going.' Of course we'd no longer be 'in government' but the important thing would be that the Iraqis would still have the benefit of our expertise.

At the end of March 2004 two senior officials came to visit us in Basra. Their mission was to meet the staff, assess how the CPA was performing and report on who and what would be needed from the British point of view after 30 June. I knew it was a crucial visit, as it would decide the fate of my team and, far more importantly, the future of the attempt to rebuild southern Iraq. I went to see Patrick Nixon. 'Patrick, I'll get my team together so we can we can discuss what to tell our visitors – otherwise they might get a confusing message,' I told him. It seemed me vital we all kept to the same message otherwise they wouldn't have a clear picture from which to draw conclusions.

Patrick disagreed with me. 'That would be counter-productive,' he told me. 'They should just see it as it is.' I wasn't happy about this. The visiting Whitehall team would just get a snapshot of our work, and as far as I was concerned I was going to make damned sure that they were going to get the snapshot we wanted them to see.

I ignored Patrick' s advice and called a team meeting one Monday morning. 'The purpose of the meeting is solely to discuss the forthcoming visit,' I told my assembled team. 'There will be no other business. This is probably the most important visit we will have,' I continued. 'It's all about what this organisation will become. Our message is that our successors need adequate resources – and that means people. In my view the Iraqis are not in a position to take over power until the end of September at the earliest so we need to manage the transition.' I said that we needed to highlight areas that Whitehall might particularly care about – health, water and electricity. I decided not to try and fight for every part of the team because we already knew they wouldn't be interested. But if we could at least focus their minds on some key issues, such as the importance of the ports, we might be able to steer them in the right direction. Perhaps we could get them to meet us half way.

Many of the team were very apprehensive about the visit. After all the hard work they'd put in and the dangers they'd faced in the heat and dust of southern Iraq, they were being asked to sit down with two London-based civil servants and effectively sing for their supper. There was another complication too. We were all on six-month contracts, many of which were due to expire at the end of April. So some faced

the prospect of having to go home well before the handover –
unless those contracts could be extended.

My own meeting didn't go well. I'd asked Pat and Katrina to
make themselves scarce at the appropriate moment so I could
see the civil servants on my own. It kicked off with an assur-
ance that the British government was committed to southern
Iraq. Next came an explanation about a £5 million initiative
with the BBC to encourage independence within the media.
Then one of the civil servants described the plans for transition.
First she told me that the CPA in the south cost too much and
so Whitehall had decided it must fund its own activities after
30 June – and not in any joint venture with other nations. I
couldn't let this pass without comment – after all the US was
currently picking up the bill for the camp not the British.

'If the UK decide to take their advisory team within its own
consulate then surely the cost of life support will increase
rather than decrease?' I argued.

'In London we feel it best that each nation involved in CPA
South should make up its own mind about what they should
do after transition,' she continued.

'But this is the UK military sector, and therefore the other
nations will be following our lead,' I explained.

'It's been decided that a consulate should be established
here in Basra,' she replied, 'and we shall have a normal consular department within it, as well as a Transitional Advisory
Team or TAT team for six months – so that there's a transition
before normal consulate operations can be resumed.' She then
explained that beneath the ambassador or consul general
there would be a consulate team, a trade and industry team
and a development team. The TAT team would ultimately
work with the US-run PMO.

I was incredulous. 'So you really think that within six
months this will be a normal consulate carrying out normal
consular activities?' I asked. I wondered privately how many
British tourists there might be in Basra who would need the

consulate's services. She avoided my question and instead turned her attention to my advisers.

'The team is too big,' she said, 'and the focus of co-ordination of the development effort will be in Baghdad, not in Basra. CPA South will be either subsumed into another organisation or wound down.'

Next my visitor outlined the areas that DFID was proposing to support after transition. These included schools, health, water, power, transport, irrigation, quantity surveying and contract management. Trade and industry, she said, would be moved to Baghdad. 'We may re-activate work with small and medium enterprises at a later date,' she added. I felt a growing sense of unease. When I saw the organisation chart that they'd brought with them it was clear this was less a consultation and more a done deal. On the chart the oil, sewerage and sanitation, transport, housing, roads and bridges and telecoms sectors had all been crossed out. These are some of the key areas for the development of any economy. It was a huge blow but not in truth a huge surprise. I'd guessed that London civil servants would focus on areas where each department felt most comfortable – namely the areas of policy and security, and those that were humanitarian in nature and which aimed to alleviate poverty. The problem was that this was neither a coherent strategy for the civilian sector nor did it offer any real help to the military in finding an exit strategy. Put another way, it didn't make a lot of sense.

However, I wasn't keen to pick a fight at this stage. I praised their plan to put in finance staff for the governorates. But I said there would be far too few of them. 'They will just get swamped,' I said. I also pointed out that simply relying on the PMO to get on with reconstruction on its own was a big mistake. From my own experience of US contracting and reconstruction I knew that the large schools, hospitals and other facilities that were being built weren't being integrated into the existing Iraqi economy. Sooner or later a new plant or machinery would break down through a lack of spares, training or operating budget.

'They have few if any plans to work with the Iraqis directly, except employing them as sub-contractors. I'm worried that they have little or no knowledge of the local directorates that we have,' I said. 'They are focussed on construction and therefore many of their projects just won't be sustainable.' As I spoke I was jotting down my thoughts in my notebook. Alongside 'Transitional Advisory Team' I'd added: 'not enough people means a nightmare and mission failure'.

My visitor then turned to the current work of my team which she felt 'lacked focus and direction'. I'm not sure whether she meant this as an attack on me but it certainly felt like it. She added that part of the problem was that we in Basra hadn't been working via the British civil servants in Baghdad. I tried to point out that we were a multi-national outfit at CPA South and it wasn't actually the job of our Italian, Danish, Czech or even our British staff to report to a British government office based in Baghdad. But she carried on and said that as 'consultants' we'd focussed too closely on projects alone. Apparently we should have been concentrating on 'institutional capacity building'.

I was dumbfounded. We'd explicitly been *instructed* by Paul Bremer and the CPA hierarchy in January to focus on projects. Moreover the reason we'd had to handle so many projects was because the Iraqis hadn't shown any particular aptitude for doing it themselves. And as for 'institutional capacity building' we'd been doing that from the start by working alongside the director generals and the ministry officials and helping them to start the process of rebuilding their own teams. Admittedly none of us had PhDs in the subject. Instead we'd just got on and done it. I was also struck by the emphasis on the word 'consultants'. Clearly we weren't felt to be part of the Whitehall club. I was hurt and angered by their approach. They acted as if they were the professionals coming in to take over from a bunch of amateurs. I felt insulted not just personally but for my team as well. By the time the meeting ended I feared the worst. They'd clearly already made up their minds on their line of action.

After they'd completed their short 'fact-finding' mission our visitors gathered us together in the main conference room one morning to tell us what they'd concluded. As around 40 of us filed in, our ports adviser Peter Bingham glanced across at me. 'So is it good news?' he asked.

'I'll leave you to make up your own mind.' I said carefully.

'Hmm,' he said, sensing that my guarded response spelt trouble. We were treated to a PowerPoint presentation which closely mirrored what I'd been told earlier. In effect they were telling my team that they were redundant and that much of their work had been in vain. The team of 50 advisers in the economic planning and development department was to be replaced by just seven people.

When the slide show had ended my team was in a feisty mood. 'So if my sector is not to be covered after 30 June, why don't I just leave now?' challenged one.

'It's important to continue work for the moment but this is something we could think about,' was the reply.

'What happens to all the work that we've done over the past year?' asked another.

'This is the purpose of the mapping document.' They were referring to a detailed handover document they wanted us to compile.

'What about sanitation and sewerage? There's no point in looking at only water production if you don't cover water and waste disposal. The two go hand in hand.'

'This is something that we shall look at.' they promised.

'So how many will the TAT team consist of?' asked another member of the team.

'Approximately six to twelve people.'

'This is exactly back where we started last year,' said Colin, 'too few people and absolutely no chance of achieving anything.'

'So why don't you have a larger transition team?' someone asked our Whitehall guests.

'With the transition to sovereignty, it's up to the Iraqis to ask us for assistance. We don't want to tell them what they need,' they said.

'What if they don't know what they need?' said someone.

Then from the back of the darkened room another voice muttered: 'They hardly *asked* us to come here in the first place.'

It was a hostile atmosphere and it was clear that my team hadn't been convinced by the presentation. I wasn't sure whether the officials from London had fully anticipated the impact on the team of what they said. They seemed to find it amusing that the TAT would be known as the 'TAT on the Shat' – after the Shat Al-Arab waterway that passed by our building. Oddly, just at that moment, not many of us found it very humorous. Morale was ripped to shreds. We had, as someone commented, been 'cut off at the knees'.

Immediately after the meeting I was collared by a couple of angry members of the team. 'Couldn't you see this coming? Why have we spent all this time and effort and risked our lives to just throw it all away? Why haven't you sorted this out with London?' I was their team leader and quite understandably they were blaming me for this fiasco. I apologised to them.

'I've failed you,' I admitted. 'I should have managed things differently.'

And I meant it. I realised then that I'd committed a major strategic blunder. I'd failed to manage the message that London was getting about the work we were doing. I should have made sure that what we did on the ground was being noticed in the corridors of Whitehall. Perhaps then the mandarins and politicians would have reacted differently.

It would have been unfair for me just to blame our visitors for what was happening. As civil servants they had been put in charge and were clearly doing what they thought was right. As one senior official said to me one day as I raged against Whitehall bureaucrats: 'Andrew, be reasonable, these guys don't get out of bed each morning and say "right, how can I f*** things up today?"!' And despite my differences with Patrick Nixon, I also knew that he had worked very hard to ensure Whitehall knew what was happening in the region. Yet somehow the message that rebuilding Iraq would be best served by having a tiny British civilian presence after the handover had won the day. Perhaps it was simply – as I was being told privately – that the Foreign Office lost the Whitehall battle with DFID over what should happen next. Jack Straw, the foreign secretary, had been out-manoeuvred by Hilary Benn, the secretary of state for international development. Ultimately of course it was Tony Blair's call. He must have endorsed the transition plan.

I wasn't the only senior CPA person to feel dismayed. Brigadier Peter Williams, the senior military CPA man in the south, told me: 'The British and CPA south are about to execute a manoeuvre that isn't even in the military textbook!' He was right. The military have a procedure which is called a 'rearward passage of lines'. When a unit is retreating this manoeuvre is designed to ensure that the withdrawal is orderly and constructive. In this case, however, the British Government wasn't doing that. It was simply saying: 'On 30 June we're out of here!'

I spoke with a senior official in Baghdad. He voiced the fears of many when he told me: 'Having decided not to replace the CPA we are now looking at an uncoordinated group of organisations, each of which will be doing part of the work that you and your people have been doing. The list is obvious – the World Bank, UN Agencies and so on. But the reality is that they aren't about to start doing it any time soon.' It was *just* possible, he said, that the US successor to the CPA – known as IRMO or Iraqi Reconstruction Management Office – might be willing to take on some of our work in Basra. 'But,' he added, 'I rather think that the US will take the view that if the

UK doesn't think these things worth doing in Basra – then why should they take a different view?' It was just what I feared. But though the official warned me that I was extremely unlikely to change Whitehall's mind I knew I had to try something. It was our last chance.

I decided to write to Hilary Benn at DFID to let him know what we thought of Whitehall's decision. I accepted that the various well-intentioned civil servants who had visited us had listened to our concerns that key areas of our work needed to be maintained after the handover. But I didn't think they were providing the necessary means. Having just seven people after 30 June would make British activities weak to the point of impotence. I outlined a compromise plan in which I proposed a team of 18 people covering health, education, electricity, the ports, water and sewerage, finance and planning. This would still be barely adequate, I argued, but would at least have a 'fighting chance' of success. I finished the letter by outlining what I thought was at stake. I wrote:

> We have a moral obligation to be here and I believe the Prime Minister's statement was 'for as long as it takes, not a moment more'. We all accept that [the Iraqis] are not ready to assume power and that the fledgling administration is too weak to stand alone, or else why would the military remain here? At the very moment that technical assistance is required more than ever by the Iraqi ministries, we will evacuate some 50 staff from [my] department over two weeks on or around 30 June.

> It is a catastrophe in the making and I would be irresponsible if I was not on record and didn't argue strongly for senior politicians in UK government to be aware of the implications of such a decision, politically, economically and militarily.

> At best we will be perceived to have walked away, at worst

there is a real risk that such a departure is a contributing factor in the drive towards a full-scale civil war. The problem may be security, but the root cause of much of the disorder is still the poor state of the economy. It is this situation that the religious extremists are exploiting. Why we are removing all our expertise at the critical moment is beyond me, and will potentially ensure that the UK is completely militarily engaged in Iraq for a long time to come because we fail to address the real issue which is the economic reconstruction of the country.

I still believe that this is not the outcome that UK government wants to achieve.

For protocol reasons I addressed the email to Patrick Nixon and asked him to send it on to Hilary Benn – whose email address I supplied. The following morning, I had a mail back from Patrick Nixon that simply said: 'It has been sent.' A number of my team also saw the letter. 'Well done, you represent the view of the majority here,' one of the health advisers told me. There was support from the hierarchy too. 'Bravo,' was the response of Brigadier Williams. From London itself I heard nothing. Neither Mr Benn nor any of his senior staff replied to me.

Even before our withdrawal the security situation was beginning to get worse. I wrote to a friend describing what it was like. 'Truthfully I didn't sleep much last night with so many explosions and gunfights outside the walls of the compound,' I wrote. 'RPGs have finally come to Basra and it doesn't bode well for the next few months. I suspect that I've been here too long and fear what is happening and where it may lead – civil war. Two of our CPA subordinate locations here in the south in Al-Amarah and Nasariya were attacked yesterday. The Italians have 12 injured today and there were 15 Iraqis dead after gunfights that lasted most of the day.'

I then described what, privately, we were planning to do in case we came under sustained attack at Al-Sarraji – we would stand and fight. 'In one sense I dare not brief my staff about my concerns over what is really going on because it may scare them too much. Instead we lock-down the compound and try to continue as normal.' Soon afterwards the Green Zone in Baghdad started to come under sustained rocket attack and for some days all our staff were forbidden from travelling to the capital. One day I sent all my local staff home at lunchtime after rumours started circulating that al-Sadr had issued a *fatwa* against all Iraqi staff who were working for the CPA. Though later we were never able to find out if such a *fatwa* had really been issued it felt real enough at the time. Our work was important and the local staff were essential to it but it wasn't worth risking their lives over it.

I was still exercised about Whitehall and their plans and very doubtful about the value of the 'mapping document' – which seemed pointless to me. There would hardly be anyone left to read it – let alone implement any of it. I voiced my frustrations in an email to a friend. It was 'a pointless exercise in bureau-cracy so that they can cover their bureaucratic backsides with glossy reports.' Yet even as I was writing, another crisis was starting to break that needed my full attention. The Danish shipping company Maersk was threatening to pull out of the south's main port Khor Az Zubayr, known as KAZ for short, through which most of Iraq's imported diesel and exported heavy fuel passed. My transport team and I knew that this was potentially disastrous for the south, and damaging for the whole country. One of the first steps that the military had taken at the end of the fighting in 2003 was to sign a deal with Maersk to take over the running of KAZ. This helped to ensure that the port ran effi-ciently and to reduce some of the corruption that had hamstrung the existing port authority. Now, however, US officials in Baghdad had concluded that the contract that Maersk had signed with the military was 'illegal'. Just to add to the farce, the greatest customer of Maersk at the time was the US military. Faced with this uncertainty Maersk was threatening to pull out unless their status was guaranteed and they received some operational costs they were owed. The situation was starting to fall apart. By email I opened negotiations with Allan Rosenberg, the former CPA South chief of staff who was now back at his own job at Maersk, and with the Ministry of Transport in Baghdad. It was soon clear I needed to get to the capital – and fast. So though all other CPA South staff had been grounded, I was given special permission to travel to Baghdad.

As soon as I arrived at Baghdad airport I went to look for the security detail. They weren't hard to find in their Toyota land cruisers with high-frequency antenna mounted on the front bumper.

'Hello, Sir,' said one of the team courteously, 'this is becoming a bit of a habit.'

'Yes,' I said, 'but sadly no-one seems to recognise Hercules air miles.'

He smiled and opened the heavily armoured boot for my holdall and laptop.

'How is the airport road today?' I asked.

'There were a couple of incidents this morning, so there are a few more of us today.' Looking around there were five armoured land cruisers, more than I'd seen before.

At the palace I was interested to see to see that the security cordon was tightening, with far more concrete blast barriers than on my last visit. I made my way through a 20-feet-high laminated wooden door and negotiated the maze of corridors to the Ministry of Transport adviser's office where I spoke to the chief adviser Manson Brown about the problem at Khor Az Zubayr. He was very phlegmatic. 'It would make no sense to have them pull out now – what makes you think that they will go?' I told him that I'd been speaking with their director in Dubai, Allan Rosenberg. And I also knew that the ship the *Maersk Alaska* was arriving shortly at the port.

'They'll begin loading their equipment, including all the equipment that they've provided to the port and leave tomorrow night,' I told him.

Just then Dave Nash, head of the US-run reconstruction arm the PMO walked in to the office. 'Dave, do *you* know anything about this Maersk situation?' Manson asked him.

'No, tell me,' said Dave. Manson summarised the problem and when he heard that Maesrk was about to pull out Dave was horrified.

'This would be a disaster, and it would set us back months! We need those ports.'

I seized my chance. 'Would you mind walking with me into the Ministry of Finance?' I asked him. 'We need $1 million to cover the cost of the contract – and apparently there is no money in the Iraqi Transport Minister's budget for this.'

'That's right,' agreed Manson, 'and the minister would most likely block this anyway because we're in delicate negotiations over other issues regarding Baghdad airport at the moment. So this is not a good time.' he added.

Dave and I walked to the Ministry of Finance office where we met George Wolfe, the senior adviser there. 'Hi George!' said Dave and walked straight in in his usual blunt way. 'We have a problem in the ports. Andrew can give you the background, but the bottom line is that we need $1 million by tomorrow.'

George Wolfe looked at us both. 'We can't do that,' he said. 'The next programme review board isn't scheduled until Wednesday and we're in negotiations with the Iraqis over various budgets at the moment.' He asked about Ministry of Transport funds but was told there were none available there either. It was a frustrating situation. Just about everyone seemed to agree that Maersk shouldn't be allowed to pull out. But bureaucracy seemed against us. The amount of money we needed was relatively small in Baghdad terms – we just couldn't get our hands on it. George said we had one last chance. 'The only person that can make this happen is Ambassador Bremer,' he said.

'If he tells me that I have to do this, then we'll just have to find you the money – but I have to warn you that I think you're up against it.'

Dave and I left the office while we discussed what I had to do. 'You'd better prepare a submission to go to Bremer's office,' said Dave as we walked. 'There's not much more that I can do, although if he asks I shall tell him that this is mission critical.' And as we parted Dave pressed me not to give up. Back at the Ministry of Transport office, I spent the next hour drafting a note outlining the Maersk issue. I then took it down to the British office which was next to Ambassador Bremer's office, right in the inner sanctum of the CPA. Officials there agreed to help me and introduced me to the CPA's chief of staff who listened attentively to what I had to say.

'Leave this with me,' he said. 'Are you around this evening and if so, where will we find you?'

'I'll probably be in the Ministry of Transport office upstairs,' I said.

Later that evening I received a phone call on my Baghdad mobile phone. It was Tash.

'Congratulations, you've just made CPA history. This is the fastest I've ever seen anyone get funding approval; I have the note here from Bremer's office. You've got your $1 million. It says in his handwriting simply "This must not happen" across the top of the page.'

This was excellent news. Although it was late, I called Dubai. 'Allan I've got the money,' I told him. For now at least, we'd staved off the crisis. Maersk unpacked their kit and stayed to run the port.

In the beginning Patrick Nixon had been dubious about whether CPA in Basra should get involved. 'After all, this is an Iraqi decision,' he'd told me. That was true of course – but I was working with my contacts at the Iraqi ministry and I knew that I was ideally placed to bring the various sides together and broker a deal. And to his great credit Patrick was unstinting in his praise when the deal was reached.

Soon he had another reason to offer his congratulations. While I was at the Ministry of Transport I was told there was a telephone call for me. It was the Commanding Officer of the Queen's Own Yeomanry, my TA Regiment in the UK. Somehow they'd tracked me down to this office. For a split second my blood ran cold as I feared the worst. All kinds of thoughts went through my head; it must be serious if they'd gone to this trouble to find me. Had there been an accident at home? 'I have to take this call,' I told Manson Brown.

'It's OK, Andrew, you can use my office,' he said, seeing the anxiety in my face.

I went through and picked up the call and I heard the familiar voice of my colonel. 'Andrew,' he said, his upbeat tone quickly reassuring me, 'I'm delighted to tell you that you've been nominated for an MBE in the Queen's Birthday Honours List.' I was stunned. It was completely unexpected.

As news filtered out of the award, I started to receive congratulations from all directions. My team sent me messages and Patrick sent an email with the news round to all staff. But perhaps the message I most treasured was a congratulatory email from Sir Hilary. Much of what I, and above all my team, had been able to achieve was down to his work in the hard months of late 2003 and early 2004. This praise from him meant a great deal to me. But I was still in a state of shock from having got the MBE at all, especially after all that had happened in the previous weeks. One thing I'd come to learn in Iraq was that you never knew what would happen next.

10

BOGGED DOWN IN BUREAUCRACY

May 2004

Every day in Iraq threw up new challenges and new experiences. But some days were definitely stranger than others. One morning I'd got to my desk as usual and met some of my team about some pressing economic issues. That meeting finished at 9.30 am. Now I turned my attention to the next item on the day's agenda – Oscar. For some time many of us had been worried about our cat's appearance. Though he'd been packing away all the food we could find for him he didn't seem to be getting any bigger; in fact he seemed to be getting thinner. Finally someone worked out what the problem was – Oscar had worms.

Pat and I had taken it on ourselves to carry out the vital task of worming him. I'd never done this sort of thing before. But when I picked the poor animal up and Pat tried to force tablets down his throat, we half-expected the reaction. Oscar went berserk. The office was filled with his wailing and hissing and his claws sank into our flesh. We let him go and he cowered, hurt and angry, while we considered what to try next. Round one to Oscar. David Williams, one of the agricultural team, happened to pop into the office. He took one look at the situation and gave us the benefit of his expert opinion. 'What you need to do is wear a coat,' he told us. 'That way you won't get scratched.' Despite the fact that the temperature was already getting close to 40° C in the sun outside, Pat and I donned thick gloves and anoraks as we again grappled with Oscar. This time I managed to hold his mouth open ready to pop his de-worming tablets in. Unfortunately I now had no hands free to do this. Luckily Katharina Pfitzner bravely stepped in and administered the dose. Once the tablets were safely inside the cat, we dropped him and he shot straight for the window, giving as a look of pure hatred as he flew outside. The operation had been worth it, however. Over the next few weeks Oscar started to put on weight.

The excitement of Oscar's worm treatment had barely subsided when we were suddenly involved in another, rather more serious, drama. An Iraqi from Basra had turned up at Al-Sarraji to see Rosie. He had gone to the Al-Basra governorate offices a few hundred yards from us, and clambered up to the third floor to her office. Rosie, who noted at the time that he didn't look well and was sweating profusely, told him he'd come to the wrong office and directed him instead to us. Eventually he arrived in our room and explained why he'd come. He was a small independent contractor and had carried out work on a schools project. He'd now come for his money. All the paperwork was in order so we counted out $15,000 to give him. But no sooner had Pat handed over the money then the man collapsed on the floor. We managed to get him up on a chair but it was clear something was seriously wrong. 'We need to get Jane,' I said. We were fortunate that in addition to Jane Wilshaw with her nursing experience we had several doctors. By now it was clear the unfortunate man had suffered a heart attack and the medical experts gave him mouth to mouth and compression to keep his heart going until we could fetch the CPA's defibrillator. With two or three zaps of the machine they brought him back to life. But I realised that he needed more permanent help and raced to the military brigade HQ next door. Unfortunately I couldn't get through the gates because the brigade had parked a huge armoured vehicle in the way – and neither the driver nor the keys were there. So even though there was a military medical centre just the other side of the wall from us, I had to run right round the compound to get to it. Finally I made it and explained that we needed oxygen quickly. Though the military were wary of creating a precedent – in theory Iraqi civilians had to be treated in Iraqi hospitals – they came to the rescue. They sent a team to our part of the compound to evacuate the stricken man but though he was given urgent attention he later died.

Back at our offices there was a stunned silence. For a while the area had resembled a war zone and no one quite knew how to react. Then normality began to kick in. Pat went over to the dead man's jacket and retrieved the plastic bag full of the money we'd just given him. We didn't want this to go missing in the confusion. It was later given to the man's family along with his other belongings. I also had another meeting to go to. I looked around at everyone. 'Right, I guess we'd all better get back to work,' I said as I went off to my meeting. 'OK,' said the others and they went off too, all of us deeply upset.

I still hadn't given up all hope of changing the British government's plans to reduce our deployment in the south to just a handful of staff after 30 June. Yet there were also reports that the British military were pulling out of the palace site and even rumours that the US contractors had been asked to quote a price to dismantle the Al-Sarraji camp. This was even more disastrous news. If the British military pulled out of the palace and the compound was dismantled, where could the PMO install themselves to help with their big projects for the south? In other parts of Iraq they were planning to become 'embedded' with the US military. But where could they stay in the south? The whole messy situation lacked any planning, as I confided to a senior US official I'd got to know. 'We need Washington to speak to London at a high level and sort this out,' I told him. 'Otherwise we'll literally be walking out and turning off the lights in seven weeks' time here at CPA South. Or is that really the plan?' It would be crazy to make the PMO have to build a new HQ in the south when a compound already exists. ' I can't believe that our respective governments could be that incompetent ...'

My friend agreed. 'It's all very hard to fathom,' he told me. 'No one has thought this through above clerk level.' And he promised to pass on my thoughts up the chain of command in Baghdad and also Washington.

As for the Iraqis, their view about our departure was neatly described by Jane Wilshaw. 'A member of the media was interviewing the hospital director I work with and asked what he felt should happen to the health advisers when CPA ceases at the end of June,' said Jane. 'His response was unprompted: "I think every hospital should have a Miss Jane. It is very important that we continue to receive support from professionals from other countries".'

Despite what seemed like chaotic planning, or lack of it, in Washington and London, Whitehall was nonetheless desperate to put the best possible gloss on events in Iraq. We received a request from Patrick to send him details of all that my team had achieved in the past months in Iraq and the work that was still going on. These 'good news stories' were to be passed on to London to be used to brief the Prime Minister himself. The list of success stories we produced was extensive. They included repairs to five of the six power stations in the south and commissioning a new one, the putting up of 500 pylons, restoring water and power supplies to all hospitals, rebuilding the public health laboratory and burns unit, refurbishing the blood bank, renovating the former military hospital and giving it to the civilian population, re-equipping and re-opening elderly residential care homes, male and female orphanages, deaf and mute centres, centres for the blind and child day-care centres, establishing landfill sites and urban cleaning programmes, restoring telecommunications, rebuilding banks, equipping various state-owned enterprises with much-needed equipment and many, many more examples of similar projects. They were all schemes that had been suggested and overseen by members of the team.

On the one occasion in this period when Mr Blair talked during Prime Minister's Questions about the achievements in the south, he mentioned only military projects. It came as no great surprise. The civilian work of the CPA in the south had rarely merited much attention in the media or anywhere else. Now as the organisation approached its end and nearly all of us were set to leave, it felt as if we were being written out of history.

However, Mr Blair must have been personally briefed on the work we were trying to do. His main foreign affairs adviser Sir Nigel Sheinwald had visited Basra and spent two hours in my office. He listened very attentively as I outlined my thoughts on the south, both on what we'd achieved and also about the future. He promised he would speak to people in London but wouldn't be drawn on anything himself. He was in listening mode. I think, however, it may have dawned on Sir Nigel that the future plans for the south and the likely outcome on the ground were a disaster in the making. After the meeting I simply wrote in my diary:

- flaws in UK's transition plan
- potential crisis with PMO (and the fact that the US believed that Basra was our area and therefore they were not staffing it, and sending only five people to be part of the State Department front office)
- lack of critical mass (lack of personnel)
- no real response (from either PMO or Whitehall)

Even the transition plans announced by Whitehall didn't seem to be moving. It looked as if everyone was hoping that the US-run PMO and the United Nations would step into the organisational vacuum of southern Iraq once the CPA vanished. And that the World Bank and the Japanese would provide some of the needed cash. But there seemed to be very little planning to ensure that the transition team would hit the ground running on 1 July. There was a real danger that if and when these organisations arrived, all the good work of the CPA would already have unravelled. I even suggested that my own team become the transition team until Whitehall could find more permanent recruits for the jobs.

Security, however, was fast becoming the number one issue for us. In a late-night email to a friend I described how for the first time we'd reached Threat Level Four at CPA South – the highest level. 'Everyone is wearing body armour and helmets when outside the buildings but otherwise spirits are high and work continues as normal, or at least as best it can,' I wrote. 'There was an attempt to fire seven rockets at the compound two nights ago, but fortunately only three actually left their tubes and only two detonated, albeit 50m over the other side of the wall. Basra city has been locked down today with only military units moving throughout the city, and then only in armoured vehicles. One of our CRG [Control Risks Group vehicles] from the airport was attacked early this morning by RPG and small arms fire but fortunately the RPG missed and everyone arrived here safely.

'This afternoon we rehearsed our "stand to" procedure and for a compound of 500 people, many of whom are civilians, it is difficult to do so with military precision! However, everyone was calm and it's a testament to the people that we have here that everyone went about it with a sense of purpose … Truthfully the staff have all reacted well to recent events but there are only so many near misses and "things that go crack, thump and BANG in the middle of the night" that they'll endure before they'll say "enough is enough"'. Though Basra had been immune from the level of bomb attacks that had been hitting Baghdad for months, they were growing in number in the south too now. On 21 April, for example, 68 people were killed in a series of blasts across the city. That included a group of children who died when their bus was ripped apart in an explosion.

There were various reasons for the rise in tension. At the end of April graphic stories emerged of the ill-treatment of Iraqi prisoners at Abu Ghraib, while Falluja had been identified as a major source of terrorist activity by the Americans – and pounded with bombs. Another reason was al-Sadr. He had promised a $150 bounty for anyone who killed a British or any coalition soldier, and $350 for any one they took alive. On top of that women soldiers captured could be kept as 'slaves', he announced. This kind of ghoulish announcement inevitably made an already difficult situation worse, and it meant that the local Iraqi staff couldn't come to work. In areas such as Maysan the situation was even worse. Around 70 Iraqis were killed in the course of a week trying to take the CPA compound at Al-Amarah. Some of us referred to Al-Amarah as 'Rorke's Drift', after the place where a small band of British soldiers famously held off a Zulu army in 1879. I spoke to the Maysan governorate co-ordinator Molly Phee and her deputy Rory Stewart at one of the regular governorate team conferences. They both described attacks by al-Sadr's militia the al-Mahdi. Molly said that for three days the Maysan office was under constant mortar fire and small arms fire. At the time one of the team had been speaking with his wife back in England who had said: 'I'm so glad you're near Basra and not in Baghdad.'

Katharina Pfitzner also had a tough experience on a visit to Maysan. 'There was a riot and people were throwing big stones at us and the CRG land cruisers,' she recalled. 'We wanted to get into the CPA South compound but the gate was closed because of the riot. Our CPA friends in Maysan wouldn't open the gate so we had to push back through the crowd – which wasn't so pleasant – and then we were stopped on our way through Maysan by a group of so-called "Ali Babas" who were armed. They let us go though when they saw that we were armed too and in armoured vehicles.'

The coalition and our local staff weren't the only targets. As I wrote to my friend: 'The latest trend is for key Iraqi personnel in the government departments to be kidnapped and held for payment of large amounts of cash – if they aren't simply killed for collaborating with the coalition.' Such developments made us feel angry as well as despondent. 'Frankly there are times when one wonders if they really want to have the economy redeveloped,' I said. But then I added: 'And then one remembers that these insurgents are only a small minority and the majority wants to be a modern secular state. One of my local staff phoned me and told me that many people are pleased that the UK military were exerting some strength today and they will continue to do so tonight. No doubt this will not be reported in the press – instead we'll no doubt have a piece about how badly we're all doing ...' I complained. We were certainly under no illusions that as far as the media were concerned Iraq was a 'bad news' story, and there was only one way that our work would be portrayed. 'What really gripes us here is that tomorrow in the western press there will be a piece complaining that the reconstruction effort is too slow ... and yet we cannot leave the compound, and when we do, we do so in armoured vehicles.' I signed off by telling him what we could expect that night. 'No doubt with all the military action today, there's a strong chance that the bad lads may have a go this evening. I've only tried to have an early night three times whilst here in CPA South and on each occasion we've been mortared.' Jane Wilshaw remembered an earlier evening. 'I'd managed to purchase a tray of twenty-four cans of beer on one of my visits to the military hospital,' she said, 'and we decided to have a street party outside my "hooch" or cabin. Everyone brought some nibbles and Giovanni – our cardio-thoracic surgeon – brought his guitar. He was extremely good and we all sat in a circle outside in between the rows of hooches drinking beer, nibbling nuts, crisps and dried fruit and singing Beatles songs.

'At half past midnight a rocket whooshed overhead and exploded before landing. The whole area shook – it was quite close. I've never seen ten people lie flat on the ground, then clear up and vanish to their own hooches so quickly! It's certainly one way to break up a party but not to be recommended.' Like many of us Jane had worked out a strategy for coping with the times when we had to stay hunkered down. 'I had a very comfortable little nest under my desk – unfortunately the roofs aren't re-inforced so we're advised to go under our desks. I had a small rug to lie on, my torch was nearby and I could reach the fridge from there – and always had a good book to hand.'

The security problems didn't just come from al-Sadr and other Shi'ite groups. Members of the local security forces were sometimes themselves the cause of problems. On one occasion a group of up to 15 armed and masked men from what was described as 'Iraqi Intelligence' burst into telecom offices at Manawi-al-Basha in Al-Basra province and demanded that staff hand over 150 SIM cards within 24 hours – or face violence. An urgent email came from one of the staff there to our telecom expert. I later received a copy. The site controlled the GSM mobile-telephone network for the whole of southern Iraq, 'Now our engineers are afraid to return to their jobs and so how can I maintain the site?' the manager asked plaintively. 'So we expect our network to be down if you do not take any action.' The email named the two men, one with the rank of captain, who the manager said were behind the raids.

Some incidents were even worse and personally sadder. Bob Morgan was on secondment as an oil adviser to Ibrahim al-Uloom, the Iraqi oil minister. He was delightful company and his clear idea of what could and could not be achieved in the country, was a great help to me. And as a fellow Brit – he was originally from Merthyr Tydfil – we spoke the same language. So I was looking forward to meeting up with him again for a meeting in Kuwait. He and I were supposed to be driving down together. But shortly before the trip I heard that he'd been killed in Baghdad. The 4x4 he was travelling in was hit by a RPG just yards from the entrance of the US headquarters. I had to go to Kuwait without him.

I feared that Basra was about to descend into the rioting madness of the previous summer – or even worse. I knew from my time in the City that the big market crashes occurred when a series of unrelated events coincide. And I warned Patrick Nixon that a number of different events were coming together and could spell trouble. First there were no medical supplies being delivered to hospitals locally even though there was plenty of money in Baghdad for them. The Health Ministry had only spent $40 million of its $600 million budget for 2004 – by then it should have spent $200 million. Red tape was the hold-up as ever. 'If there's another attack or major incident the hospitals will be unable to respond,' I told Patrick.

Meanwhile the DG of fuel distribution Mr Saed had been removed from his post and this had led to longer petrol queues and shortages of domestic fuel as everything ground to a halt in the absence of a director general. At the same time, the unrelated removal of corrupt officials – who had been responsible for supplies of fuel going missing – had also led to a strike by angry staff. Two power stations were also down, meaning that electricity supplies to the city were four hours on, two hours off. And finally even the solution to the water shortages was being hampered because some of the necessary pipes were still held up – by bureaucracy. 'The talk in town is that there's presently not enough water, despite our initiatives,' I pointed out. 'These are almost exactly the conditions that sparked the riots last summer.'

At the same time Pat and I were dreading the arrival of the auditors – and now they'd come to Baghdad. There were two main auditing processes. One was done on behalf of an international body made up of members of the UN, the IMF and the World Bank. The other was carried out by the CPA's own inspector general's office which reported straight to the US Congress. There was growing concern on Capitol Hill about what was happening to all the US – and Iraqi – cash that was being spent in the country. They were worried, as indeed we'd always been, that the availability of so much cash so quickly could result in poor spending. Or even worse, corruption.

In Basra our books were straight. This was largely thanks to the diligence of our main financial man Pat who made sure that the money that we processed was scrupulously accounted for by us or the Iraqis. Between us we had witnessed the distribution of many hundreds of millions of dollars of Iraqi oil money, which was paid out in wages, operating budgets and welfare payments via the Ministry of Finance, hundreds of millions of dollars paid directly to contractors, millions of dollars in donor aid programmes and as well as millions of dollars in cash that we processed for projects in the southern region. This included the $1.2 billion of Iraqi oil money we paid out in wages and social payments through the Iraqi Central Bank, the $300 million project money directly paid to contractors and the $26 milion we had processed in cash for projects. However, we knew that the auditors were making their presence felt because the US moneymen in Baghdad became even more pedantic over paperwork.

'They want us to fill out different forms,' Pat wearily complained one day after another lengthy email correspondence. 'Apparently – according to Colonel Davis – the ones that we've been using are all wrong.'

'Did you point out to him that it was his predecessor that sent us the forms?' I asked sarcastically.

'Apparently that's no excuse – we have filled out the wrong forms and they want them all changed.'

'Are these people for real?' I asked. It surprised none of us that months later a new team of officials in the comptrollers office complained that their predecessors had done 'everything wrong'.

I was still trying to persuade the PMO to focus more on what was going on in Basra. I spoke with its head, Dave Nash, about it. I admired and liked Dave a lot but I still felt that he hadn't yet woken up to what would be happening after 30 June in the south. The PMO would move in to start to spend some of the billions of dollars pledged by the US – almost all of the money spent thus far was Iraqi oil money – and find it had no infrastructure left. 'This whole structure of regions is just going to collapse – we'll be handing back the regional offices and walking off into the sunset,' I told Dave. 'The same will happen all across the country, not just in the south – you guys will have to come in and reconstruct the regions but we'll have closed all the offices.' Dave began to see there was a problem coming. He also realised that that the ports in the south were crucial to the PMO's work – much of its heavy materials would come in through there. So at last, after months of persuasion, Dave Nash and his deputy Larry Crandall finally came down to Basra for the first time.

Patrick was keen to get Dave and Larry in a round-table meeting but I wanted them to see the whole team in operation as well. 'Why don't we let them go on a walkabout around the CPA?' I suggested to Patrick. 'Let Dave and Larry talk to the team and see what they're doing.' They did and spoke to Peter Bingham about the ports and Robert Apsley about power as well as to other members of the team. Then they came in to my office for a chat.

'This is incredible,' said Dave, as he sat down. 'I think this is the only CPA office that is staffed appropriately in the entire country. I can't believe what you're doing here.' Then he looked at me and added: 'We can't let this fold, can we? This is just the organisation we should have for the PMO down here.' He looked at me even more intently. 'So what do we have to do, Andrew?' I was pleased. Dave was now clearly focussed.

It was Larry's turn to speak. 'I wonder if you could write a report from the CPA point of view outlining what you think should happen,' he said to me. 'From what you've said it sounds as if basically nothing will be happening here after you leave. Who did you say again would be taking over?

'I don't really know,' I confessed.

'OK, well go ahead and write that report,' said Larry. 'Maybe we can stop this thing.' Their appreciation for what we were doing at the CPA was great to hear and also gave me some encouragement to think that some of our work might continue. But it also added to the curious nature of the situation we found ourselves in. We'd already been praised by a UN official; Number Ten seemed to approve of what we'd done; and now the top US reconstruction outfit was saying how effective and efficient we were. So why exactly were we being wound up and reduced to a skeleton team from midnight on 30 June?

At a small round table in my office the three of us, Dave, Larry and myself, came up with possible ways we could get policy makers to change their mind about our fate. 'We mustn't let this fail,' I said, pleading for their help. 'That would be snatching defeat from the jaws of victory.' I turned to Larry. 'Larry, you guys are very well connected up in Washington circles – can't you get someone to start kicking someone in London?' He explained that they had their own problems in Washington. The PMO reported to the Defense Department in the US but now the State Department – who had a dim view of what the DoD had done in Iraq – was taking over.

'State think we have got it wrong so they want to take over – and we will be subordinate to them,' he explained.

'OK, what about the UN then?' I suggested, none too hopefully.

'Nah, I don't think we can rely on them in these circumstances,' replied Dave, as we desperately searched for answers. The UN's direct role in the country had been uncertain after two bombings outside their Canal Hotel base in Baghdad in August and September 2003 had led to the evacuation of their 600 staff from Iraq. Their rules now limited them to having only 50 people in the country at any one time.

We all realised the urgency of the situation. Surely we could come up with an answer? Just at that moment, Oscar quietly came in to the office, via the window as usual, and strolled over to the fridge where his food was kept. Suddenly our intense debate about how to save our team was interrupted by a furious grey and white bundle of fur landing on our papers. Oscar, fed up with waiting, sat and looked at me as if to say: 'Feed me!' Dave looked at me in surprise. I looked back at him. 'Sorry gentlemen, it seems I've got to feed the cat!' With that I picked up Oscar, went over to the fridge, found the food and tipped some into his dish near the window.

Dave still looked bemused. Then he said with mock horror: 'Andrew, this could only happen in the British sector … '

Oscar's intervention had served a purpose, though. It took some of the heat out of the debate and we got down to the practical steps that could be taken. I agreed that I'd write a detailed memo about the current transition plan – and what I thought needed to be done differently. Dave and Larry agreed to pass it on up to Washington. However, I'd begun to sense that we were fighting a losing battle. Later that evening Patrick Nixon commented how good it had been to have Dave Nash down to see us. 'I assume you'll be working for PMO after this?' he said with a smile. I think that was then the common assumption: that I'd stay on in Basra and switch to PMO.

'Patrick, I don't think it's that cut and dried!' I replied. I knew from the discussion I'd just had that Dave and Larry had their own battle to fight with the State Department. And just as I'd never got a response from Hilary Benn, no one in Washington ever gave me any feedback on my memo either.

The people I felt most concerned for on a personal level were the Iraqi local staff – there were about 40 of them in all working for the CPA in Basra. Those I knew best such as Abdul and Ahmed couldn't believe we were all going. 'Mr Andrew, you can't leave now, we still need you in our country!' Abdul told me. I sat down with them and explained the situation.

'We're not going to abandon you, that's the last thing we're going to do – the US and the UK are committed to you,' I told them, though even as I spoke I wasn't sure I really believed what I was saying. These people were putting their lives on the line every day simply by coming to work for us and yet the organisation was just about to close the doors, turn out the lights and leave.

Aran Maree described it very well. He said it was as if the west had come to build a bridge between the two civilisations and that we in the CPA were the scaffolding across the river to build that bridge. 'But now the guys from London are knocking down the scaffolding,' he said. 'And the whole thing will fall into the river. It's OK for us,' he added. 'But the Iraqis who've committed to us and helped have to scramble back to their side or fall in the water.'

The sense that we were near the end of something grew as one or two of our staff started to leave. One of those leaving early was Colin McBride, who'd been with us almost since the beginning, and whose tour of duty had come to an end. It was sad to be losing someone like him so soon. His wit and singular way of looking at the world had helped keep us going during bad moments and his departure came as a blow to all of us. However, it was his own choice to go early. He knew that we were phasing out the departures gradually and, as head of the utilities team, Colin felt that keeping some of the functional experts in place such as Wally and Robert would be more productive.

As the handover got closer some of us made sure that we experienced as much of Iraq as possible while we still could. Jude Dunn, who in fact stayed on after 30 June, felt that one of the highlights of her work with the finance team was the occasional chance she had to get out and see something of the country. For some time she'd wanted to visit an orphanage. 'It was a bit of a personal mission for me,' she explained. 'Being the child that I am I'd brought a couple of bin bags full of toys with me when I came to Iraq. These were the teddy bears and all those cuddly toys that you collect over the years – I wanted to give them to children here,' she said. 'I'd spoken to one of the interpreters about it and they mentioned this place in Nasariya. So for my trip there with the Treasury I took along my bin bags of toys and after a working visit to a police station I went with a guy called Harry – who also worked for the CPA – to the orphanage. There were about forty children in all, of all ages from babies upwards,' said Jude. 'Everyone was very pleased to see us and Harry had brought some footballs as well which went down very well. I made sure that each of the children got a toy – they didn't seem to have any toys of their own.'

As they drove away Harry said how sad it was that the children might not get to keep the toys. Jude knew what he meant. 'We couldn't be sure that the toys wouldn't be taken off them and sold in a market,' she said. 'Unfortunately that was the way things were. But for me it was like making a contribution. I'd been there for more than a year and in a bizarre way I'd grown quite fond of Iraq and Basra. There were some horrible times and some very challenging times. But you also got to meet some very nice people.'

Although most of us were appalled that so few staff would be left after the end of June, at least an organised withdrawal or 'draw down' had been arranged. The advisers were to leave in phases as projects were finished. With the exception of Colin the heads of teams and groups generally stayed on the longest.

This process at least gave some order and structure to the final weeks. There were still grave doubts, of course. The London civil servants seemed very proud of the big handover document that they'd asked us all to produce, to keep alive the institutional knowledge we'd built up. It's a great idea on paper – but unfortunately on paper is where it stayed. Who on earth was going to read a 700-page document prepared by 50 people? Who was the target audience in any case? The much-vaunted transition team – the TAT on the Shat – hadn't even been recruited yet. Perhaps someone back in Whitehall read it. In any case, what a document lacked was the linkages and personal contacts. Arab society and business works on relationships. 'Mr Waleed, I'm leaving now but this is the person who will be replacing me – he and I have sat down for two weeks so he knows all I know.' That was the kind of conversation we should have had. *That* would have been transition. Not producing a 700-page document few people would read.

For a brief period at the end of May Whitehall's interests in the CPA were represented by a London-based official, standing in for Rod Matthews who was off on holiday at the time. Unfortunately his visit coincided with some serious attacks on the Al-Sarraji headquarters. The temperature was now reaching 50 °C and the violence had grown. Suddenly and unusually we were taking live mortar rounds in the compound in daylight and we were forced to rush for cover into protected buildings and hangars. The atmosphere was very tense for a few days.

Whitehall suddenly became terrified about the security situation. A high-priority order came through from London to the CPA HQ. Patrick Nixon immediately called a staff meeting and there he broke the news. 'In view of the security situation Whitehall has decided to bring some staff home earlier than planned – they intend to leave only those whose presence is essential to the completion of projects. All of you are asked to leave Iraq by 10 June,' he informed us. As we listened in horrified silence he went on: 'I know that this will be unwelcome to many of you. I can only say that the decision was taken at the highest level – and shows that that Whitehall takes its duty of care seriously.'

We could hardly believe it. We'd suffered a few bad days but security was no worse now generally than it had been for months. When our London visitor flew back home I suspect he must have told people what the security situation was like; how we had to wear flak jackets all the time and so on. And it was true the attacks *had* been bad for that brief period. Though security was always on our minds and often impeded our work, much of the time we felt relatively safe. Yet I knew from a friend in London that in various Whitehall offices the chatter and gossip there was all about the mortars landing and how dangerous it was. So perhaps our London visitor – who hadn't been used to life at Al-Sarraji – had unwittingly set off alarm bells about the dangers of Basra after his brief visit. Now all our carefully worked out plans to manage our departure and complete projects – including major ones for the ports and for Basra airport – were in jeopardy. We were being told to pack our bags and leave. Once again London had acted in a knee-jerk fashion.

The military have a principle that is known as an 'OODA loop'. This stands for Observe Orientate Decide Act. For soldiers it's critical that they act and react more quickly than the enemy. However, one of my military friends said that for Whitehall the OODA acronym stood for something else – Observe Overreact Deny and Apologise! Over the next few days about 25 people – more than half my remaining team – were bundled into land cruisers and driven down to Kuwait to catch a plane. What had started out as an orderly withdrawal was now turning into a rout.

11

DEPARTURE

June–July 2004

We faced a major problem now that so many of our team was being ordered home early. The department had been committed to about 400 projects, scores of which were still not finished. So there was a headlong rush to complete them. But to do that we didn't just need the people – we needed cash too. It was no good waiting until after 30 June for funds to be processed to pay contractors for the work they were carrying out. Once the handover took place we'd have no legal authority in the country. Our signatures would be worthless.

One option was to hand over the projects and the financial authority to the Iraqis. The danger with this was that the ministries were still often split by disagreement. There was a strong risk that the projects would just get caught up in endless haggling between different factions and would founder in red tape. There was even the possibility that certain Iraqi officials would stop the projects, claiming they didn't like them – and then quietly pocket the money. This wasn't the kind of legacy we wanted to leave to the vast majority of law-abiding Iraqis. We wanted to leave them projects that were completed and which worked.

I reckoned we needed about $32 million in cash; and the only place to get it was Baghdad. We'd then have to bring it down to our office to pay the contractors on the projects. With the current security situation it was a high-risk strategy. There was also the question of what would happen to the rest of the cash if we didn't manage to spend it all. Who would take charge of it after 30 June – and who would be accountable if it went missing?

'I've decided I'm going to go to Baghdad to bring back that money,' I announced to Pat one day in our office. Pat looked panicked. 'But you can't, it's too risky,' he complained. 'We'll be accountable for it,' he pointed out. 'What happens if it goes missing?'

'Don't worry, I'll take this one on the chin myself, Pat,' I told him. 'I'll take full responsibility.' I certainly didn't want him to be at risk from any gamble I took in getting the cash. Pat had been a loyal ally as well as a scrupulous financial controller from the early days. It was one of our only major disagreements but fortunately we were able to settle our differences amicably. But we needed to get that cash in our possession in Basra – if we had the money with us, London would have to take notice of it. I feared that, given half a chance, Whitehall would otherwise go for the easy option and close down any unfinished projects during these last few weeks. And then re-assign the unspent money back to Baghdad. In a few cases that did in fact happen but I was determined that it shouldn't be the general rule. Once it was in our office, the cash was a form of insurance policy that meant that London, Baghdad and Washington would have to allow the projects to be finished.

The next problem was physically how to get the cash. I needed to go to Baghdad to get it signed off at the US Comptroller's office. The problem was that London had issued an edict banning any of us from travelling. Baghdad was currently suffering one of its many periodic eruptions of serious violence. It was a total lock-down. No one could move without the express permission of London. This was crazy – how could London know if it was safe to get to Baghdad from Basra or not? In any case I simply had to go – I was convinced the projects depended on it. So I went to see Patrick in his office and painted a pretty stark picture. 'If we don't get this money now then our entire effort at trying to buy consent from the Iraqi people is going to collapse,' I told him. 'We're running out of time.' Patrick told me that London considered the route from Baghdad airport to the city centre so dangerous that no one should go on it.

'But with you we'll make an exception,' he continued with a wry smile, 'seeing as how you need the money.'

In Baghdad the CPA staff had learnt to live with the grim security situation. Tash told me how one night she'd been woken up in her trailer by an unusual noise. 'I thought "that's very strange, I wonder what that was?" I couldn't work it out but everything seemed fine so I went back to sleep,' said Tash. 'I woke up next morning and looked up at the ceiling and saw a hole in it. In the roof of the trailer. I got out of bed and a bullet dropped out of my sheets. It was happy fire … and the bullet had come through the roof and landed in my bed. It was the kind of thing you might mention at breakfast but after that you would just carry on. As long as you were OK you just carried on.'

I realised myself how dangerous Baghdad had become as soon as I arrived. As always I applied my armoured-car test – the more that accompanied you, the more dangerous it was deemed to be as you sped from the airport towards the relative safety of the Green Zone. And this time I was to have nine armoured vehicles around me, each of them heavily plated and weighing about 2.5 tonnes each. 'God this is serious,' I muttered to myself as I approached one of the vehicles. 'Which one do I get in?' I asked a nearby US soldier.

'It don't much matter,' he drawled laconically, though whether out of confidence or fatalism I wasn't quite sure.

It was a mad journey. Just three of us were being taken from the airport, protected by nine vehicles and the heavily armoured soldiers inside. We were flung from side to side inside as the vehicles raced along the road, swapping positions constantly to create confusion among any would-be attackers. It was a bit like a scene from Wacky Races except that the weapons and armour around us were anything but cartoon-like. Eventually I arrived at the palace complex in one piece and headed straight for the comptroller's office. I knew it would be tricky to persuade them to sign off the funds. And I wasn't disappointed.

I launched into my spiel about how I needed $32 million to ensure our projects were completed. I hadn't got very far when the powerfully built and grim-faced US army colonel put up his hand to interrupt me. 'Let me stop you there, buddy,' he said in his very deliberate way. 'I'm afraid we can't give you the money.'

'But why not, I'm from Basra and we've received lots of money from Baghdad in the past,' I protested.

'Because we haven't got any of your files,' the colonel explained, talking as if he was addressing a five-year-old. 'We don't know if you've closed out the projects you've already received money for.'

'We have a whole room full of files in Basra.' I said.

'Well you need to bring them to Baghdad so we can see all the folders,' he said, looking at me without the slightest sign of emotion on his face.

'But it would need a truck to bring all those files to Baghdad – and that would probably get hijacked on the way,' I pointed out. 'Why don't you just send someone down to inspect them – it would be easier. And you'd be most welcome.'

'We don't do that,' replied the colonel, un-amused. It was true and that was part of the problem. They never left Baghdad and didn't believe that anyone knew what they were doing unless the receipts and project records were physically put in front of their noses. We were at an impasse.

'This is bureaucracy gone mad.' I told him. 'I'm the fund custodian for CPA South, I've been here for a year, I've handled millions of dollars – so why don't you believe who I am and what I say?' The colonel was unmoved. For good measure he also informed me that all the projects we'd done so far wouldn't be valid because they'd all been done on the wrong forms. And he showed me the correct ones.

'But these forms didn't exist when we started.' I pointed out. 'You put this system in afterwards.'

'You still have to put them all on these forms – otherwise they won't be legal,' the colonel told me. I was getting nowhere fast.

In a desperate last attempt to budge him I started to spout titles and qualifications at him. 'I'm registered with the UK Financial Services Authority and my finance man Pat is a registered chartered accountant,' I told him. 'So we must be keeping proper records – mustn't we?' Amazingly it seemed to do the trick and the colonel's attitude began to soften. Eventually after more haggling we reached a deal.

I signed a piece of paper promising that our precious files would be brought to Baghdad. I also had to put my name to another document which authorised me to carry the money with me (despite the fact that I'd been doing this for nearly a year already). In exchange the money I needed was signed over to me. We kept our side of the bargain and a couple of weeks later the files were sent up by a Hercules transport plane to Baghdad. Some time later they were mislaid and for a while the comptroller's office would insist that we'd 'stolen' $26 million. The whole affair was a black comedy.

Back in Basra the team was beginning to disappear fast. At the weekly staff meetings Patrick handed out certificates for those who were about to leave. This was recognition of their work from the CPA and its many member countries. It was an odd feeling. The organisation was vanishing in front of us and yet we knew the job was nowhere near finished. Wally Weeks came at the end of the list when the time came for him to receive his certificate. 'There was a lot of mirth when I finally collected my certificate and my name was read out,' said Wally, who had been christened Warwick. 'Being the Wally of the project was a humorous moment for everyone I think.'

Since we didn't know how long any of us would be around, quite early on a huge farewell bash was held in the Iftar tent in the compound. It was a chance to say goodbye to a lot of people. Meanwhile Raneen, Abdul and Ahmed organised a departmental farewell lunch for me and my team. They brought in lamb and rice and sultanas and tabbouleh as well as the local delicacy – a fish called *mazgouf,* which swims in the Shat and is traditionally roasted over an open fire. I must admit I usually refused to eat it no matter how many times it was offered to me. I knew what else swam in the Shat – raw sewage! However, the rest of the spread was great – we had kebabs too, and the local unleavened bread. To drink we had the usual staples of the Middle East – Coca Cola, Pepsi Cola and SevenUp. There were nearly 50 of us sitting around the table in the compound's main conference room. It was a quiet occasion. We all knew then it was coming to an end. Wally stood up during the meal and said a few words. He and his water and sewage team were already known as the 'dirty dozen', and so he now described us all as the 'dirty four dozen'. 'I knew it would be the last time we were all together,' said Wally later. 'But I assumed that one of the big wigs would be there to say a few words. I only spoke when I realised that no one else was going to … so my language was from the hip.' Then I stood up. I thanked everyone for their commitment and for laying their lives on the line for the cause.

I told them: 'Take a good look around you. I don't think you will ever work with a team of such calibre in such circumstances again – nor be in a situation like this. And I concluded: 'You should all feel proud of what you have achieved.' I meant every word. Ahmed, Raneen and Abdul had helped arranged the lunch and taken so much trouble over the food – even that wretched fish – because they too wanted to say thank you to the team. To us, the Iraqi members of our teams weren't just employees – they'd become our friends too. And unlike some in the coalition, we didn't regard them simply as 'local staff'; they were 'our staff'. Whenever I heard someone from outside our department refer to them as 'only Iraqi staff' I would always contradict them. 'No – they're part of our team,' I insisted.

I experienced a mixture of moods. Part of me felt that we were being betrayed. I think that some in the team felt the same way. There was a great deal of talk at the time among the bureaucrats in London about wanting to 'normalise' relations with Iraq. By this they meant having an Iraqi embassy in London and a British consulate in Basra. All the different nations were retreating into their own buildings. As for the rest of it – the teams we'd built, the work we'd done with the Iraqis – all that was going to vanish in the face of this bureaucratic desire to 'normalise' things. Our work was going to disappear in the face of red tape and, I felt, indifference. That, for me, was the toughest thing of all. At times I wondered if I actually lived in a different world from the bureaucrats. Maybe we had dreamt it all. My middle name is Barrie after my distant relative, JM Barrie, the creator of *Peter Pan*. Just as he had imagined that world, had I too simply imagined all that we'd done in Iraq? And was it now simply going to vanish with the wave of a bureaucrat's pen?

But I was plagued, too, by self-doubt. As all around me people left I suddenly wondered whether I'd had got my approach all wrong. Perhaps, I found myself thinking, I should have done things very differently. I knew that some of the civil servants would concur – they'd already told me that we'd got it wrong. Yet when I spoke to the Iraqis who worked with us and those we dealt with they were far more positive about our work. Their support reassured me. They persuaded me that our approach had made sense, so I determined to keep working to the bitter end. The Iraqis had put a lot of faith and trust in me and my team and we didn't want to let them down. I didn't want to give up just because some civil servants in the UK government said we didn't know what we were doing.

Sadly, the transition arrangements were threatening to degenerate into farce. Whitehall had appointed new consultants whose brief it was to look at their oft-mentioned 'institutional capacity building'. Helping Iraqi officials to learn how to run ministries, departments and a whole host of other organisations was of course work we assumed we'd been doing since the previous summer. One of my team sent a message around to the remaining members of the team that made us smile with both amusement and exasperation. 'New consultants have arrived,' he announced. 'And guess what, they asked three questions. One – what do you all do? Two – what should we be doing? And three – Do you want a job?'

It was a classic. These consultants had been sub-contracted to carry out this work in Iraq. But they very soon realised that the best-placed people to do much of their work were ... members of my team, the same team that was being disbanded by Whitehall. Indeed, it had often been made very clear to me that one of the reasons we hadn't been able to do our jobs properly in Iraq was because we weren't specialists. We weren't 'developmentalists'. Yet here we were in the summer of 2004 and the specialist consultants from London were now asking to hire us – because apparently we knew what we were doing.

As the handover date fast approached, London finally agreed that we needed a small handover team to look after the finances in Basra. I wanted to be part of that team so I could make sure that all the money was properly accounted for. After all, I'd taken responsibility for it. There was one last kick in the teeth, however. My main contact in London, who was handling all our contracts, gave me a call.

'I'm really sorry, Andrew, but we'll no longer be able to pay you at your current rate if you stay on,' he told me. 'Why not?' I asked.

'As you're no longer running a department you'll be paid according to the rates of a finance officer for the first two weeks of July,' he told me. I felt sick. It was nothing to do with the money – it was just the pettiness and penny-pinching bureaucracy that really got to me. The British government had spent hundreds of millions of pounds invading Iraq. Yet now I was being told I had to lose my pay grade for two weeks at the end of my contract because 'it was not appropriate' to pay me more. It wasn't his fault, of course, it was the heavy hand of Whitehall that was behind it. However, I decided not to make a fuss at this late stage. By now I just wanted to get the job done.

I still had unfinished business with the US-led PMO. The organisation now knew it needed help in the south if it was to work there and Dave Nash knew that the CPA infrastructure was about to come crashing down. There was talk of the PMO hiring me after the CPA vanished. And I thought working for the PMO might be one way of seeing the job through properly. I had got to know Dave's head of regions, a man named Buddy Allgood. Buddy used to cycle everywhere around the Green Zone and was just what Dave needed for the job – a real 'go getter'. He told me one day 'Andrew, I never give up' and I believed him. Buddy's plan was to have some key staff in the old governorates – he would have preferred Iraqis with western backgrounds if he could have found them – and to have a person based in Basra co-ordinating the region. He wanted me to do that job. He was very flattering. 'Andrew, you are the guy who knows everyone in the south, and it's all about relationships,' he said.

I didn't need too much persuading. 'I've done it before,' I assured Buddy. 'I know what's needed. The only thing is that we can't do it with just four people.' He promised to see what he could do about the numbers. And he also wanted other members of my team who were still around – people such as Rosie, Dominique and Kevin Thomas, the fuels expert – to join the governorates as he was unable to find any Iraqis to do the job.

'But there's one problem,' said Buddy. 'And that is that we're capped on salaries.'

'I'm not sure how well that will go down with the team,' I said. 'And it's getting more and more dangerous to work in Iraq. But I'll speak with them.' So I talked to some of the others about working as part of the new PMO team in the south on reduced rates of pay. 'It's not ideal, I know,' I told them. 'But let's run with it for six months – at least it will be some form of transition,' I suggested, aware that Whitehall's own transition plans were making painfully slow progress. 'And transition is what we need – even if it is a heck of a pay cut!' It seemed we had the makings of a new outfit – a new, much smaller version of my old team but working for the PMO.

So at 10 am one morning I was in the offices of PMO when Buddy told me that I was hired. I was to be regional co-ordinator for the organisation in the south. 'Great news,' I told him. 'I look forward to working with you.' At about 4 pm that same afternoon Buddy tracked me down to another office in Baghdad. His face immediately told me something was wrong. He was visibly embarrassed.

'What's the matter, Buddy?' I asked.

'This is very un-American,' he told me,' but the Ambassador has just vetoed your appointment and those of your team. I know this is absolute madness but he will not have the American reconstruction effort in southern Iraq managed by anyone other than an American. I'm so sorry.' It was certainly the shortest time I'd ever held a job. For a few moments I didn't know what to say – I was gobsmacked.

'Buddy, you know what,' I finally managed to say, 'I'm not that surprised. All I can say is good luck!'

I'd had enough. I didn't feel like playing any more. If this was how the British and now the Americans were going to carry on then they could go to hell as far as I was concerned. There must be a better way of doing it, I thought. Perhaps I would set up a private company and maintain the direct links with the Iraqis – meanwhile those bureaucrats in Washington and Whitehall could let the place go to hell in a handcart. I hitched a lift on the next Hercules out of Baghdad and headed back to Basra.

The mood in the south was grim. Many of the team had already left and the rest were preparing to leave. Only a handful were going to stay on, including Jane Wilshaw from the health team. But things were getting more dangerous and she'd just been caught up in a serious incident. She'd been driven by the Control Risks security team to the city's teaching hospital for a meeting to discuss the best way to continue training and supporting the development of the doctors. 'We had just got to the gates when there came a peremptory call over the intercom for us return to base,' said Jane. 'The security team looked a bit shaken but they skilfully did a U-turn and raced back to the CPA. I tried to ring the hospital director to warn him we'd been diverted but couldn't speak to him direct,' said Jane.

'Twenty minutes later he rang me back to thank me for calling – he understood why we'd been diverted as he was dealing with the consequences. Apparently an old saloon car had been spotted driving up and down that road. It was filled with incendiary devices, which eventually blew up. Someone was definitely watching over me again that day. It was the second time in the same week that the hospital had been at the centre of an attack. That was quite scary.'

But about the same time Jane experienced a very different – and more typical – side of the reaction of most Iraqis towards us. One of her regrets – and that applied to many of us – was that we rarely had a chance to see how ordinary Iraqis lived. 'I think that they wanted to invite us to their houses and they wanted to show us their culture but for security reasons they couldn't,' she said. However, as the CPA's final days neared, Jane's interpreter, Hassim, organised an impromptu party for those in the organisation he'd worked most closely with. 'His mum had prepared some food for us to eat,' said Jane. 'Normally we weren't supposed to have food brought in case we were poisoned, so this was highly illegal! But on this occasion we got the food in and we had a wonderful feast,' said Jane. 'It was almost Mediterranean-like – lots of dips and spreads and salads. It was a taste of what it might have been like in other circumstances.'

One of the few people to be staying on was Katharina who was to work as a finance project manager with the Americans. 'It felt lonely with so many people gone,' said Katharina. 'It was depressing to see that all the efforts and work and resources we had were now gone – and the progress made would be destroyed.'

Meanwhile the experienced Wally Weeks, who had worked all around the world, summed up the mood: 'Many people just didn't want to go home – they felt that there was still so much more work to do. In fact, generally speaking, they were quite devastated when it came time for them to leave. That may surprise most people who watch the TV news and see all the dreadful things. But the fact remains, people were disappointed at going.'

The hardest part was having to sort out the future of our Iraqi staff. Raneen had come to me in mid-June. ' Mr Andrew, who will we be working for?' she wanted to know, understandably enough.

'What do you want to do?' I asked her.

'I just want a job,' she said. 'What would I be good at?'

'You are an excellent assistant, and you run this office very well,' I said. 'Why don't you work for the British consulate? You've always wanted to work for them.'

'If you think this is best then I shall do this,' she said, putting her trust in me. It was probably one of my most difficult moments of the whole year because it was so personal, so close to my heart. These were my people and I didn't want to see them in the wrong jobs, or hurt in any way.

'Sir, maybe I should work for the British,' said Ahmed. 'Mr John [Dyson] has asked me to work for him. What do you think?'

'I think you need a role where you can think,' I told him. 'You are very intelligent and you need to be able to use that brain of yours.' Although I had reservations about Ahmed working for the new consulate, I had even greater doubts about him working for the Americans. He was occasionally quite out-spoken and could get himself into trouble.

Finally it was time to say goodbye to them. Raneen came in to the office. 'Well then, this is it. It has been a pleasure working for you and I hope that one day that we can work together again,' she said. She was smiling and putting on a brave face.

'Raneen, we've come such a long way since you came to the old CPA building with your brother,' I told her. 'Thank you for everything you've have done. Please keep yourself safe.'

Then it was Ahmed's turn. 'Goodbye, Sir,' he said. 'I'm sorry that you could not do more and that you have to go. You were one of the ones who cared – I will not forget you – and by the way I want an invitation to your wedding some day. You know there is still an Iraqi girl here that would suit you,' he said smiling. I thanked Ahmed in return.

'You've taken many risks to work with us. I shall not forget you,' I promised him. 'Please keep yourself and your family safe. If there's ever anything that you need, you just have to get in touch.' We then shook hands, a very British gesture which seemed quite inadequate. With tears in his eyes, Ahmed turned and left. It was a very emotional moment.

I also found it hard to say goodbye to Pat. He'd been my right-hand man almost from the start. However, he'd made it clear that he'd had enough and didn't want to stay on. He wanted to close the books and be gone. It was all, as he put it, 'bollocks'. There was no big farewell, it was just a case of 'well

OK, see you then'. And he went. I think that was the moment when I really knew it was about to end.

The handful of us left were now desperately trying to get the projects completed and the money accounted for before the handover. On the 28 June I was sitting at my desk writing away when the chief of staff Peter Duklis wandered in.

'I thought you'd like to know, Andrew,' he said.

'Bremer's handed over early – it's happened today!' And that was that. Ambassador Bremer had handed over early and immediately left the country to help reduce the violence that was expected to greet the transition. So instead of being a momentous high-profile occasion the handover became a non-event. This wasn't an organised or dignified withdrawal. It was a full-blown bureaucratic retreat. In the south this meant that the Iraqi ministries were now in full control. A few hours ago I'd held one of the most important and powerful jobs in southern Iraq. At the stroke of a pen I was now just another civilian foreigner.

For five days after the handover Basra was under a full lockdown. This was another attempt to reduce the risk of disruptions. But as soon as I was able I flew back up to Baghdad on business. After the Maersk crisis, our ports adviser Peter Bingham and I had been working for some time to put the port on a more secure footing for the future. We wanted to put its running out to competitive tender on the international stage. At first there had been opposition to the idea at the Ministry of Transport. But when I explained the advantages long-term of having a private firm run the port, officials began to change their minds. 'You mean, Mr Andrew, that this company will take over responsibility for paying the workers and dealing with them?' one senior official asked me, the look of pleasure spreading across his face as the realisation dawned on him. But first I needed to sort out some details with deputy transport minister Attah in Baghdad. He had become a very useful ally and colleague.

As I landed for the final time in Baghdad I could see the change since the handover. People in the Green Zone were busily emptying offices, bundling files into boxes and loading them onto vehicles. There was a feeling of anti-climax, almost indifference. This once all-powerful organisation had suddenly just vanished. There was a power vacuum. Yes it was true that more US civil servants were arriving – from the State Department: and of course the Iraqis were now officially running the country. But it felt like witnessing the fall of a city.

When I went to visit various CPA departments at the palace in Baghdad there were still US soldiers on the gates. But inside I just saw row upon row of empty desks. It was an empty shell – the whole organisation had been cratered. I hurried next to see deputy minister Attah, whose offices were outside the Green Zone. I'd hoped that I could persuade him to go to Amman to be present at the port's tendering event. But I knew that he had to stay in Baghdad since he was still unsure who his new minister was going to be. He greeted me warmly as ever and was in an upbeat mood. 'Yes it's a pity we have lost all our advisers,' he told me. 'But we still have you, Mr Andrew!'

I looked at him. 'Not for much longer,' I informed him. 'In just over a week from now I'll be gone too. The UK government hasn't extended my contract.' However, I said I was sure the minister could manage the tender process on his own.

'We must see what we can do,' he said, referring to the possibility that I might stay on.

The few of us who remained in Basra had no visitors – we had no authority, no money other than what was already allocated, so why would anyone need to visit? Overnight the bond of co-operation had been broken. In one sense this was a great thing. It meant that the Iraqis were at last in charge of their own destiny. The problem was that they weren't ready to take charge. The damage caused by Saddam's system of government, the long war with Iran, economic sanctions and the aftermath of the invasion couldn't be repaired in just a year. We knew that and, more importantly, they knew that. For weeks now the directors general had been saying this to me, Wally, Colin and others. 'You are our advisers, we need your help – we don't want you to leave now.' And we didn't just help them with their own work. We were also their bridge to Baghdad. When the officials in Basra found it hard to get something they needed out of Baghdad – as was frequently the case – we were an alternative line of communication. We could step in, talk to the minister and make things happen. That line of communication had now been abruptly severed.

The Al-Sarraji site was also undergoing abrupt change. Now that the multinational CPA had vanished, each of the nations who wanted to maintain a presence in southern Iraq had to find a new, separate home. The result was a land grab. The Danish targeted the old Basra governorate building, the British wanted to set up a consulate in another building, while the old CPA site was to become part of a new US embassy for southern Iraq. Overnight the Americans moved in and began to strip the place bare. As we attempted to work normally, trying to sort out the remaining finances and balance the books, the organisation was dismantled around our ears. They clearly wanted us out of there as soon as possible. One US official informed me that they'd put a metal bin near two palm trees for our use. 'Burn everything unless you really need to keep it,' he told me.

That, I knew from experience, was the American way – in finance as well as in this situation. Destroy the paperwork. One advantage of this approach was that if anyone afterwards tried to accuse you of anything you could turn around to them and say: 'Prove it!' However, I had nothing to hide. And if someone came along with any queries later I wanted to be able to show them what we'd done. 'But I have all these folders and files I want to preserve,' I protested. So the official allowed me to fill up a big wooden chest.

The chest had our team's name 'Economic Planning and Development' stamped across it and I packed it with our old maps, charts and files, though I stored some of the more sensitive files on disks and kept them with me. One day I stopped what I was doing and looked at it. The work of 50 people for a year in one of the most difficult, challenging and dangerous operations imaginable had been reduced to the contents of an old wooden box.

The British civilian operation was now taking on its own character. Rod Matthews, who had been in charge of projects and reconstruction at the CPA, was now the head of DFID's operation for the south. I went to see him about some issues that related to his old job. 'I need clarification on some of these projects – we need to close them out,' I said to him, painfully aware that I was no longer director of a CPA department but simply a finance officer.

'I'm sorry but I can't help you, Andrew,' Rod told me. 'I'm now head of DFID here and I no longer have that old job.'

The British presence was moving too, to the building that the military had been using as a quartermaster's store. That was to be the new consulate while the officers' quarters became the consul general's residence. The new consul general was a very pleasant man called Simon Collis. Patrick Nixon had already left, just after the handover of power. We'd said goodbye to each other and parted on cordial terms. After a bad start we'd managed to forge a reasonable working relationship.

There was a ceremony on the day the consulate officially opened. The the union flag was run up the flag pole and briefly got stuck on the way up. 'I hope this isn't an omen of what is to come,' I whispered to an army friend next to me.

The time had now come to pack my belongings. I had two large carpets and a metal trunk full of documents to take with me, as well as my laptop, rucksacks and black bin liner full of clothes. I told Control Risks that I'd need a couple of wagons to take all my stuff, which had to be taken to the border and then driven on down to Kuwait. One of the few people left in the office apart from me was another stalwart of the finance team, Tony Bennett. But it was when I threw the last items from my desk into my bag that it hit me. 'Hang on, this thing is really finished, isn't it?' I thought to myself. I looked at Tony. 'See you in London!' I said and walked out of the offices for the final time.

The Control Risks land cruiser was at the entrance of the compound waiting to leave and I was just putting on my flak jacket when one of the security staff turned to me. 'Andrew, I bet you're not sorry to see the back of this place!' he said with a grin.

I smiled. 'Actually I am sad to go – this place has been a little bit of history,' I replied wistfully. With that we sped off down RPG alley for the last time. As we drove along the main road towards Kuwait I looked back at the city one more time. 'Have we really made a difference?' I wondered.

Fatigue suddenly overcame me and I slept all the rest of the way to the Kuwait border where I was to be met by a car from the British Embassy. My metal trunk and carpets were loaded on to a lorry heading for Kuwait City. Crown Agents had arranged it on my behalf – though I had to pay – and I signed the consignment note as the goods were put on board. Suddenly I remembered something else. 'Here, you'd better take this,' I said pulling off my flak jacket and handing it to the driver. Ever since I'd been in Iraq wearing a flak jacket had become second nature to me, as it had to so many of us. It was a kind of comfort blanket. Now I'd worn it for the last time. 'My god,' I said to myself. 'This really is it. I've left Iraq.' And I walked slowly to the car that was waiting for me.

EPILOGUE

There had been no real handover in Basra – after all, we'd had no one to hand over to. The multinational CPA had simply dissolved and the member nations and their staff had retreated into separate embassies and consulates. But in October 2004 the Foreign Office decided to hold a series of 'brainstorming' sessions in London to 'tap into people's experiences' of working in Iraq, as they put it. One session was on the role of ministries in Iraq – the ones we'd been working with for more than a year. Among the topics for discussion was: 'What should we be doing to support them?' It was, I reflected, a little late in the day to be asking that. I was unable to attend the meeting and I'm not sure how many others made it. I doubt they'd have been enticed by the email invitation, which told us to 'bring your own sandwiches' to the session. To this day I still haven't been debriefed by anyone about my work in Iraq.

Soon after leaving Iraq, I went to my cousin's wedding in Lebanon and then visited Jordan. After that I flew to Australia where I took a complete break for three months. I visited the Great Barrier Reef, learned how to dive and completed the RYA Day Skipper course in sailing. It was a chance to have a real rest and clear my mind. For a month I rented a flat in

Sydney and it was then that my thoughts started to focus on the future. I'd kept in touch with JoAnn Foster from the engineering firm the Foster Group who were building the power station in Samawah. She was keen for me to help them with that project and other deals. I was also keen to stay involved in the region. What was happening now in Iraq was a complete mistake and I felt we in the west had a moral obligation to try and get it right. We couldn't just walk away because a British government department said it didn't suit them.

I set up a UK-registered company, Gulf Capital, based in Amman in Jordan. The Foster Group helped us organise our office. It was strange being back in the region in a different role. Before I'd been on the 'government' side looking out. Now I was on the contractors' side looking in. The first job we did was to make sure the Foster Group got their next round of money to finish the Samawah power station. The Americans were having second thoughts about the project. They said there wasn't enough money left. But at a meeting with US officials I told them that it would be a disastrous move to stop it now. 'Letting this project collapse after spending twenty-four million dollars simply because there was no maintenance contract would be quite ridiculous,' I insisted. Fortunately they carried on with it and it is now – finally – nearing completion.

Going back to Iraq was an even stranger experience. I visited Basra and Samawah as well as talking to Iraqis in Kuwait and Jordan. I felt like an outsider now – not with the Iraqis but with other westerners. In Baghdad there was an unofficial club of contractors and officials. If you were inside that that club in the Green Zone you could do business. For those of us left outside it was virtually impossible to break in. Iraq itself seemed stuck in a time warp. Nothing had moved on since we'd left – they were still trying to tackle the same problems. And Iraqi politics had brought any economic activity to a standstill. The British meanwhile were seen as increasingly irrelevant because they had no money. The message I got from the Iraqis was very clear – if we didn't have any money they wouldn't bother to talk to us. As a former Iraqi finance minister put it when I met him at the Four Seasons Hotel in Amman: 'No money, no play'. I met the same attitude when I tried to help my old contact Mr Waleed – the head of South Oil. He rang me and said he wanted to visit oil experts and installations in Aberdeen and see how they worked. However, the DTI wanted him to visit corporate offices in London. There was a compromise under which we and the DTI were supposed to organise the trip together. But at the last minute government officials announced that there would be no time to visit Aberdeen after all. I wasn't surprised – the DTI seemed to regard us as 'upstarts'. What saddened me was the way in which Mr Waleed asked my company for £80,000 to send him to Aberdeen on a separate trip. 'But what will I get out of it?' I asked him.

'First spend the money and send us – then we will see,' was his reply.

I could hardly blame him. The 'hand-out' culture had arrived. The Iraqis now felt that all they had to do was hold out their hands and they'd be given money. And it was we in the west who had helped create that donor culture. Instead of concentrating on creating the right conditions and infrastructure for Iraqi business to flourish, we'd thrown money at projects and problems. The Iraqis had got used to that. Under the previous regime it had been Saddam Hussein who had controlled all the money and handed it out as he saw fit. Now the coalition had behaved in a similar way. Little wonder the Iraqis just kept asking for more. And little wonder too that in Kuwait, Jordan and Iraq we now see local business people operating classic 'churn and burn' tactics. They talk to a western company, see what they can get out of them, and when they've got what they can they move on to another one.

The inevitable result is donor fatigue. People are less interested in spending money in Iraq because they see little is changing on the ground. The coalition authorities hoped that their policy of 'spend, spend, spend' would create the right conditions for local businesses to flourish. But in fact they have achieved the precise opposite. Their donor policy has crowded out legitimate inward investment. And once the donor culture is established it's very hard to get rid of. We'd warned from the start that the priority in southern Iraq should have been to encourage economic infrastructure – not simply to 'buy consent' by showering money around. Our fears were brushed aside.

Corruption, too, has become a major issue. During 'our watch' in the south we kept a tight control over funds and saw relatively little corruption. But a friend who worked in Basra some time later found that fraud was rife. The westerners who controlled the cash were unable to get out of the bases because of the worsening security problem. This meant that they had to rely on photographs and documents to 'prove' that the buildings, bridges, and roads were being built as promised. 'A whole new industry in forged documents, receipts and photographs had grown up,' said my friend. 'They were ingenious, though not always very thorough in the fraud. I said to one of the Iraqi officials one day "if you are going to show me fabricated photographs of the project at least show me photos of the same place!" The pictures he was showing me the project being completed came from at least two separate locations.'

In 2006 my company Gulf Capital did manage to close one deal in Iraq. We'd arranged for the first slice of corporate finance for a wireless communications project. It was one of the very few deals that was done in Iraq in 2006 and could lead to an investment of up to $500 million. We used a bank in Kuwait and it showed that our business model of getting inward investment could work. But it was a very hard transaction to pull off. Conditions have become so tough now it's almost too difficult to do business there. The only real success stories are the security companies who have government contracts.

At least Gulf Capital presented a chance for some of the old team to work together again. Peter Bingham, the ports adviser, has been working with me – though now in London. For a time Brigadier Peter Williams was a director of the firm; he is now working as a strategic consultant for a large oil company in Nigeria. The heroic sergeant Ian McClymont – who left the regular army – worked for my firm briefly, though has since been working as a security consultant in Africa.

Some of the old team have also gone back to Iraq. Water specialist Wally Weeks returned to Basra, this time with the engineers Mott Macdonald, and another of the water team, Dougie Smith, also went back. Projects manager Rosie Knight worked in Baghdad, then for the UN in Erbil in northern Iraq. Pat McLaughlin, too, spent a brief period back in the country. My old friend Tash Coxen, who had left Baghdad on 28 June with the handover, now works as a freelance consultant in post-conflict situations and has been back to Basra. Ed Lock, who helped me plan my team of advisers, has been working in security in Baghdad while David Amos, who had such a huge influence on my work in Basra, became head of Control Risk Group's Iraq operation. Katharina Pfitzner stayed in Iraq until the spring of 2006, working for the Americans and then for a security firm. The head of the agricultural team, Ole Stokholm Jepsen, also stayed on in Basra, his work funded by the Danish government. He has remained as committed as ever to Iraq – and its future. 'We must stay on as long as possible if the Iraqis want it, no matter how difficult it may be,' he told me from Basra. 'This is a very new and fragile democracy in an old society and in a region where many neighbouring countries' leaders are very scared of this development – and therefore trying to help abort it at birth.'

Other former advisers have gone further afield. Colin McBride has been working with DFID official Rod Matthews in Afghanistan while Robert Apsley went to work for a multi-national in Pakistan. Jane Wilshaw went back to her director of nursing position on the Isle of Wight but retains a keen interest in events in the Middle East. Dominique Hope and Jude Dunn have both decided to return to university. Among the most senior staff Sir Hilary Synott retired after leaving the CPA in February 2004 but does some consultancy work. Janet Rogan became number two at the British Embassy in Tel Aviv.

Many of the UK team members from CPA South were recognised in the Queen's Birthday Honours towards the end of 2004 for the contributions that they'd made to the operation in Iraq.

Oscar the cat was last seen still living at the old palace in Basra.

The western members of the CPA at least had a choice about where they went after the organisation was closed down. Our Iraqi staff had few options. Their country has now become a place of sorrow and danger. Anyone who has worked – or still does work – for the British and other members of the coalition have become targets and are being hunted down by death squads. Religious extremism has taken over in the south fuelled, as we had feared, by economic stagnation.

Ahmed didn't stay long working with the British in southern Iraq. He quit after just two weeks as he said he'd been asked to investigate passport applications and asylum claims. 'If I'd done all this they'd have killed me,' he told me in an email. As it is, Ahmed has become a hunted man anyway because of his previous connection with us. He has sent all of his family abroad to safety. Meanwhile his wife goes alone to the shops while Ahmed stays at home behind locked doors. He's scared that if he ventures out he'll be murdered.

That is what happened to Judge al-Latif's chief of staff Hasim as early as July 2004. He was gunned down in Basra because he'd worked with us. It was Hasim who had said to me one day before we left: 'Mr Andrew, you cannot leave, you have been here for one year – we are only just getting to know you.' He was a delightful man. Rosie Knight's interpreter was also murdered in January 2006. Another of our interpreters fled to Kuwait for his safety and even Abdul – who still works for western organisations – has judged it safer to live in Jordan.

They are all depressing stories. Perhaps the bleakest, however, is Raneen's. She continued to work for the British consulate in Basra and found great personal happiness when she married. Her new husband was an Iraqi who also worked for the coalition, in his case the Americans. Her happiness didn't last long. One day in July 2006 she and her husband were out shopping in Basra when they were attacked. A gunman wielding an AK47 opened fire at the couple from point-blank range. Her husband died on the spot while Raneen was hit three times and left for dead on the street. She was rushed to Basra's main teaching hospital which is about 150 metres from the palace compound. Doctors battled to save her life.

When the British authorities got to hear about what had happened to Raneen they sent a military team to the hospital to check how she was. She was too ill to be moved and so they had to leave her. Unfortunately their visit also meant that Raneen was now still in danger from attack. If the extremists who had carried out the shooting didn't know before that she'd survived, they did now.

The first I heard about it was when Abdul contacted me on behalf of Raneen's family. They asked me to get involved. I immediately sent a message to everyone I knew saying that Raneen had been shot and needed help. I received a phone call from a consular official in Basra who'd had seen the message. 'What are you doing sending this out?' I was asked. 'Who are you to be getting involved in this?' I explained that, as the person who'd hired her, I was the reason that Raneen was working for the British.

The situation dragged on for a few days with Raneen still critically ill and little sign of rapid action to help her. I felt I was getting nowhere fast and decided to call Sir Hilary Synott. 'Raneen has been shot and we need to get her out of Iraq,' I told him. Sir Hilary got to work immediately. Meanwhile Rosie Knight, who was in Kuwait at the time, lobbied the British ambassador there.

To their credit Whitehall now sprang into action. I was even told by one official: 'But Andrew, you're pushing at an open door!' Maybe, I thought.

In the meantime Raneen's family hadn't waited for officials to act. They were so worried that the extremists would come back to finish her off that they moved her to a safe house even though she still had bullets in her lung, back and shoulder. When a Whitehall official rang me to tell me that Raneen was still too ill to be moved I had to inform them that she had already left the hospital . . . 'She's being targeted by the insurgents who are trying to track her down,' I told them. 'Here are the numbers where you can get hold of her family.' Eventually Raneen was taken to the relative safety of the British military hospital at Shaibah near Basra. Later she was evacuated by the British government from Iraq and taken to a hospital elsewhere in the Middle East.

I went to visit Raneen in hospital and it was heart-breaking. She tried bravely to joke with me from her hospital bed. 'I hoped you would come and visit me, Mr Andrew,' she told me. 'I am still waiting for an invitation to your wedding one day!' She smiled and I smiled back at her. But I could see the changes in her and they weren't just physical. When she started work at the CPA Raneen had been full of bounce and hope. Like so many Iraqis she was glad that we were there and delighted that she could play a part in our work as she looked forward to democracy and freedom. Now she'd lost all her sparkle. As she looked back at me her eyes were lifeless. Something inside her had died.

Like the other Iraqis I have mentioned, Raneen and her husband were targeted simply because they'd worked for us. My friend Aran Maree talked about how we'd tried to build a bridge between our two worlds – and then hastily had been told to take down the scaffolding. We'd managed to clamber safely back to our side but Aran had always said that the Iraqi staff would be at risk of 'falling off'. What had happened to Raneen and the others showed just what 'falling off' meant in practice. They were paying a very heavy price for working with us.

What makes the suffering of people such as Raneen even more galling is that the coalition has since dramatically changed its approach to rebuilding Iraq. When the CPA closed, my team and I were told that individual countries operating from their own offices would do the work better. More than a year later, however, in late 2005, this policy was abruptly reversed. Coalition military and civilians banded together to form what are called Provincial Reconstruction Teams (PRTs) across Iraq. In May 2006 one was set up in Basra. When he inaugurated one in October 2006 the US Ambassador to Iraq, Zalmay Khalilzad, described their aims. 'The objective,' said Mr Khalilzad, 'is for US and coalition partners, military and civilian, to work with Iraq's provincial governments to develop a transparent and sustained capability to govern, enhance security and rule of law, promote political and economic development and to meet the basic needs of the community . . . The PRTs use all of our tools, military and civilian, to get behind the ideas the Iraqis feel are most important to build their national institutions to offer a better hope for the Iraqi people's economic future.'

The PRTs are mini-versions of the CPA in all but name. Those very words could have been a mission statement of the team of advisers that I'd led in Basra. The coalition had done a complete U-turn. It now realised that it needed a regional multinational team after all. And above all, it realised it had to tackle the economy – the area we'd long told our Whitehall masters was the one that most needed urgent attention.

It's not just the wasted time that hurts. It's the loss of knowledge and key people. When I spoke with someone connected to one of the new PRTs in the south (now working out of Kuwait for security reasons) I gently pointed out that it's the ministries rather than the local Iraqi councils who are the key players in the economy. He looked at me in amazement. 'Who are they?' he wanted to know. This was the very problem others and I had faced and then overcome after July 2003. No lessons had been learned. Clearly the much-trumpeted 'handover' document hadn't been widely read.

By 2006 the British consulate in Basra was still technically open but with a much reduced staff. Movement is either by Warrior armed vehicle or by helicopter at night. As a friend who visited Basra recently said to me: 'How would I measure success? Judge for yourself – when I was here in June 2003, I was having dinner in downtown Basra and shopping unaccompanied in the souk. Three and a half years later, when I visited Basra recently, we never left the compound and when we did move, only to enter or leave the country, we were banned from any movement by road and we could only fly at night in a darkened helicopter, firing flares to prevent us being shot down.'

In a conversation with a PRT source I was told: 'Well, of course, Andrew, no one has paid any attention to the economy in the south since the invasion.' I could have wept with frustration. As we'd all feared, our work in Basra hadn't just been forgotten – it had been erased from history.

As for me, I still intend doing business in the Middle East and still have the same vision about bridging the gap between the developed world and emerging markets. I still believe that private enterprise has a vital role to play in improving the lot of people's lives in those regions. But my time in Iraq has taught me to be patient. It's a long-term affair.

As for the work of the CPA, did we succeed? No, of course not. But I don't think we failed completely either. By the time we were told to pack our bags and make way for the 'professionals', southern Iraq had shown some signs of progress. After the mess and muddle of the early weeks of the occupation we'd managed to bring some direction and order to the reconstruction of this shattered country. We'd worked closely with the Iraqis and those labours were beginning to bear fruit. We'd shown passion and commitment. As Rosie and Tash said, we'd left behind our friends and families and put our lives at risk for the sake of something worthwhile.

Then, we were told to leave. Many of us felt deeply let down. We knew what we could still offer to the country and its wonderful people. We knew, too, the risk and suffering that would follow if we left abruptly. Our worst fears have come true. Friends such as Raneen have been forced to pay a terrible price. Looking at what Basra and Iraq have become today, my greatest feeling is one of overwhelming sadness. Whilst we in the west grow tired of newspaper and television reports of escalating violence in Baghdad and throughout Iraq, we should perhaps pause to put this violence in context of our own experience. The tragic suicide bombings in London on 7 July 2005, which killed 52 commuters, and in New York on 9 September 2001, which killed 3,030, are the equivalent of one day and one month respectively of the carnage and casualties that continue in Iraq. And this is a conflict of our making. I fear for the new Iraq that's being created, the people we have left behind and the deadly scenes that are being played out every day. I just pray that our efforts have not all been in vain.

London, December 2006

WHO'S WHO

Some names have been changed for security reasons.

Abdul	My interpreter.
Mr Abdullah	Director general for telecoms
Ahmed	My interpreter, sometime entrepreneur and computer programmer.
Mr Ali	Director of the Central Bank in Basra and Mr Raffaq's replacement.
Colonel David Amos	Deputy Brigade Commander of 19 Mechanised Brigade, responsible for Operations Support in the Brigade HQ, including civil military operations (CIMIC). The immediate boss of Major Michael Hostrup, he also commanded the Light Dragoons Regiment.
Robert Apsley	The Economic Planning and Development team's power expert.
Philip Ashton-Johnson or 'AJ'	Fellow Yeomanry major I travelled out to Basra and shared quarters with. Worked as a liaison officer.
Paul Attenborough	The Economic Planning and Development team's industrial and heavy-industry consultant.

Andy Bearpark — Senior British civil servant, director of operations for the Coalition Provisional Authority in Baghdad, one of Paul Bremer's right-hand men.

Hilary Benn — British Secretary of State for International Development, head of DFID.

Tony Bennett — Member of the Economic Planning and Development finance team.

Peter Bingham — The Economic Planning and Development team's ports expert.

Bjorn Brandtzaeg — The Economic Planning and Development team's trade and industry expert.

Brigadier Bruce Brearley — Deputy Divisional Commander of MND(SE) based at Basra airport. Replaced Brigadier Gregory as Senior Military Adviser to CPA South.

Ambassador L. Paul Bremer III — US senior representative in Iraq and Head of the CPA in Baghdad throughout its tenure until June 2004.

Manson Brown — Senior US Coastguard Officer, head of CPA Baghdad transport team and chief adviser to the Ministry of Transport in Baghdad.

Major Frances Castle — In charge of 19 Brigade's administration and pay and an invaluable source of information when I first arrived.

Colonel Peter Duklis — Director of Regions for CPA South, then Chief of Staff following the departure of Allan Rosenberg in December 2003.

Corporal Jude Dunn — TA corporal who used to work in a bank in the UK. Paid Basra's wages for us.

John Dyson — Foreign and Commonwealth Office Management Officer and veteran of many overseas missions, created our purpose-built office and camp complex.

Major Hugh Eton — Chief of Staff of the Basra-based 19 Mechanised Brigade HQ to which I was attached initially.

Daniela Fiori — Specialist in the SME sector, member of The Economic Planning and Development trade and industry team.

Nigel Forrest	The Economic Planning and Development team's finance and economics expert.
JoAnn Foster	Chief Executive Officer of The Foster Group, responsible for installation of a 40MW turbine in As Samawah province.
Sir Jeremy Greenstock	British Ambassador to Iraq, his office was next to Ambassador Bremer's in CPA Baghdad.
Brigadier Andrew Gregory	Deputy Divisional Commander from MND(SE), seconded to CPA South, acted as deputy to Ambassador Ole Olsen, the Head of CPA South before Sir Hilary Synnott.
Mr Hassani	Governor of Al-Muthanna and Samawah.
Stuart Hills	Lieutenant within UK military specialist CIMIC Group and worked alongside Charles Monk as the Education Adviser within CPA South.
Dominique Hope	Arrived as TA Major and converted to civilian specialist contract. Member of the Economic Planning and Development team, first in trade and industry then business development.
Major Michael Hostrup	The Danish officer who was initially given 'my' utilities job.
Ole Stockholm Jepsen	The Danish adviser on farming and irrigation issues for CPA South.
Rosie Knight	One of the early arrivals at CPA South. A specialist civilian contractor and projects manager for the Al-Basra governorate team.
General Graham Lamb	General Officer Commanding (GOC) of Multi-national Division South East [MND(SE)] based at Basra airport from June–December 2003.
Governor/Judge Abdul al-Latif	The first Governor of Basra, nominated by local councillors and elected by the people of Basra in elections held in summer 2003.
Captain Ed Lock	British officer and the Economic Planning and Development team's electricity expert.
Ambassador Mario Maiolini	Italian Ambassador, Sir Hilary Synnott's deputy, shared an office with the senior military adviser in CPA South.

Dr Aran Maree	An old friend, cardiologist and the Economic Planning and Development team's social services expert.
Rod Matthews	British civil servant in charge of DFID's reconstruction programme in Iraq.
Colin McBride	TA Major and Head of the Economic Planning and Development utilities team incorporating oil, water, electricity and transport. Awarded an MBE for his work for CPA South.
Brian McCarthy	Was a TA corporal, then the Economic Planning and Development team's waste-management expert.
Sergeant Major Ian McClymont	A regular army soldier attached to 19 Brigade; set up a one-man outreach post outside our compound.
Pat McLoughlin	Member of the Economic Planning and Development team; chartered accountant who became my right-hand man.
Pradeep Mittal	Research analyst from India, member of the The Economic Planning and Development trade and industry team.
Brigadier Bill Moore	Commander of 19 Mechanised Brigade with responsibility for Basra province from June–October 2003.
Rear Admiral David J Nash	Director of the US-run reconstruction arm the Program Management Office (PMO) in Baghdad.
Nei-San	Head of the Japanese CPA mission in Basra
Patrick Nixon	British Ambassador and Head of CPA South from January–June 2004 after Sir Hilary Synnott.
Ambassador Ole Wohlers Olsen	Danish ambassador and head of CPA South before Sir Hilary Synnott.
Katharina Pfitzner	Finance specialist and key member of the Economic Planning and Development finance team.
Molly Phee	Maysan governorate's co-ordinator
Christopher Prentice	British Ambassador to Jordan

Mr Raffaq	Director general of the Iraqi Central Bank in Basra.
Raneen	My wonderful assistant; brutally attacked for working with the coalition in 2006.
Janet Rogan	Foreign office official who had volunteered to work in Iraq as Deputy Regional Co-ordinator within CPA South from May–August 2003.
Allan Rosenberg	Danish CPA South Chief of Staff from May–December 2003.
James Sharp	The Economic Planning and Development team's telecom expert.
Sir Nigel Sheinwald	Member of British cabinet, Tony Blair's chief adviser on foreign policy.
Grand Ayatollah Ali Sistani	The most senior Sh'ia figure in Iraq
Phil Smith	Specialist finance consultant working for DFID in Basra on reconstruction of banks in June/July 2003.
Dougie Smith	TA sergeant major who worked with Wally Weeks in the Economic Planning and Development water team.
Rory Stewart	Deputy to Molly Phee, the Maysan governorate's co-ordinator. In April 2004 he transferred to Nasariya to become the Deputy Regional Co-ordinator of Nasariya province in the Italian sector.
Jack Straw	British Foreign Secretary
Sir Hilary Synnott	Head of CPA South from August 2003 to January 2004 after Ole Olsen. Former ambassador to Pakistan and second most senior British diplomat in Iraq.
Kevin Thomas	The Economic Planning and Development team's fuels expert. He was awarded an MBE for the work done for CPA South.
Jon Walden	A TA officer and logistics specialist who worked for the British Crown Agents, which was responsible for administration of our contracts.

Mr Waleed	Director General of South Oil, which produces approximately 70% of all of Iraq's oil.
Wally Weeks	The Economic Planning and Development team's water expert. He was awarded an MBE for the work undertaken in Iraq for CPA South.
Michael Whitehead	The Economic Planning and Development team's health expert from July–October 2003.
Brigadier Peter Williams	Deputy Divisional Commander of MNDS(SE) from December 2003 to June 2004, head of Operations Support and the CPA's senior military adviser, following in the footsteps of Brigadier Andrew Gregory and Brigadier Bruce Brearley.
Allan Williams	The Economic Planning and Development team's construction expert with significant experience building various airports, including the new Hong Kong airport.
David Williams	One of the Economic Planning and Development agriculture team, working with Ole Jepsen.
Jane Wilshaw	Specialist consultant in the nursing sector sent by the UK Department of Health. Member of the Economic Planning and Development health team.
George Wolfe	Senior adviser at the Ministry of Finance in Baghdad from April–June 2004.